CROSSING
THE LINE

Martin Dillon worked as a BBC journalist for eighteen years, producing award-winning programmes for television and radio, and has won international acclaim for his unique, investigative books on the Ireland conflict. Conor Cruise O'Brien, the renowned historian and scholar, described him as 'our Virgil to that inferno'.

CROSSING THE LINE

MY LIFE ON THE EDGE

MARTIN DILLON

MERRION
PRESS

First published in 2017 by
Merrion Press
10 George's Street
Newbridge
Co. Kildare
Ireland
www.merrionpress.ie

© 2017, Martin Dillon

9781785371301 (Paper)
9781785371318 (Kindle)
9781785371325 (Epub)
9781785371332 (PDF)

British Library Cataloguing in Publication Data
An entry can be found on request
Library of Congress Cataloging in Publication Data
An entry can be found on request

Interior design by www.jminfotechindia.com
Typeset in Adobe Caslon Pro 11.5/15 pt
Printed and bound by TJ International Ltd

Cover design by Fiachra McCarthy
Cover back: Martin Dillon

To my wife

Violeta

A stocking leaves a shapely leg.
Over the head, it bends the nose.
Eyes partially blinded,
twitch in the gauze.
The mouth sucks in nylon,
ears pinned back, hearing impaired.
A knot on the skull hides humanity.

– Martin Dillon, 'Non-Heads'

Contents

Foreword

Journalism is apparently the first draft of history so presumably the journalist's memoir can be the second. If Martin Dillon's remembrance here achieves equivalent significance to his original reportage, then this book should be of historical import.

In the 1960s the half-century-old partition of Ireland into two states, one post-colonial, the other neo-colonial, began to sunder. Once more, and to the great chagrin of London and Dublin, the Irish problem had to be solved again.

Northern Ireland was being ambushed by a series of forces past and present; the Vatican Council's ecumenical movement impacted on its historic Protestant fundamentalism; the new era of foreign direct investment began to undo its traditional discriminatory worker practices; the rising Catholic birth rate was threatening its gerrymandered artificial majority and, most significantly of all, there was the impact of the 1947 Education (Northern Ireland) Act.

This act, which created free second-level education, in time overwhelmed the old Orange state, unleashing a first generation of middle-class professional Catholics who, unlike their fathers and grandfathers, were not prepared to take no for an answer.

It all began with street protest but very quickly the guns came out and, as though out of the history books, stepped the old ghosts of Republicanism and loyalism. It was planter versus Gael – twentieth-century style – with Molotov cocktails, Armalites, Semtex and 'Romper Rooms'. Few knew then that a thirty-year conflict was beginning.

The young Martin Dillon had just got his first typewriter when the first stones were thrown. For the decades following, he was to both live in this battlefield and report it. This memoir is suffused with encyclopaedic small-print local knowledge and has all the energy and urgency of a journalist who had no home to go to at closing time since his home was also in the trenches. Dillon's reportage came as much from his Belfast-born DNA as from his journalistic instincts.

As the troubles grew, Belfast soon had its colony of journalists – most were brief visitors – but for Dillon, merely counting the stories in and counting them out would not satisfy his appetite. He began to poke and peep into the hidden places and the secret practices that all of Northern Ireland's many armies – legal and illegal – were hiding. His old contacts book should go to some journalistic museum.

It is no exaggeration to say it but there were times, especially in the 1970s, when after dark some of the streets in Belfast were among the most dangerous places in the world. Apart from anything else, here was a journalist who took huge risks in asking the difficult questions.

In the end, as Dillon had always suspected, one day he would have to pack his typewriter and notebook and leave before they came for him. Even for veterans like him, the delicate balance between getting the story and not getting yourself killed was a daily and frequently exhausting calculation. Judging from this memoir, he got out just in time.

From the very beginning, there were two simultaneous and parallel wars ongoing in Northern Ireland; the visible one that was all over the tea-time news, and the invisible one that would sometimes emerge briefly, leaving behind tantalising fingerprints and glimpses of hidden agendas.

Here was a battlefield where the politicians ceded control to the spooks, where the state's writ barely ran, and about which the less the good citizens of the liberal democracies were supposed to know, the sounder they were supposed to sleep in their beds at night. This was Dillon country and as he followed its mysterious trails, he was among the first to raise the deeply troubling question of the legality of the state's dirty war.

At their very best, journalists are worker bees, hewers of information and carriers of facts, especially the very few who will not take no for an answer. They should be pains in the arse for any establishment, and

Dillon was one. You'll find him all over these chapters, the hack armed only with a pen and facing the high walls of official denial.

In his 1990 book *The Dirty War*, Dillon had opened the first ever window on the secret counter-insurgency war that the British state fought in Northern Ireland. This was a campaign drawn on classic Brigadier Frank 'Kitsonian' parameters that, even to this day, is still reluctant to give up some of its ghastly secrets.

Even today as more and more secret agents are uncovered and led out, blinking into the sunlight, or as veterans begin telling their stories for the first time, the visible extent of the dimensions of the secret war grow year by year. Perhaps the most extraordinary thing about the truth is that eventually, however long it takes, it will always come out.

But across thirty years, with its vast network of agents and intelligence agencies, the complete story of the dirty war remains to be told. Shoot-to-kill; the running of double agents; the manipulation of paramilitary killings; the secret importing of weaponry; the unexplained deaths; to this day the incident files remain bulging with unanswered questions.

Within that extraordinary hall of mirrors, it is to Dillon's unique credit as a journalist that he was among the first to begin lifting the stones and looking underneath. It was difficult and dangerous work, even the journalistic establishments were timorous near this terrain and Dillon's courage and dedication should be recognised.

Dillon was also the scribe who revealed to us some of the most deprived human animals who ever existed, in his 1989 book *The Shankill Butchers*. His telling of how a group of bog-standard, working-class men in a United Kingdom urban jungle could spend their evenings in drinking clubs featuring their unique floor show of the torture and throat-cutting of their Catholic neighbours still makes the blood run cold. In some places, such a group might constitute a club for playing darts or for pigeon racing, in Northern Ireland here was a club for the enjoyment of serial killing.

Lenny Murphy the Shankill butcher who slashed his victims' throats; Michael Stone the loyalist paramilitary who attacked a funeral with hand grenades; Freddie Scappaticci the double agent in the Provisional Irish Republican Army, known by the codename Stakeknife: Dillon's cast of villains across this memoir takes some equalling.

There are other chapters, too, on his childhood, his failed religious vocation and a tender memoir of his famous great-uncle, the artist Gerard Dillon.

Gerard's brush left behind indelible images for us of his era, his great-nephew Martin's pen has drawn hugely significant questions marks across another era. The artist with his colours, the artisan with his words, the Dillon DNA has hugely enriched us all.

Tom McGurk, August 2017

Prologue

Growing up in 1950s West Belfast, it was natural to feel trapped by the physical contours of the city and stories of its troubled past. In the Falls area, Black Mountain rose above the narrow, intersecting streets of Protestant and Catholic enclaves. A few years before I came into the world, the mountain offered nightly shelter for families hiding from German bombers pounding Belfast. The city being an industrial hub for the British war effort suffered terribly during the Blitz whereas the Nazis spared Dublin because it was neutral territory.

My grandfather, Patrick Dillon and his brother, John, fought bravely on the Normandy beaches, yet their sacrifice was somehow diminished in Protestants' eyes because many Catholics throughout Ireland were branded as anti-British. That perception of Catholics was not entirely true but, like so much history in Ireland, myths trump facts. Interestingly, more Catholics than Protestants on the island fought and died in the ranks of the British Army in the Second World War. It is equally the case that there was profound anti-Britishness throughout Ireland, which Republicans transformed into a pro-Nazi mentality.

It was manifested in the refusal of the Dublin government to cede important ports to Britain to make it easier to defend Allied shipping in the Atlantic from German gunboats and submarines. Members of the IRA even met leading German military figures, convinced if Germany won the war the IRA would be considered a friend and ally. The most egregious example of pro-Nazi sentiment was the decision by Irish leader, Éamon de Valera, to open a condolences book at the German Legation in Dublin so people could express their regret at the death of Adolf Hitler.

In my youth, I knew little of the intricacies of the war period as they related to Ireland, yet I was familiar with my tribe's attachment to

Irish history. I refer to 'Irish history', and not 'the history of Ireland', to confirm that what I learned from an early age was either written or passed on orally by those defining themselves as Irish. In Belfast, you learned history sitting on your grandmother's knee, or in my case from the De La Salle Brothers in St Finian's primary school on the Falls Road, where my fellow pupils included Gerry Adams, a future IRA leader.

In St Finian's, the past was a potent recounting of Ireland's brutal colonization by the British. Tales of the slaughter of men, women and children, ordered by English generals like Oliver Cromwell, made Irish rebels of old and IRA gunmen of the twentieth century seem god-like and heroic. Built into the narrative was an understanding the Northern Ireland State was illegal, and its institutions, especially the judiciary, as well as the Royal Ulster Constabulary and its paramilitary force, the B-Specials, were mechanisms for oppression.

Our eyes were directed towards 'The South' as the finest example of how people lived in freedom. Some Catholics from my grandparents' era referred to that part of the island as 'The Free State', which was its official title after independence from Britain in 1921. It remained within the British Commonwealth until 1937 when it was declared a sovereign nation with the Gaelic title, Éire. In 1947, it became the Republic of Ireland, but most Northern Protestants continued to call it Éire as though in doing so they were reinforcing the point it was Irish and separate from British-controlled Northern Ireland. In my childhood, I never heard a Protestant refer to it as anything other than Éire or 'The South'. Calling it 'The Republic of Ireland' or the 'Irish Republic' was taboo among many Protestants. 'The South' was shorthand for a political perception that the South and the North were equal entities, which of course was silly, given the fact that Northern Ireland comprised only six of the island's thirty-two counties and was not a sovereign state. Power over it lay with successive London governments. It was, therefore, hardly surprising Northern Ireland's children were confused when the other part of the island was treated to a variety of names. As a child, I imagined the border separating the two parts of the country had to be so high no one could see over it.

Being a newly created state, the Republic of Ireland was not as wealthy as Northern Ireland, which was heavily subsidised by the British Exchequer. Nevertheless, Belfast Catholics were quick to point out that Catholics south of the border were 'richer' because they could freely express their political opinions, practise their faith openly and play Gaelic games on Sundays. In contrast, in the North, or 'The Black North' as many Catholics across the island called it, Protestants held power through gerrymandering, discrimination in public housing allocation and the use of the Special Powers Act, a piece of legislation that provided the majority Unionist government of Northern Ireland with excessive police powers, including the use of internment without trial. Unlike Catholics, Protestants called Sunday the Sabbath and celebrated it by closing everything but churches. In parks, children's swings were locked, and elsewhere, cinemas, pubs and shops were shuttered. My lasting childhood image of Belfast city centre on Sunday afternoons was a sad and profoundly silent place. Still, a few Catholic districts in the west of the city were especially noisy on Sundays, when Gaelic football or hurling games were played in Casement Park in the Andersonstown area, or in two smaller parks off the Whiterock Road.

When major Gaelic games were scheduled, the pavements on the Falls Road filled with throngs of men and boys, too poor to pay for a bus ride. Though my father was one of those men, he claimed shoe leather got him to the game quicker than a bus. The return journey was often depressing because local football and hurling teams rarely matched the skills of teams from the island's other provinces. I was always bemused by the playing of 'The Soldier's Song', the Irish national anthem, before games because the majority of spectators knew only a few familiar lines or phrases of it in Gaelic, especially the closing lines, which were always sung with gusto. Had the games been held in Dublin, more people would have been able to sing the entire anthem in Gaelic. As a friend of mine later explained, Catholics in Northern Ireland liked everything Gaelic except the language, while Catholics on the rest of the island learned Irish at school and rarely spoke it.

I often overheard adults talking politics in my childhood, but it was in primary school where history and social awareness were defined for me. I took the De La Salle Brothers at their word when they taught me history because they had a most persuasive way of getting their message across. They used thick leather straps to beat knowledge into your hands or legs if you displayed little aptitude for learning or if your attention waned during lessons. I acquired one of their straps decades later and its construction impressed me: several machine-stitched layers and a perfectly formed handle. It was indeed a formidable weapon when wielded by a Brother keen to dispense raw justice. The prospect of being battered with a strap encouraged me to pay attention in class. When my homework required me to learn chunks of Patrick Pearse's speech over the grave of O'Donovan Rossa, I devoted hours to the task.

Catholics of Ireland revered Pearse, considering him one of the most prominent revolutionaries of the 1916 Rising in Dublin, which paved the way for the eventual end of British rule in twenty-six of Ireland's counties. Jeremiah O'Donovan Rossa was a rebel from an earlier generation and the first Irish Republican to organise the dynamite bombing of English cities in the 1880s. After he died in exile on Staten Island, New York, in 1915, the Republican movement shipped his body home for a majestic burial. It was a stunning public relations coup for a movement which needed a spark to ignite a dying political passion.

Pearse, a schoolteacher, poet and devout Catholic, was chosen to deliver the graveside oration in Dublin's Glasnevin Cemetery, where O'Donovan Rossa was buried. The oration would become the centrepiece of Irish Republican rhetoric and, in the decades following, the Christian and De La Salle Brothers made sure every pupil familiarised themselves with it.

By their promotion of Pearse's idealism in the Northern Ireland of the early 1950s, the Brothers became the vanguard of the blood sacrifice tradition of an Irish Republicanism that would find fertile ground two decades later in the emerging Provisional IRA. When the Provisional IRA took to the political stage in 1971, some of my classmates from the early 1950s played prominent roles, in particular Gerry Adams. Four decades later, when I went to interview him, he invited me to go next door to St Finian's, our old primary school, to look at some photos of us when we were students there.

As we walked through the narrow stone entrance of the school, which had remained unchanged architecturally for half a century, I expected to inhale the smells of stale milk and urine, which permeated the schoolyard all those years before. Now, the crates of empty milk bottles were gone, but the toilets still faced some of the classrooms. Students met Gerry Adams with smiles while I received curious stares when we entered the main building. Boys as young as five gave him admiring glances and reached out to shake his hand. After we looked through our class photos, he whispered with a wry smile it was time for the Angelus. I was somewhat speechless, having forgotten the prayers of my childhood. But, when the bells of nearby Clonard Monastery rang out, memories of me reciting the Angelus floated back. It was a prayer devoted to the time the Virgin Mary was visited by the Angel Gabriel and told she would bear a child. In the 1950s, pupils stood up in every classroom throughout Ireland to recite it. I now found myself standing alongside Gerry Adams at the head of a class of seven-year-old boys, their hands clasped in devotion. He led the prayer while I bowed my head, embarrassed as I stumbled over the words. A line of it struck me as emblematic of what I was witnessing, 'And the word was made flesh and dwelt amongst us.'

Gerry Adams and the pupils spoke it with such requisite reverence, their eyes closed, heads bowed ever so slightly. When the prayer ended, boys reached out to touch Gerry like pilgrims touching a relic in the hope of being transformed. They were thrilled to be close to their hero in the flesh and were trying to come to terms with the sheer joy of it. The historian Thomas Carlyle said history is like a letter of instruction handed down to us. It is charred and burned and pieces are missing, making it difficult to read. In Ireland, people never faced that problem. The oral history tradition, which was handed down to them and fed their understanding of the past, was vivid and seemingly complete. Looking at Gerry Adams and his young admirers, I saw how the past was made more enticing by the presence of a living icon instead of the dead ones whom I was once encouraged to imagine. As I left St Finian's that day, I thought of the 'Angelus bell o'er the Liffey swell ringing out in the foggy dew'.

We are witnesses of Time with a duty
to reflect the past without bitterness.

– Martin Dillon

PART ONE

ONE

Belfast – Early Family Roots

My mother insisted she preferred her children on her knee than on her conscience. It was her way of saying she agreed with the Vatican's ruling that artificial birth control and abortion were mortal sins. As a consequence, she had ten of us, starting with me, Martin, and my fraternal twin, Damien, followed by seven girls and the last in line, a boy named Patrick. The girls were Frances, Ursula, Mary, Monica, Imelda, Attracta and Bernadette. Starting with the eldest, I learned to rhyme off their names in that order.

Irrespective of my mother's commitment to Church dogma, she really wanted lots of children, and like many Catholic women of her generation she never considered motherhood a burden. I tend to believe my parents paid little attention to the Catholic version of birth control called the rhythm method. My mother believed it was God's will she had a large family. For her, marriage and the sex act were not only about pleasure but also about procreation.

While born Mary Teresa, she was always known as Maureen, one of eight children born to Edward Clarke and Margaret Clarke, née Carson. Her father, Ed Clarke, was a troubled individual, who was abusive towards his wife and children. Some people said he was angry with the world because one of his legs was shorter than the other, which required him to wear a heavy, ugly boot. It left him with a pronounced limp, and sometimes children poked fun at him in the street. He was from Ballymanagh, a townland close to Ballina, County Mayo, in the West of Ireland. He became estranged from his family at an early age and ran off to London where he worked for a decade in the famous Saville Row garment district, becoming an expert men's tailor. Years later, he moved to Belfast where he met and married my grandmother, Margaret Carson. They settled into No 4 Ross Place, a two-level, brick house opposite St Peter's pro-cathedral in the Catholic, Lower Falls area of West Belfast.

Ed's story of how he left his family was shrouded in mystery, and my mother's narration of it when I was young had all the ingredients of a nineteenth-century novel. According to her, he was wrongly accused by his father of stealing family savings and was so incensed by the accusation he left home, giving up his right to inherit a mansion and a large farm with racehorses. My mother was often the butt of jokes about her description of the Mayo Clarkes. My father hinted that the Clarkes' West of Ireland home probably looked like a mansion to my mother when compared to her tiny house in Belfast.

It took me decades to learn he was wrong. He had no knowledge of Mayo in the 1920s and 1930s when my mother spent summers with her father's family. In fact, my father only went to Mayo in the late 1960s, and by then, there was little evidence of the mansion or the racehorses. Only while writing this book did the truth emerge about the Mayo Clarkes. Painstaking research by my cousin, Eddie Clarke, revealed Ed's family members were big landowners from the middle of the nineteenth century until the 1930s. They lived on a large spread called 'Brickfield', named after a brick-producing factory they owned. The soil on the western end of their property was the best in the region for not only making bricks but also delph and china. They were known as the 'Lord Clarkes' because only English Lords had their kind of wealth and a large stable of racehorses.

She often used colourful language to enhance her stories about the Clarkes. By the time I was old enough to enjoy her stories, her father was dead, and she had lionised him to erase every unsavoury aspect of his personality. She ignored the heavy drinking and gambling that led him into debt and almost bankrupted him. As a consequence, the small family home in No 4 Ross Place had to accommodate his tailoring business, his wife Margaret, their eight children, and Margaret's older sisters, Sarah and Bridget Carson. He even conducted the tailoring from a downstairs backroom during the day, depriving the family of privacy in their daily lives. My mother overlooked the hard times he heaped on her and her siblings because she believed he redeemed himself by giving up alcohol and gambling before he died. She saw salvation in his ability to conquer his demons, and it allowed her to highlight his reformation when I was old enough to ask questions about his darker side.

My mother's storytelling ability was just one aspect of her vivacious personality, which endeared her to the young men of her generation. She later admitted she wasn't the most beautiful girl in St Peter's parish but she was the liveliest, with a great sense of fun. Photos of her when she was eighteen show a girl with a full figure, a radiant smile and a shock of auburn hair. 'My hair was my crowning glory,' she would say as she got older, adding, 'and my pins weren't too bad either'.

My father first set eyes on her in 1939 when he was fourteen and she was sixteen. He was a regular visitor to 4 Ross Place because her brother, Gerard, was his best friend. The two-year age gap allowed her to dismiss him as 'the kid'. It upset him because he had a secret crush on her and was too embarrassed to admit it. Instead, he publicly chided her for trying to look pretty, and that caught the attention of her older brother Willie Joe, whose moniker was WJ. He was an astute young man, who would later set up his own tailoring business on the Falls Road. For some time, he had observed young Gerry Dillon's fascination with his sister and realised he was besotted with her.

'He who slights the meadow buys the corn,' WJ told him one day, using a proverb that went to the heart of the issue.

A short time later, my father plucked up the courage to ask my mother for a date. She turned him down, saying, 'You're just a kid. I wouldn't be seen dead going out with you till you're eighteen.'

While she genuinely thought Gerry Dillon was too young, her rejection of him was punishment for the times he loudly made fun of her appearance. He took the put down in his stride and continued to arrive at her home every evening on the pretext of looking for her brother. She never wavered in her refusal to go on a date with him until the evening of his eighteenth birthday. They went to a local ice cream parlour and briefly to a dance studio. Decades later, my mother joked with me that there was 'no hanky-panky' during their first date, and he behaved like a 'scared kid'.

In 1943, my mum had just celebrated her twentieth birthday when cancer struck her father. To help her mother financially she worked in a factory, making items for the war effort. Her father died when she turned twenty-one, and she married my father four years later in 1948. They spent the first six months of their marriage living with my grandmother Clarke and her sisters, Bridget and Sarah. They then rented No 7 Ross Place, across the street from No 4. They were in their new home three months when my twin, Damien, and I were born. It was 2 June 1949, and my father was 24 years old. In his brother Vincent's eyes, his days as 'the fancy-free kid' were over though he didn't quite know it. According to Vincent, my father did not realise how living opposite his mother-in-law and her sisters made him the focus of their scrutiny.

He began training as a watchmaker and lived a quiet life until he joined colleagues one evening after work, returning home drunk. My mother was emotionally devastated. Perhaps suppressed memories of her late father's drunkenness and abusive ways were suddenly unlocked. She ran across the street into No 4 and began crying uncontrollably. Her mother decided this was a marital problem that had to be nipped in the bud and walked straight to my grandmother Dillon's, a mere five minutes away in Lesson Street. Granny Dillon was a tall, dark-haired woman in her early forties who gave birth to my father when she was twenty. Her name was Frances, and her children called her Francie as though she were their sister or friend. Sadly, she would die of cancer on her forty-ninth birthday, five years after I came into the world. She possessed a gentle personality and was highly respected as a caring mother. When she learned her newly married son was drunk she was horrified.

The two grandmothers made their way to 4 Ross Place where they drank tea and discussed strategy. According to my uncle Vincent, they let my father 'stew in his own juices for several hours until he was sober enough to take his medicine'. The medicine took the form of a long lecture about life and his responsibilities as a husband and father of twin boys. My father later admitted, 'Awaiting the arrival of my mother and mother-in-law was punishment enough.' He said he felt like Kafka, facing the wrath of two determined women. In Kafka's case it was his lovers, Stella and Vanessa. In my father's, it was two traditional Catholic grandmothers who knew my mother was pregnant with her third child.

They must have scared the daylights out of him because he joined the Pioneers, a Catholic lay organisation of men who pledged not to drink alcohol so they could be closer to God. He also became a member of the Society of St Vincent De Paul, dedicated to doing charitable works and helping the poor and sick. My father was recognisable as a Pioneer by a heart-shaped pin displayed on his jacket lapel, signifying dedication to the Sacred Heart of Jesus. For a young man who had never been troublesome or fond of alcohol, being a Pioneer was a mammoth step towards a more conservative lifestyle – a step he later considered served him well, as he fathered eight more children. With such a large family there was no room for alcohol or for 'good times with the boys', he would later say. His decision to 'take the pledge' provided my mother with reassurance he would behave himself. Twenty years later, however, he put the Pioneer pin in a drawer and began a love affair with French wine, a passion he shared with my mother until her death.

My childhood memories of my mother can best be summed up with the words, 'dedication' and 'love'. She was dedicated to her growing family and to her Church, and she loved her husband, children and God with much the same intensity. She had an ability to describe situations and people with exactitude and wit, allied to a peculiar idiomatic use of language and imagery, a talent I may have learned from her. Her ability to find humour in the midst of hardship never ceased to amuse and intrigue me. With ten of us children sharing one bedroom, she would joke with friends, saying she, 'stacked us in beds and cots like a deck of cards'. Her command of language, coming from a young woman with little formal education, was impressive. When a friend suggested she must surely be proud of the success of her ten children, she replied, 'Yes I'm proud of all of them. But some have the spark of genius, and the rest have ignition trouble.'

In my formative years, I was very close to her even though my father watched over my school homework and took me for long walks over Belfast's Cave Hill and in the Divis and Black Mountains. I saw in her a gentleness and an inner strength I rarely witnessed in other women later in life. She managed to maintain a youthful spirit, matched with boundless energy. Twenty-four hours after the birth of one of my sisters, she was on her hands and knees scrubbing the floors of No 7. Her greatest joy was her belief she was married to the 'best-looking guy in Belfast'. She insisted he was the spitting image of Cary Grant. With any saved money, she paid her brother, Willie Joe, to make tweed jackets, which my father wore until they were threadbare.

She never offered me an explanation for her yearly pregnancies. But after the birth of two of my sisters, my father felt it was time to bring me and my twin, Damien, then aged seven, into his confidence. He took us for ice cream and it became an annual ritual I later noted in a journal:

THE DAYS OF ICE CREAM AND MYSTERIES

There was nothing mother ever said to encourage questions. She had the same rounded belly and ungainly walk, but we knew something was happening. Father, too, was silent until it was time for ice cream. It always seemed like summer when he clasped our hands, dragging us into his longer strides. A secret was in his dark features and in the heart beating steadily behind his woollen shirt and tweed jacket. He ate his ice cream without ever licking it. 'Your mother's going to have another baby, and its God's will,' he would mumble. God and my mother! It was too miraculous to contemplate. And what of my father's will? I couldn't quite formulate that question in the days of ice cream and mysteries. I would have to find out for myself.

My parents were deeply attached to Catholicism and a strict observance of its rules. I have often asked myself whether their devotion, which bordered on the obsessive, was a response to deep convictions or the proximity of our home to St Peter's pro-cathedral. The whole family attended Mass and Communion every morning. I firmly believe she thought it elevated us religiously to a cut above the rest.

'A family that prays together stays together,' my mother would assure us, restating the Catholic Church mantra of the time. Sadly, it would prove not to be the case. When we got older, many of us drifted apart, some of us never to speak again because of perceived slights and inheritance disputes.

One of the curious things at that time was the excessive amount of time my father spent in Fr Armstrong's confessional every Friday evening. Subsequently, I learned any confession with Fr Armstrong had the potential to be a lengthy experience, more akin to an interrogation. He liked to talk and was curious about the minutiae of the lives of his penitents. As an altar boy, I had first-hand experience of his eccentricities, or more pointedly his obsessive-compulsive behaviour, especially when he handled the bread and wine during Mass. Later, I would recall these early experiences with Fr Armstrong:

THE ALTAR BOY

I poured water into Christ's blood as the chalice turned 180 degrees in Father Armstrong's gnarled fingers. He talked into it before holding it aloft, waiting for its energy to find the rest of us. When he wiped it clean, not a speck of the Body or Blood was left behind. I carried it into the sacristy, its coldness expelling warmth in my tiny hands, terrified to look inside for fear a voice would speak to me from Calvary.

When I walked to my grandmother's in No 4, I would gaze up at the twin spires of St Peter's towering over the Lower Falls. I asked my uncle, WJ, why the spires were so tall, and he jokingly replied they were there to remind Protestants in the nearby Shankill area we Catholics existed. Protestants, I felt, needed no reminder since there was a Protestant church fifty yards from my home on nearby Albert Street.

It still puzzles me why St Peter's needed such towering spires in a tiny area like the Lower Falls. It was perhaps as much a political as it was a religious statement in a city where two communities shared a competitive fervour. When I was seven years old, I developed a fear of those sometimes dark, foreboding spires, each capped with a metal cross. On wet days when rain made it hard to see the tops of them, I held my mother's hand tightly on the way into church. My fear was heightened by a large hawk that visited the spires from time to time and left pigeons' carcasses splayed across the church steps.

Most days, my grandmother Clarke's sisters, Sarah and Bridget, sat by the fire in No 4, praying for the 'conversion of Russia from Communism' and for the 'black babies in Africa'. My aunts raised other monies for the Church, believing they would be used to convert 'Communist heathens' in Russia, once a 'God-fearing nation', which had to be restored to the faith.

'Why aren't we praying for the Protestants on the Shankill Road?' I once asked Aunt Bridget.

'We're not!' Her reply was sharp and was intended to blunt my inquisitiveness.

'Why not? Uncle Willie Joe calls them heathens too.'

She fixed me with a disapproving stare before responding. 'You didn't hear right. Your uncle probably called them hooligans, but they are probably heathens as well. Then again, that uncle of yours wouldn't know the difference.'

She briefly allowed herself a smile, thinking my curiosity had been satisfied. But children have a tendency to be persistent.

'Shouldn't we just pray for Protestants to become Catholics?' I asked, somewhat sheepishly.

'No. You see, the difference between Protestants and Communist heathens in Russia is that the Russians were once Catholics, and Our

Lady will return them to the faith. Protestants don't have the faith and never had it.'

'Couldn't we give it to them?'

'Yes, if they were willing to become true converts!' With that she waved a finger at me to be silent as she reached for her beads to mumble a decade of the rosary.

In my youth, I spent a lot of time in my grandmother Clarke's, while my twin preferred to play with friends in the street. My grandmother and her sisters rarely discussed their family history, but I often heard them describing the terrible events of 1920–2 when Catholic and Protestants slaughtered each other in what became known as 'The Pogroms'. My aunts knew families that were murdered in their beds in the dead of night, and decades later their memories of the period still haunted them. Catholics believed their community bore the brunt of 'The Pogroms', but the reality was different. Of the 500 dead in Belfast, approximately 42 per cent were Protestants. Thousands were also injured on both sides, leaving a bitter legacy.

In my youth, I saw a great deal more of my mother's siblings because they visited No 4 when going to or leaving Sunday Mass in St Peter's. I liked St Peter's, but I also had a curious attachment to nearby Clonard Monastery that had a lot to do with my mother's sister, Vera, who lived on Clonard Street. She never seemed to mind when I stopped off on the way to the monastery to ride the rocking horse and play her piano.

Trips with my twin, Damien, to Aunt Vera's took on a special significance after we grew a little older and became conscious of our mother's yearly, unexplained pregnancies. Since no one discussed the origin of life with us, my brother and I had some unusual theories about childbirth. We were particularly fascinated by Aunt Vera's extra-large breasts, which she made no effort to hide. On the contrary, she wore dresses and blouses enhancing her more than ample cleavage. Given we had never seen a woman's breasts, or for that matter a naked female, the sight of Aunt Vera's cleavage was sublime and a little confusing.

After one particular visit, I told Damien I might have solved the mystery of where babies come from – the deep crack between women's 'diddies'. He ridiculed me, saying our cousin, Don O'Rawe, who was two years older than us, had been assured by his mother that babies were born under cabbages. I decided to confront the issue head on.

'What if Aunt Vera bends over some day and a baby falls from the crack between her diddies when we're eating her sandwiches? What are we gonna do then?' I asked my twin.

By the look on his face I knew my question troubled him. The following day, we went to see our cousin Don, and I presented him with my diddies theory. He thought it was hilarious, but nevertheless insisted that I take him to Aunt Vera's so he could have a closer look at her bosom. Damien agreed, and off we went to her place. We sat on the floor, knowing a lower elevation would provide Don with an unobstructed view of her cleavage when she bent over to give us treats. When she bent down to hand Don a biscuit, he let out such an audible gasp she asked him if he was troubled with wind. He shook his head and stared at the biscuit, unable to find the strength to eat it. He still had hold of it when we thanked her for the snack and said our goodbyes.

On the way home, Don came up with a piece of logic that made perfect sense at the time. Women with bigger 'diddies', he insisted, had bigger cracks between them and therefore gave birth to bigger babies. He had been truly sold on my theory, and I was thrilled. For all my prurient interest in Aunt Vera's bosom, she was one of my favourite aunts because she was kind and colourful.

TWO

Ancestral Eccentricities

My mother's older brother, John, fascinated me most. He was tall and bald, with peculiar, deep indentations on each side of his forehead. He wore wire-rimmed spectacles and resembled the renowned Irish writer, Samuel Beckett. He chain-smoked unfiltered Park Drive cigarettes, chewed gum, made long speeches no one seemed to listen to and drank tea from a large mug. When adding sugar to his tea, he loudly announced each teaspoon of sugar, only stopping when he reached ten. He claimed to like tea when it was strong enough for him to stand on it. He would lift me high in his arms and give me two gentle pecks on my cheeks, exclaiming, 'Jelly and custard!' My twin and I got the jelly-and-custard treatment each time he saw us.

He was thirty-six but looked older than his years and seemed somewhat detached from the world around him. He frequently used combinations of complex words and quoted extensively from the writings of Marx, Lenin and Engels. While those names sounded exotic and foreign to me, he also talked a lot about a certain James Connolly and, because Connolly was an Irish name, I assumed he was referring to a friend or neighbour. Years would pass before I understood the Connolly in question was the Irish revolutionary socialist executed by the British for his role in the 1916 Rising in Dublin.

On our eighth birthday, Uncle John took Damien and me on our first Sunday morning stroll along the Falls Road to Milltown Cemetery, Belfast's main Catholic burial ground. The trip soon became a weekly routine, beginning before midday Mass and ending two hours later. Every time we walked through Milltown's heavy wooden gates and arched stone entrance, Uncle John would point out the oldest headstones. Many were granite or marble, from 50 to 100 years old, commemorating prominent Belfast Catholics, whose wealth came from bookmaking and alcohol. In contrast, the Protestant City Cemetery, a short distance away, had more ornate headstones, honouring people who had amassed wealth from linen mills, shipbuilding, land ownership and politics. Catholics were essentially second-class citizens and their opportunities to generate wealth and move up the social ladder were restricted to a few business models and trades.

After inspecting several small tombs near the entrance, we visited some family graves, beginning with the Carsons. He never prayed but insisted we say an Our Father followed by three Hail Marys at each family member's grave. He always showed us the Republican Plot and begin a familiar rant about the failings of Irish Republicanism, which he claimed was now dominated by 'cowards' and 'dog-collared bastards'; the latter term he used for priests. For him, James Connolly was the only true Irishman, who would have transformed Ireland into a Socialist Workers Republic if the British hadn't 'murdered' him. Instead, his death led to the emergence of a narrow-minded, Catholic Nationalist Ireland.

On the journey home, our uncle's speeches became more intense and rambling. We never interrupted his tirades, believing they were part of his personality. Minutes from home, his ranting always tapered off, and he became jovial and funny. It seemed like an alarm went off in his head, telling him it was time to revert to his other persona. He would take a rounded bubblegum, known as a 'Bubbly', from his pocket, tear it into two equal pieces and give one to each of us. It was his idea of a bribe, and it worked because we never told our parents or our grandmother about his odd behaviour.

In those early years, I never heard my parents criticise my uncle or make fun of him. I was too young to realise just how different he was from the other adults in my life, but I trusted and loved him. He had idiosyncrasies and obsessions but wasn't sectarian in a society ridden with religious prejudice. He insisted his political views were based on socialist principles that appealed to Catholics, Protestants and dissenters alike. Much of what he said did not make sense in my childhood.

I was unaware he had once been a prominent IRA activist. Like many Belfast Catholics of his generation, he was a teenager when the IRA secretly recruited him. He fell under the influence of older men with a history of political violence, and it took years for his parents to learn of his IRA affiliation. By then, he was too deeply attached to the organisation to heed the pleas of his family to leave it. His mentors, to whom he pledged total commitment, were IRA veterans from both sides of the Irish border. They treated him to political lectures and trained him in guerrilla warfare. Irish Republicanism so dominated his life, he ignored the effects of police scrutiny on his parents and siblings. It mattered little to him when the police launched regular midnight raids on his home. He was holed up in a safe house somewhere in Belfast. Sometimes, he watched the raids from the bedroom of an elderly female's home across the street.

In January 1939, while Britain faced the prospect of a war in Europe, the IRA planned to strike at its old enemy – England. It was a reckless and unjustified endeavour driven by bitterness and a crazy belief the British could be forced to abandon Northern Ireland. The IRA leadership decided the most successful strategy was to bomb Britain into submission. When the British received an ultimatum to leave Ireland or face the consequences, they dismissed it as farcical. But the danger was real. To the British government's shock and horror, bombs exploded in eight major English cities, including London and Liverpool, on 17 January at 6 a.m. Units from the IRA's Belfast Brigade took responsibility for some of the explosions and for many more that followed.

The bombing campaign was ultimately a failure. It antagonised many Irish in Britain, who soon found themselves under suspicion and ostracised by their English friends and neighbours. Good police work led to the rounding up of IRA operatives throughout Britain, and my uncle John was among them. Due to lack of evidence, he was deported to Dublin after he claimed Irish citizenship. The IRA promptly sent him north to re-join its Belfast Brigade. He was quickly re-arrested in a massive round-up of IRA activists, sympathisers and left-wing trade unionists, all of whom were imprisoned without trial on an old naval vessel, the *Al Rawdah*, anchored in Belfast Lough.

Two years later, he was transferred to Crumlin Road Prison. While there, he protested his confinement without trial, refusing to vacate his cell for the preferred safety of the open yard during German air raids. He tried to encourage other IRA prisoners to join him, but they refused. Prison warders, the majority of whom were Protestant and anti-IRA, vented their anger at his rule breaking by assaulting him in his cell. Their brutality left a lasting impression on my mother, who accompanied my grandmother during prison visits. They were not permitted to see him after beatings. Instead they were handed his bloody clothing and told to take it home and wash it.

By the time Uncle John left prison in the spring of 1944, nothing remained of the young ideologue of the pre-war era. He returned to No 4 Ross Place deeply depressed and rarely went outdoors. Before long, he began denouncing the IRA, its Belfast leadership, the Catholic Church in Ireland and the Vatican. His anti-Catholic rhetoric puzzled his family, but they weren't unduly concerned by his antipathy towards the IRA. Belfast's IRA leaders knew all about John's terrible prison treatment, yet none of them visited him after his release.

As the months passed, his bitterness increased. He would look out from the living room window into the street, hurling abuse at the priests of the parish and the IRA. Somehow, all the knowledge he had acquired from reading socialist literature and attending political lectures in prison transformed him from a Catholic Nationalist into an atheistic socialist. His disintegrating personality also made him a disgruntled and angry individual. Ironically, his striking political transformation was a reflection of a similar metamorphosis, which infected the IRA less than a decade later. In the 1950s, the organisation transitioned into two factions: one advocated traditional Irish Republicanism, while the other promoted a Connolly brand of socialism with some Marxist-Leninism included for good measure. That metamorphosis within Republicanism was particularly manifest in prison debates in the mid-1950s when Republican veterans expressed disillusionment with the IRA's attachment to Irish Catholic Nationalism. I believe, however, the genesis of that political divergence can be linked to an earlier period when my uncle and a small number of Republicans emerged from prison articulating what many Catholics branded a 'godless philosophy'. In my uncle's case, his newfound socialist ideals sounded like a reasonable alternative to Republicanism when he spoke about it in short bursts. Over time, the bursts lengthened and his mind gave way to depression and a mental chaos exemplified by obsessions with the Pope, the IRA and the British Royal Family.

My grandmother Clarke blamed her son's depression and 'craziness' on the beatings he received to the head from prison warders. After my grandfather Clarke died of cancer in May 1944, his wife and her sisters, Bridget and Sarah, could not cope with John's noisy outbursts, which sometimes lasted the whole day. Frustrated, they turned to Dr Gray, the family's physician. He regretfully told them he could not do much for her son and referred him to a psychiatrist. Had Uncle John been alive today, he would have simply been medicated. Sadly, he lived in an era when the world of psychiatry had a horrific solution to mental illnesses – the pre-frontal lobotomy. This was the cause of the two peculiar indents on Uncle John's skull, which caught my attention as a child. The lobotomy left my uncle worse off mentally and increased his paranoia.

Months after doctors performed the procedure, Uncle John returned home without medication. Three years later, he entered my life as the 'custard and jelly' uncle. Sadly, our relationship was short-lived because he was cruelly snatched from my life one Sunday afternoon, following a trip to the cemetery. I watched terrified from our doorway as two male nurses in white linen coats dragged him out of No 4 in a strait jacket. They bundled him into the back of a van with metal grills on the windows and slammed the doors shut to silence his cries. When I asked my father why my uncle was being taken from us, he claimed he had threatened my grandmother, and it was better for him to be in a secure place where he would be properly looked after.

Doctors confined him to Purdysburn, a hospital on the Saintfield Road outside Belfast, where he had been institutionalised years earlier. The facility, also known as the Villa Colony, had opened in 1895 as an asylum for the 'lunatic poor'. For the next three years, two Sundays per month, my father, Damien and I visited my uncle. We brought him unfiltered Park Drive and Woodbine cigarettes, a packet of Virginia tobacco, a bottle of lemonade, several containers of cigarette-lighter fuel and six Bubblies.

I can still recall my first visit. Men and women wandered aimlessly throughout the grounds, some talking loudly to themselves the way Uncle John did on our Milltown trips. A few stared at us, wild-eyed, but bowed their heads when we returned their gaze. I stayed close to my father, fearing we would never get out of there alive. He said the strangers were like our uncle and meant us no harm. We found Uncle John in a large brick building that smelled of urine and disinfectant. He was thrilled to see us and lost no time filling his pockets with the gifts we brought him.

'Can't be too careful,' he smiled, dutifully concealing cigarettes inside the lining of his jacket. 'They're all nuts in here, and they'd steal the eyes outa yer head.'

He was funny and lucid for an hour until he lapsed into a familiar rant about the IRA, the Pope and the Queen of England. After two years of Sunday visits, it became clear his continued confinement angered him. He talked of plans for a new life, stressing no one had the legal right to keep him locked up. He declared his intention to settle in The Irish Free State, promising to make his home in Dublin or Ballina. The way he spoke implied it was going to happen soon. My parents and family insiders dismissed his plans as 'wishful thinking', pointing out he could be released only if my grandmother signed the necessary legal papers and she was unlikely to do that because she was too frail to cope with him.

It shocked everyone when he walked out of Purdysburn three months later and vanished from sight. Local police launched a manhunt but abandoned it after forty-eight hours. Ten days later, my grandmother received a postcard from Dublin with 'I'm free in a free part of Ireland' written on the back of it. A letter followed in which he revealed he had simply 'strolled out of The Burn' and took a train to Dublin, outside British jurisdiction.

The most astonishing aspect of the escape was his legal knowledge. While in Purdysburn, he discovered if he could live for six months outside the institution without committing an offence he could not be institutionalised again against his will. The only way he could do that was to leave British jurisdiction for that period of time. The money for the trip to Dublin came from cigarettes Uncle John sold at a discount rate to the 'screws'.

Seven months after his escape, he did the unthinkable and returned to Belfast. Right away, he travelled to Purdysburn, dressed in a second-hand tweed suit and a pair of leather brogues. In the main office, he brazenly demanded payment for the three years he toiled in Purdysburn's vegetable gardens. It was not a large sum, but he informed the staff he was entitled to it, and, being fully aware of his civil rights, would take them to court if they did not pay him. He even produced a letter from the Irish police confirming he had been living lawfully in Dublin for over six months. He correctly pointed out he had proven he could function as a useful member of society. Neither the screws nor psychiatrists had the right to detain or institutionalise him, he declared. Having delivered his demands, he made a little tour of his usual haunts in the asylum and shook hands with patients he liked.

'The inmates thought my return was second only to the Resurrection of Jesus Christ,' he later told me.

Within a week of Uncle John's return, the institution paid what they owed him, and he was back in No 4 with his mother. In the years following, he received no offers of treatment from medical professionals. Nevertheless, he functioned as a useful member of society, working occasional jobs and living with his mother's sister, Bridget, after his mother passed away in 1962.

In the mid-1960s, he made several trips to see relatives in the US and had no qualms about staying at the YMCA in New York. He also worked as a porter in London hotels for three years to finance multiple trips to East Germany and Russia. In 1972, when I was a young journalist with the *Belfast Telegraph*, I received a postcard from Moscow displaying Lenin's corpse in a sarcophagus at the Lenin Mausoleum. On the back of the card was written: 'Dear nephew Martin, at last I've seen Lenin. Isn't he a lovely corpse? I'm now off to East Berlin. See you soon.' He signed his name in Gaelic.

I was a bit concerned about the card, knowing some Loyalists working in the *Telegraph* might associate anything from Russia with the Official IRA whom they regarded as a bunch of Marxists. I mentioned it to my uncle when we next met, and he fixed me with a wide grin.

'You missed the point,' he told me. 'There were revolutionaries in Ireland long before these Provisionals, who are now claiming to be our saviours. In fact, you might be surprised just how many Protestants working beside you in the *Belfast Telegraph* are descendants of the Presbyterian rebels of 1798. There's more than a little revolutionary spark in the Protestant and Dissenter traditions, you know.'

My love for my uncle and his eccentricities made me conscious since childhood of the importance of being tolerant and compassionate. Too often, I witnessed my contemporaries dismiss my uncle as crazy, dumb or dangerous. On the contrary, he was funny, eccentric and insightful and never presented a threat to me or any strangers. That did not excuse what he may or may not have done while he was in the IRA. When I look back at his life, I find him to be a striking example of a political romantic, seduced like so many of his generation by tales of gunmen, heroes and assurances that force alone would bring about a United Ireland.

His older brother, Willie Joe, or WJ, was one of the notable eccentrics of his generation in West Belfast. He was a tailor, who learned his skills at his father's knee in the back room of No 4. After his father died, WJ moved the family tailoring business into a shop 200 yards away on the Falls Road. He had inherited his father's West of Ireland flair for colourful language and through the years developed a keen interest in the history of Ireland. He insisted on using the term, 'the history of Ireland' because, according to him, it encompassed two traditions on the island, namely the Catholic Nationalists and Protestant Unionists, whereas 'Irish history', by its terminology, was restricted to material written only to glorify Nationalist culture. History, he once told me, required from honest historians a firm degree of balance and detachment. He was fond of quoting from the works of both historical camps and loved expressing his personal political thoughts in verse, which he read to friends and customers alike. It was rare for him not to have at least one of his latest poems in his jacket whenever customers entered his shop.

By the time I was eight, he was a successful tailor with wealthy Protestants and Free Masons for clientele. He drove a Jaguar, and in the working-class Lower Falls neighbourhood his display of wealth made him a celebrity. He often stood at the door of his shop, shouting greetings to everyone who passed, and if a person stopped to exchange pleasantries, WJ reached into his jacket and proceeded, without encouragement, to read his latest poem about a long-forgotten episode in Irish–British history or a current international event. The reason he attracted a lot of attention was his business slogan, 'Tailor to the Intelligent Man', which appeared in local newspaper advertisements. He even had it emblazoned on the gable wall of his house. If you ask me, the slogan should have read 'Intelligent Tailor to the Ordinary Man', but his version denoted his natural wit.

Aside from tailoring, WJ loved gardening, cooking and all things French. By chance, an elderly Frenchman living in Belfast was one of his clients, and through him he learned to speak French fluently. I was twelve when he first took me to his rented, whitewashed cottage in the townland of Raholp about forty miles from Belfast. WJ called it 'St Patrick's country' because Patrick settled in nearby Saul on arriving in Ireland. At the rear of the cottage, WJ planted a large garden where he grew vegetables and herbs used mainly in French cuisine. He was the first person I ever saw cook with wine, and he used it liberally. His early influence encouraged me to take a keen interest in French cooking and French wines.

Unfortunately, his role as 'Tailor to the Intelligent Man' ended all too soon in the 1970s when the Troubles reached into the Falls area. He was forced to close his business because his Protestant clients, who had contributed significantly to his livelihood for over two decades, were too frightened to enter a Catholic district controlled by the IRA. He opened an ice cream parlour on the borderline of Catholic and Protestant enclaves on the Springfield Road, but mobs soon fought pitched battles near his new business, and he had to close it too. As he got older, his years of weekends spent cooking elaborate meals in his country home came to an end. Nevertheless, until he died in his mid-seventies, he continued to cook French meals and to tend a small vegetable garden in his West Belfast home.

The Clarke clan had a big influence on me in my childhood and early-teen years but so too did the Dillon family, which I believe raised the eccentric stakes even higher. My grandfather, Patrick Dillon, and his seven siblings lived at 26 Lower Clonard Street, not far from the Clarkes. It would be cumbersome for the reader if I referred to my grandfather's siblings as Great Uncle Gerard, who became a famous Irish artist, or Great Aunt Mollie. I shall simply call them Uncle Gerard and Aunt Molly, as I did in my childhood.

Apart from memories of Patrick Dillon, whose love of fishing I inherited, my most vibrant memories are of his younger siblings, Joe, Molly and especially Gerard, the baby of the family born in 1916. Their mother was, by all accounts, a formidable woman steeped in a strict Catholic tradition, yet she allowed them to be nonconformist in their social behaviour and fashion. She encouraged them to love drama, music and dance and ran a little theatre in their tiny home in the Lower Falls. Neighbours regarded them as 'odd' or 'strange' children because they were constantly 'in costume', delivering Shakespearean monologues, singing Irish ballads or dressing up as Arabs and clowns. Uncle Gerard told me his mother produced some of her 'little dramas' outside their house and embarrassed him by insisting he play female roles. He never forgot the first time he walked outdoors dressed as a girl. He became a laughing stock for the boys in the neighbourhood.

My great-grandmother ran the Dillon household, and she dominated her husband as she did her children. Her husband, especially late in life, was a gentle, almost withdrawn figure, who sat in a corner of the living room reading the newspaper from cover to cover, trying to appear invisible. He and his wife did not see eye to eye about most things, and their bitter disputes were political, often at her instigation. She was an Irish Republican, who liked to voice her distaste for all things British, whereas he was proud of his service as a British soldier in the Boer War. He cared nothing for talk of a United Ireland and told her the IRA was full of murderers and criminals. He would say if he had his way he would hang them all. When friends arrived at the house and he was absent, they concluded he had gone to the local pub to avoid a tongue lashing from his strident wife.

The artist, George Campbell, who regularly visited 26 Lower Clonard Street when my Uncle Gerard was young, told me my great-grandfather had been a heavy drinker and an abusive husband in the early years of his marriage. As he got older, he mellowed and frequently expressed regret for his past sins. Life had not been easy for my great-grandmother. In the early 1920s, women had no rights, and too many husbands abused their wives. Wives had virtually no recourse to the law, and their priests and ministers turned a blind eye to the issue. Gerard put his thoughts about this on paper years later:

According to my mother, any woman who did her duties and kept her dignity in spite of the hammerings her husband gave her was a saint. 'That wee woman's a regular saint,' she would say about a woman who had just left the house. 'She'll get a big crown for it when she dies.' She was talking as much to herself as to us. 'Another woman wouldn't stick it, she'd just up and fly away, but she'll be rewarded. God is good.' It was difficult for me to imagine all these 'wee women' as saints. I could not see some of them in crowns – some of them were ugly and wore shawls, and didn't comb their hair and snuffed and wouldn't suit crowns at all. I thought and thought how could you be sure you would become a saint when you died? The only thing was to grow up a woman, get yourself a bad husband, never neglect Mass, Confession and Holy Communion, and have loads of children. That was according to my mother. But how could I grow up to be a woman?

His sister, Molly, was only eight when Gerard was born, but she quickly saw herself as his protector after she dropped him on his head one day while playfully tossing him in the air. At first, she thought she had killed him. But when she discovered he was alive, she formed a special bond with him. She claimed she cared so much about him that she had an urge to tell the nun in charge of her school she couldn't love God without first loving her 'little Gerard'.

She and Gerard were very attached to their sister Teresa, who suffered from tuberculosis. Teresa never left the house and lay in a bed near a window from which she could see her siblings performing their dramatic roles on the pavement and roadway. She was twelve when she died, and her passing forged a unique bond between Gerard and his sisters, Molly and Annie. This closeness to his sisters, rather than to his four brothers, encouraged boys his age to regard him as effeminate. However, his dislike for the rough and tumble of male play may also have helped shape that perception of him. In some respects, he resembled his older brothers, Joe and Vincent, who were both effete and uninterested in sports. In contrast, the two eldest boys, Patrick, my grandfather, and John, were as tough as any their age. They joined the British Army, and John was a professional soldier for most of his working life.

I first met Aunt Molly when I was sixteen. She stayed at our house in Chestnut Gardens. I was struck by her masculinity and her love of tweed suits. Within a week of her arrival, she had changed the names of my seven sisters. It was not an uncommon thing to do in the Dillon clan because Joe had changed his name to Brian when he first moved to London, claiming Brian sounded more Irish than Joe. For Molly, the Catholic names of four of my sisters, Imelda, Attracta, Bernadette and Ursula, were 'common, much too Catholic and inappropriate'. She renamed them Barbara, Amanda, Samantha and Jane. When my aunt announced she was returning to London a month into her visit, my mother was relieved.

My earliest memory of meeting Uncle Joe dates back to 1958, when I was nine and he was fifty-five. He had been back in Belfast for a decade, having lived in London, and was in his celibate, churchgoing state. He called his Dachshund, Heine, his constant companion, and the small family Dillon house at 26 Lower Clonard Street was his home. I formed a close friendship with my uncle and regularly ran errands for him. He was slim and dapper, and sported a year-round tan that I now believe was as much due to make-up as his love of sunbathing through spring and summer. Indoors, he wore an expensive silk dressing gown with matching pyjamas and slippers, or an embroidered smoking jacket and well-pressed trousers. His rounded, half-rimmed gold spectacles were as well polished as his bald head. My most vivid memories are of entering his house to the sounds of opera or classical music playing on a wind-up gramophone and the smell of ground coffee brewing in an Italian percolator. His daily routine included a walk with Heine round the drab streets of the Lower Falls and the nearby Dunville Park. His gait was as eccentric as his personality, and he minced rather than walked, always dressed in a finely tailored suit with polished, laced shoes. Looking back, I suspect he would not have been out of place on the Boulevard Saint-Michel in James Joyce's day. He had very few paintings by his brother, Gerard, in his small 'kitchen house', but the blind on his downstairs window was a painted canvas – a gift from Gerard. I can recall Uncle Gerard arriving one summer day to wallpaper the tiny living room and staircase. He completed the task by using watercolours to draw heads and abstract shapes on the wallpaper.

Owing partially to his dream of becoming a professional singer, Joe had moved to London when he was younger. While he'd been blessed with a superb tenor voice, he lacked the money to pay for classical training, and his ambition quickly evaporated. Still, his love of opera brought him into contact with creative, bohemian types and provided him with a busy social life. This allowed him to live freely as a gay man – something he kept secret from his family back home. Ironically, after he returned to the family home in Belfast years later, he had a falling out with Gerard when they discovered they loved the same man – a prominent, married pianist. Initially, the pianist had a secret affair with Joe for several years until he met Gerard at a party Joe was hosting, and he fell madly in love with him. The pianist dumped Joe and began an affair with Gerard that lasted for a decade. The pianist was Joe's last lover for reasons he never explained.

But other more compelling reasons may have prompted him to change his life so drastically, to the point he became celibate and a regular churchgoer. His health was declining, and he was obsessed with his mortality. He feared the dark and began a pattern of staying up till four in the morning and sleeping until midday. In some respects, I believe the early religious indoctrination he received from his mother found him again and convinced him Catholicism would bring him peace. Further, celibacy undertaken as a penance would save him from God's retribution. The man, who once considered the priesthood, was undertaking the priestly requirement of a life without sex.

Of course that metamorphosis was nowhere on the horizon earlier in his life when his sister Molly joined him and Gerard in London, saying she, too, needed to escape the parochialism of their native Belfast. She chose London primarily to fulfil her dream of becoming a female underwear designer.

By any stretch of the imagination, the siblings made a strange trio. Joe was lean, sophisticated and high-camp, while Gerard was small but robust and slightly effeminate. Molly was very butch and loved wearing tailored men's suits. Much to Gerard's dismay, she still regarded herself as his guardian and emotionally smothered him with her forceful personality. In the late 1940s, after their parents died, Joe declared he was tired of the London scene and returned home.

THREE

Gerard Dillon:
The Making of an Artist

In his early teens, Gerard was highly influenced by Molly and Joe, two siblings determined to pursue creative careers. As a boy, Joe had expressed a desire to be a priest, but in his teens he chose instead to pursue a career as an opera singer. Molly dreamed of being a costume designer and Gerard, who loved drawing and painting, had ambitions to become an artist. Gerard had to settle for a job as a house painter, but he confided to Molly that it enabled him to learn to use paint and colours.

By then, he was a shy 18 year old with a gentle personality and a sense of humour that hid a deep secret. He was gay and troubled by awful feelings of guilt, stemming mostly from a religion that branded homosexual acts mortal sins – the kind of sins that would send him straight to Hell. In an effort to deal with his emotional pain and apparent 'sinfulness', he naïvely turned to the Catholic Church for help. During confession in Clonard Monastery, he sought absolution for harbouring deep emotional desires for young men. The priest angrily told him it was not enough to confess his sins. If he did not change his ways, he would burn in Hell for all eternity because his desires were 'unnatural'. When Gerard explained he could not change how he felt, the priest threatened to physically eject him from the confessional. He warned Gerard that he could be excommunicated. The experience left Gerard disillusioned with Catholicism, and he decided churchgoing was no longer for him.

Feeling trapped on all sides, he followed his brother, Joe, to London where he worked as a house painter and undertook a range of construction jobs, sometimes labouring alongside Joe. It wasn't long before Gerard learned his older brother was also gay. But it was a topic they didn't discuss, and Joe denied Gerard access to his gay circle. Gerard later confided in George Campbell that he felt Joe did not want to be responsible for him. Joe was either reluctant to encourage Gerard's homosexuality or feared Gerard would outshine him in his social milieu. The latter was probably closer to the truth because one of Joe's boyfriends left him for Gerard soon after they were introduced. The loss, or 'steal' as Joe saw it, hurt him deeply and encouraged him to build a fence round his private life.

As soon as Joe returned home to Belfast, Molly and Gerard moved into the same building. They had separate apartments because Gerard wanted his privacy. Life near Molly turned out to be more than he bargained for, and the small price he paid her for his apartment cost him his privacy. Since he was her tenant, she felt she could arrive in his place unannounced, pour herself a drink and sit down. If he was relaxing with a friend in the garden, she would often open her window upstairs and eavesdrop on their conversation. She might make obtuse observations about a bird or a strange cat on the garden wall as a way of inserting herself into their discourse.

Eventually, he managed to escape her clutches by renting an apartment in a quiet, upscale part of London. It gave him more privacy, but it did not reverse his tendency to conduct many of his sexual encounters in the shadows. He also continued to work hard, mostly doing odd jobs. Though he didn't have much money, he saved what he could to buy paints and canvasses and to travel to the West of Ireland, a place he fell in love with on his first visit there in 1944. After experiencing the Blitz of London, the exquisite landscape of Ireland's rugged west captivated him.

On 13 October 1944, he wrote a letter to Madge Connolly, a friend in London, containing illustrations. It is a letter I treasure. In it he described a trip he made to Inishmore, one of the Aran Islands, with his friend, the artist George Campbell:

Well pet, I got to the Aran Islands for three weeks – my God it was the most glorious holiday I've ever had, I think. What a change away from the world, complete and absolute peace, living a very natural, almost primitive life from day to day, not knowing what day of the week it is, hearing no news except a scrap when the boat arrived from Galway once a week … I painted life on Inishmore and had there good luck to sell two watercolours to visitors to the island. It helped me along. We stayed with Pat Mullen who has a lovely house on Frenchman's beach. He has plenty of books naturally, and some lovely records – the New World Symphony – lots of Beethoven, Brahms, Sibelius and others and scores and scores of Irish dance music and ballads. We had a few dances in Pat's during our stay. It was not unusual for Pat to come home at 12.30 a.m. and drag us out of bed to have a dance – bringing along with him a young island girl. There is no woman in the Mullen house – just Pat and his son, PJ, who is a male edition of Barbara. He is great fun and was a wonderful companion, very simple and childlike – with a wonderful sense of humour. He is absolutely unspoiled tho' he has been in the Merchant Navy.

There was a genuine innocence in the way Gerard described dancing in the early hours to recordings of Irish music. It was something he inherited from his childhood. He liked nothing better than a traditional Irish get-together with music and people reciting passages from their favourite plays. All his life, he had a love for Irish folk ballads and classical music. It was a passion he shared with his brother, Joe, and with George Campbell, who played guitar like a true flamenco musician. In another part of the same 1944 letter, he explained why the West attracted him:

Travelling nowadays is the only drawback. It takes the train (a 3rd rate train too, very uncomfortable) 6 to 7 hours from Dublin to Galway – and later it took the Steamer nine and a half hours from Galway to Inishmore. Of course it was a wonderful experience. They (the islanders) were getting ready for the yearly fair in Galway. The steamer stopped at Inishmore first because it cannot go into the coast because the water is too shallow. So it was wonderful to see the huge Aran men rowing those very fragile curraghs out to the boat – two men rowing and one at the back swimming with a cow – holding on to its horns – poor cow looked so pathetic being dragged through the waves. Then a big rope was placed round their bellies and they were hoisted on board – then another and another. The curraghs came as quickly as they could and no sooner was a cow on board than off they went to make room for another curragh and another cow. And the excitement of the men all shouting to one another in Irish. It was like a foreign country indeed – and their queer mode of dress. Then the same performance at Inishmann (an adjoining Aran island). Some of the Aran men and women came aboard with their belongings to go to the Fair at Galway.

There was a terrific bit of excitement at Inishmann when everything was on board and all the curraghs had gone back but one. It overturned with one man in it and the sea was very high. It looked like the end of it as he was washed away to the back of the steamer, a long way off. These men live in the sea and by the sea, yet they cannot swim. He kept cool and held an oar under each arm – so it kept him up on top. The islanders on board started to keen (wail) and cry in despair, calling loudly to the island where the curraghs had gone back. Then there was a wonderful race by other curraghmen out to rescue him, which they did. So the steamer sailed on to Inishmore. The first few days we felt strange in Pat's because he didn't expect us until the end of September. So we did the next best thing – we looked after ourselves with PJ's help. The islands are desolate – all rock – small, very small fields and stone walls and terrific grey cliffs facing the outer Atlantic – 300ft high – with mountainous waves thundering over them.

Gerard loved the simplicity and ease of the people of the Aran Islands and the community on the tiny island of Inishlacken where he lived with George Campbell. Inishlacken not only captured his imagination but served as an inspiration for some of his most significant paintings. To get a complete understanding of what lay at the heart of his love of the West, one has to look either at his paintings or at his letters, including this unpublished one from 13 October 1944. In it, he both sketched and described the appeal of Connemara's rocky landscape:

> The stony parts are the parts for me. If you closed your eyes and suddenly opened them, you'd think you'd been transported to the moon. It looks as if some strange gods had been playing stone throwing games, like children do, with an old tin can as a cock-shot, until all around is strewn with stones. These god-like stones are huge boulders standing up all over the place, with here and there peeping behind them little cabins and long cottages, white, stark and elfin-like intruders in this strange stone world. The light is wonderful here. Rocks, stones and boulders change colour all the time. Sometimes they are blue green, other times pink, violet, creamy white and cool grey. Behind and around everywhere, the Twelve Pins (Mountain range) tower up to the rolling clouds. They are forever changing colour too, one peak at a time, so that you can see at times a green peak, an orange-brown one, blue black, purple and grey peaks – it's terrific … a changing landscape … It's the difficulty to paint this place that makes it so fascinating. It has so much to give. The fields are small and irregular, marked off by lace-like stone walls. Each field can be a different colour. A field yellow with a violet stone fringe, a brown field with a creamy white border, an emerald one with a grey-green wall and so it can go on and on endlessly.

Deep down, Gerard was a romantic, imbued with a deep love of nature and idealism. Had he not been an artist, I believe he would have been an established poet or short story writer, and the West would have featured prominently in his writings. My father had some of his short stories, one of which brilliantly described life in Lower Clonard Street. Sadly, after my father's death in 2007, those short stories somehow vanished.

My uncle's landscapes confirm how much he adored the wild, natural simplicity of Ireland's west and how it contrasted sharply with his depictions of a desolate Belfast and London in the 1940s and 1950s. Decades later, these paintings were the most sought after by collectors, but I personally preferred the later works he created in a surrealistic vein. They employed the compelling images of Pierrots, or French mimes, hiding behind masks. Behind those masks lurked sadness, loneliness and confusion – mirroring Gerard's own alienation from the world and the confusion he felt in his personal life. Many of the works, mostly oils and collages, exude an emotional power which evokes strong feelings. He depicted his own drama, as well as human folly. He dressed his Pierrots extravagantly, revealing his love of the theatrical and the dramatic.

I did not see much of my uncle when I was a boy, but he kept in touch with my parents, writing letters to my mother and to his brother Joe. I was especially conscious as a child of their preoccupations with mortality and their frequent use of the words 'cancer' and 'coronary'. The death of my paternal grandmother disturbed our family deeply. Francie, as my father and his siblings called her, was a devout woman who refused to take pain medication when she was dying of cancer. She believed her suffering was atonement for her sins, meaning it was potentially a passport to get her through Heaven's gates.

More tragedy struck when Uncle Joe had a slight heart attack. From that event until his death, he feared he would die at any moment, alone during the night. He visited my parents every evening, staying late to listen to classical music on a wind-up gramophone and drank lots of tea. He would often leave at two or three in the morning.

In 1961, news reached my parents from London that Uncle Gerard was unwell and suffering from chest pains. I was eleven and soon to embark on a career path Uncle Joe had once considered for himself – the priesthood. There was already one priest in the Dillon family whom I had never met, Uncle Joe's brother, Vincent. He was a Passionist Father, based in Latin America, and he rarely visited Belfast. My mother described him as tall, dark, distinguished and highly intelligent, though she made it clear she was not his greatest fan. She joked he was more like a passionate Father than a Passionist Father.

She was astonished when he strolled around Belfast dressed like a rich, tanned foreigner in a well-cut suit and no clerical collar. The word 'effete' comes to mind when I look back on how she described him. My Uncle Gerard's biographer, the distinguished art historian, James White, told me over dinner in my home in 1991, he was assured by impeccable sources that Uncle Vincent, the priest, was also gay. George Campbell also confirmed it for me. Gerard, Joe and Molly were gay, so the news about Vincent hardly came as a surprise to me. In contrast, however, the two other Dillon brothers – my grandfather, Patrick, and John – were heterosexual, as was their sister, Annie, who immigrated to Canada and died there.

Uncle Joe supported my decision to enter a seminary at Romsey in Hampshire, England. He bought me new clothes and provided my parents with financial support to pay the monthly tuition fees. A decade later, Uncle Gerard shared with me that if he had been living in Belfast when I was eleven, he would have made sure my parents 'never offered me to the Church'. In his view, the priesthood was not a career for any sane or creative individual.

A major change occurred in Uncle Gerard's life in 1968. The lease on his London flat expired and George Campbell persuaded him to move to Dublin and buy a house with Arthur Armstrong, a Northern Ireland painter they both knew well. Gerard considered Arthur an ideal companion because he had 'no notion of marrying'. He and Gerard bought a house in Ranelagh, a short distance from George and his wife Madge's place. Dublin had a bohemian spirit, as well as a vibrant art scene, and Gerard soon felt much better physically and emotionally living there. That was good news considering a year earlier he had written a sombre letter to my father after being hospitalised for a month with coronary problems. In it, he wrote, 'I feel like I've walked the path of life onto the lane that leads to the tomb. There's no doubt about that. Looking around me here, I can see that death has put his hand of each of us.' Living in Dublin meant Uncle Gerard was subjected to daily radio and television reports about the deteriorating political situation in Northern Ireland. At times, the media accounts zapped his creative energy. His presence in Dublin, however, gave me the opportunity to spend some time in his company.

In April 1971, Uncle Gerard visited Belfast to arrange an exhibition of his works in the Caldwell Gallery. While staying with his friend, the pianist, Tom Davidson, he had a mild stroke and spent several weeks in the Royal Victoria Hospital. I visited him there, and to this day I treasure the memory of sitting on the edge of his bed, chatting about my job as a news reporter. He warned me to be careful on the streets and expressed deep sadness about the bitterness enveloping his hometown. I reassured him he would recover quickly and we would soon be seeing each other in his home in Dublin. He tried to appear confident, but I read fear mixed with sadness in his eyes. In a gesture, which spoke to his desire to be walking in the fresh air, he pointed to the daffodils outside his window. Embarrassed by the way the stroke had twisted his mouth, he was happy to have me do the talking. Within a fortnight, he was transferred to the Adelaide Hospital in Dublin, and I travelled with my parents to visit him at weekends. His illness did not dampen his sense of humour because he drew a sketch of himself with tubes up his nose. During one of my visits, he was thrilled to learn his Belfast exhibition was a huge success.

'How is Moneybags?' he asked me when I walked into his hospital room one morning. It was his nickname for George Campbell, who had a knack of selling more work than Gerard. I told him George was fine and had promised to visit him despite his phobia about hospitals.

'That's not the only phobia he has,' noted my uncle, in no way offended by George's unwillingness to visit him. George did indeed have many phobias, though perhaps that is not the best way to describe some of his eccentric behaviours. Each morning, even in late spring, he insisted on wearing a jacket before he sat down to a breakfast of tea and toast with honey, followed by a Spanish cigarette. He would complain about Dublin's air, saying it ruined his sinuses and gave him chills unlike the clean air of Spain, where he lived four to six months annually. After breakfast, he used to put on his beret and fill his pockets with old batteries to throw at neighbourhood dogs while he strolled to the centre of Ranelagh to buy the *Irish Times*. He disliked the mutts who poked their heads between garden fences to bite him.

When I was in public buildings with George, he always refused to use lifts, complaining he suffered from claustrophobia. He made me promise to make sure when he died he was 'really dead' before anyone put him in a coffin. He was afraid of being buried alive. In the event of his demise, I should install a window in his coffin lid and place in his hands a bottle of John Powers Gold Label whiskey and a glass. Then I should insist his coffin be buried upright with the window visible above ground to assure friends he had entered the afterlife with 'the right priorities'. Hospital visits and wakes rated highest on his list of phobias.

One afternoon, the hospital allowed Uncle Gerard to leave for a few hours. At his request, my father and I drove him into County Wicklow to see Sugar Loaf Mountain. He was frail and did not talk much. At one stage, he asked me to buy him an ice cream, saying it would remind him of his childhood when 'a day out was only special if there was ice cream'. That got me talking about my childhood in Belfast and how I loved a shop in Sandy Row where the owners displayed a massive, beautifully decorated chocolate egg in the window every Easter. Uncle Gerard loved storytelling and wanted to hear more of my childhood memories. That afternoon, all of a sudden he nudged me.

'Tell me the one about the perfume,' he said.

It was a story my mother had told him years before, but he wanted to hear my version of it. I began describing how as a boy I saved the few pence or shillings I earned for cutting sticks for my grandmother's fire and running errands for my elderly aunts and their friends. In January 1959, I began saving earnestly to buy our mother a special Christmas present as a thank you for her hard work and kindness. I decided I had found the perfect gift for her when I spotted a bottle of perfume in a chemist's window in Albert Street. I passed by the shop at least once a week to make sure it was still there.

One day I plucked up the courage to go into the chemist. Instead of asking for the price, I announced I was going to buy it for my mother for Christmas. I must have impressed the shop assistant and shop owner because they waved pleasantly to me when they subsequently saw me passing by. A week before Christmas, I counted my pennies and shillings, which I had successfully hidden in a box on the roof of our outdoor toilet. But the moment I came within sight of the chemist, my hands began to tremble. What if the perfume cost ten times what I had saved? There was nothing for it but to seek Divine help. So I made a beeline for St Peter's where I said a decade of the rosary. By the time I left the church, I was brimming over with confidence, which evaporated the moment I walked into the chemist's.

'You're here for the perfume for your mother,' said the owner. I nodded and spread out my assortment of coins. When I had placed them in an order of value, the perfume was packaged and handed to me. I whispered 'thank you' and left as quickly as my legs would carry me. On Christmas Day I gave my mother the gift. She gasped when she opened the package.

'Gerry, I can't believe it. There must be a mistake. Maybe you should go down to the chemist,' she told my father.

Two days later, he went off with the perfume and returned grinning from ear to ear.

'There is no mistake. Your son bought it,' he said.

When my mother unwrapped the package a second time, to my horror I saw it was not the bottle of Chanel No 5 I had been admiring all year, but my mother didn't seem to care. I discovered later the shop owner told my father he knew I wanted the Chanel No 5, but thought my mother would be pleased with a less expensive but fashionable product. When I subsequently told my mother what I thought I had bought her, she said forever more she would remember only that I bought her Chanel No 5. Uncle Gerard loved the story, and it struck me his attachment to it was connected to the love he had for his mother.

Weeks after enjoying his company on the car ride, his condition appeared to improve. There was even talk of him going to London to stay with friends, and my father said he would accompany him. Sadly, on 12 June, his condition deteriorated, and he asked for a priest to hear his confession and give him the Last Rites. He died on 14 June, and in accordance with his wishes was buried in Milltown Cemetery, Belfast. He had stressed throughout his life he did not wish to be buried in a neat, tidy cemetery of the type he associated with London. Milltown was the antithesis of that.

In the aftermath of his death, decisions were made, which I feel should be known, especially to those who may write about him at some time in the future. During the final year of his life, he worked hard, using a large press to make etchings. Presumably, the strain of using the heavy press contributed to his declining health, especially in the spring of 1971. He never finished his etching series. But according to James White, who produced an illustrated biography of Gerard a short time after his death, the artist, Arthur Armstrong, who was sharing a house in Dublin with my uncle, spoke to John Kelly, Director of the Graphic Studios where Gerard worked. Kelly told Arthur there were more than fifty plates Gerard had etched and they 'should be cancelled by scratching an X across each plate so if anyone wanted to make a print in the future the mark would show'. I never saw the fifty plates, but I did see plates my father later had in his possession, which were from a small series Gerard had all but finished. Arthur Armstrong convinced my father, in his capacity as one of Gerard's heirs, to scratch those plates so they could never be used again. According to Armstrong, Gerard had always felt that when European artists died, they left behind plates that were used to create prints much like hand bills. It was Gerard's philosophy anyone who bought a painting, drawing, watercolour or etching by him should be able to recoup their outlay by selling it in an emergency. I vehemently opposed the destruction of those plates, even when my father insisted he knew Gerard's mind. My father said he was doing it on the advice of Armstrong. My father made X scratches across the plates and later gave them to my brother, Dr Patrick Dillon.

When I went to Uncle Gerard's house after his funeral, I found someone had rifled through his belongings. His sister Molly thought it was George Campbell's wife, Madge, looking for Gerard's will, concerned about how it might impact the life of Arthur Armstrong. According to Molly, Madge was anxious to find out if Gerard had left his part of the house to Arthur, who was not in a position to pay the market value for Gerard's half of it if it was not bequeathed to him. By viewing the will, argued Molly, Madge would be better placed to give Arthur advice. There was no evidence to support the allegation, though Madge declared after my uncle's passing she would do whatever was necessary to protect Arthur's rights. Uncle Gerard had promised my parents they would inherit everything he had. Weeks before his death, he told my mother he had written a will but none was found when we searched his possessions. Everyone in the Dillon family was convinced my uncle had intended to leave everything to my father, and they left my father to sort out Gerard's affairs. My father allowed Arthur Armstrong to buy out Gerard's 50 per cent interest in the house at a knock-down price.

All Molly wanted from her brother's estate was twenty-five oil paintings from Gerard's West of Ireland period. My father simply gave her the works, but she then insisted on having his diaries. I was first to read the diaries in the days after my uncle's death. My father read them much later and, contrary to my advice, erased all comments in them about Molly and Vincent, hoping to save them embarrassment. He also blacked out criticisms directed at some leading figures in the Dublin art world. On learning of the dairies, Uncle Gerard's brother, Fr Vincent, who was by then retired and living in Texas, asked Molly to send them to him. I suspected then, and still do, he was anxious to discover if they contained any scandalous revelations about him. Because of this, his relationship with my parents suffered when the diaries were passed to Molly. The rift between Vincent and my parents was so deep he never got his wish to be buried in Belfast with Joe and Gerard.

Molly subsequently claimed she sent the diaries to Fr Vincent Dillon, but there was no proof she ever did. I was not made aware of everything my father erased in the diaries. I believe there were at least two journals that were undated. I told my father I was sure Molly returned to London in the weeks after my Uncle Gerard's death with one or two of these journals, which were additional to the ones my father passed to her months later. My father did not wish to challenge her. When she learned that the diaries I read in the days after my uncle died contained revelations about his sexuality, she demanded them from my father. I never saw those writings again.

In fact, no one in my family ever saw the journals after they were in Molly's hands. She was evasive when I asked her about them a decade later. When I pressed her, she hinted they had been destroyed, although she refused to be specific. They were not among her possessions after her death, and there was no evidence Fr Vincent ever had control of them. It is possible Molly lied about having sent them to her brother in Texas. She may have destroyed them because she was reckless with some of Uncle Gerard's possessions. While sorting out papers and art works in the days following his funeral, she lit a small bonfire in his garden and proceeded to burn letters and more disturbingly drawings, which she felt did not measure up to his talent. She was a single-minded, capricious and wilful woman. She was the type of person one could not reason with, a fact Gerard found out to his cost when he lived with her in London.

Before Uncle Gerard's death, his Dublin art dealer, Leo Smith, launched a clever 'wine-and-dine campaign' to court my parents, certain they would inherit a large art collection. Leo owned and ran the Dawson Gallery, one of Dublin's finest and most celebrated galleries. He was a shrewd, sophisticated man with a wealth of knowledge of the art world, having worked for years in Bond Street in London. According to George Campbell, the fact he was gay partly determined his close, personal rapport with Gerard. When Leo dined with my parents, he sometimes exhibited his artsy, bohemian side and treated my mother in particular to scandalous stories and risqué jokes about well-known Dubliners. He adored the letters she wrote to him and was fond of quoting lines from them to business acquaintances. He convinced my father if anything happened to Uncle Gerard he was the person to secure his legacy. It would be important he stressed, to ensure only one person managed and sold the work Gerard left behind. It was clear from Leo Smith's comments to my parents that my uncle had told him he was bequeathing his work to my father.

Leo explained to my father he had handled the estate of Jack Yeats and other prominent artists. In the process, he learned that when an artist died his reputation went into decline because the market was flooded with his or her creations by heirs determined to make a quick buck. As a consequence, the value of the work plummeted, and the artist's reputation suffered for decades or in some cases went into a serious decline. Gerard's legacy would be assured only if his paintings were released for sale over time to maximise interest in them, thereby enhancing their value. As Leo put it, the ultimate goal was to honour Gerard by 'handling his work in a fashion that solidified his place in the history of Irish art'. The logic appealed to my father, who loved Gerard and always wanted him to be considered one of Ireland's 'greats'. Shortly after Uncle Gerard's death, my parents told me they were convinced Leo had the ability and respect for my uncle to handle the art he left behind. Clearly, Leo Smith's campaign in the months before my uncle's passing had proved successful.

What happened next constitutes, in my opinion, one of the hidden scandals of the Irish art world. On learning my father had given Aunt Molly twenty-five oil paintings, Leo Smith flew right away to London and bought them from her at a knock-down price, knowing she was living on a pension and needed the money. This angered me when I found out about it years later. Leo's main objective, however, was to get his hands on the rest of the art Uncle Gerard left behind. He persuaded my father, against my judgment and that of a close family friend, who also happened to be a lawyer, that he was ready to buy the work and do all the wonderful things only he could do with it. Of course, he would have to get it at the right price, he pointed out. Hundreds of works were removed from Gerard's home and transferred for safe keeping to the Killiney home of a leading Dublin solicitor. They included major oils, watercolours, drawings and mixed media. In the meantime, Leo Smith put in motion a strategy to ensure he could purchase them at a price that suited him. He began by enlisting the help of his friend, James White, an international art expert and former director of the National Gallery of Ireland. White, who would later publish, *Gerard Dillon – An Illustrated Biography*, knew and personally admired Gerard's work to the extent most people deemed him the sole expert on him. It was a clever move by Smith because any valuation by White of Dillon's works would not be challenged should my father decide to seek an alternative valuation from another expert. Leo Smith, I believe, was confident my parents and Gerard's sister, Molly, would not question White's judgment. He was right.

White subsequently valued the work in a way that ensured Leo Smith acquired it for a ridiculous price. I recall seeing White's valuation document and being appalled by the prices he attached to some of the work. Etchings, for example, were listed at fifty pence. I am confident a copy of White's valuation, as well as numerous other documents related to my late uncle's life and work, were among my father's possessions before he died in 2007. For the purpose of this book, I asked the executors of my late father's estate, my brother, Dr Patrick Dillon and my sister, Ursula Mc Laughlin, about the archive of documents related to Uncle Gerard. They told me no such archive existed even though I had seen parts of it with my own eyes.

My father could have bought the Dillon collection instead of permitting Leo Smith to purchase it. In fact, a family friend offered to loan him money to buy it, but by then Smith had done a marvellous job of convincing my parents and Molly only he could deliver Gerard Dillon's proper legacy. I cannot be exact about the overall value placed on Gerard's work, but I believe it did not exceed £6,000. Not long after Leo Smith acquired the collection he died on his way from a funeral in Dublin. Ironically, he left no will and the collection was passed to his heirs to sell as they saw fit.

Before James White died, I had an opportunity to talk to him about my uncle's unusual relationship with Leo Smith. I remarked how George Campbell had, once or twice, hinted that there was much more he could say about it. White smiled in a way that suggested he was the keeper of secrets. He admitted that Leo and Gerard shared a habit of 'cruising' for lovers in Dublin's docks area. He suggested they may even have done this together on some occasions. According to White, Leo and Gerard were very close but had never been lovers, even though Leo loved and desired a physical relationship with Gerard. Unlike Gerard, Leo was indiscreet and liked to confide in White. Gerard was secretive. White admitted my uncle never opened up to him about his sexuality. I have often wondered how and why White became Leo's 'confessor'. One thing that stands out about White is how he genuinely feared, when writing the book on my uncle, that if he spilled all his secrets about Leo and Gerard, he risked being ostracised by his contemporaries. Nevertheless, he managed during his research for the book to encourage close friends of Gerard's to talk to him off the record about matters that had remained hidden for decades, including the closeted lives of Gerard's siblings, Joe, Molly and Vincent. I regretted that White lacked the tenacity to publish what he learned, knowing it could help future art historians.

FOUR

George Campbell's 'Non-Heads'

After Uncle Gerard's death, I visited Dublin a lot, staying mostly with George and Madge Campbell. George also visited me in Belfast, where I drove him through districts marred by the Troubles. My tales of riots and gun battles provided the inspiration for a little known series of paintings he made about the Troubles. A typical evening with George in Dublin involved a leisurely stroll with him and Arthur Armstrong to Madigan's pub on Morehampton Road. After the pub closed, we always went to George's, each of us carrying a half bottle of spirits. Arthur preferred Powers whiskey, while George liked vodka. I usually bought gin or whiskey, depending on my mood. It was the same routine George and Arthur had often followed with Gerard on nights he was not hiding from them.

On these evenings out, Madge stayed alone at home drinking whiskey and watching television. When we got back, she made tapas while 'the lads', as she called us, retired to the front room. Once drinks were poured, George became our DJ, selecting vinyl discs from his huge collection of flamenco and classical music. I never tired of the experience because it had its eccentric twists in the end. Madge would serve tapas and argue loudly with George about his music selections, calling him a 'nasty old bollocks' or 'old fart'. We were careful never to favour either of them in their disputes because Madge was just as likely to turn on the person who came to her rescue.

Many times, I found myself alone with George in the early hours, sitting on the floor while we reminisced about Uncle Gerard. At some point, George would put on his favourite LP of David Oistrakh playing the Adagio from the Bruch Violin Concerto No 1. We would both cry for a friend we missed a lot. Over time, George's sense of loss became more pronounced whereas Arthur rarely expressed regret at my late uncle's passing.

Arthur Armstrong was tall, skinny and had a sickly appearance. George gave him the nickname 'Skinny' and often joked about his talent for being inconspicuous. Madge adored Arthur, lavished affection on him and treated him like her child even though he was in his fifties. She never ceased reminding him to take his vitamins and encouraged everyone to pamper him. She never chastised him for the amount of Powers whiskey he consumed because she was fond of a fair old tipple. There was a funny side to Arthur I truly enjoyed, and it related to his dry, conversational mannerisms and his attachment to the 'juice of the barley'. One evening, Madge arrived from the kitchen with tapas and reprimanded George for his choice of music. He stopped the music and announced he had begun painting a new series of works he called 'Non-Heads'.

He said the series reflected his personal distress about the terror campaign in Northern Ireland, especially the grisly sectarian murders, which had become commonplace. He believed that while killers sought to dehumanise their victims by the act of murder, they, too, were dehumanised. He was particularly intrigued by the fact terrorists hid behind masks made from nylon stockings, woollen balaclavas and hessian bags. In his opinion, the mask transformed the terrorist into a 'Non-Head', reflecting an abstract, gruesome and dehumanising persona.

'I began painting Non-Heads to get the terror out of my own head,' he declared loudly, after pouring the last drops from his vodka bottle.

It was clear Arthur had heard nothing of George's rationale for his Non-Head series because he was busy replenishing his glass with whiskey.

'A Non-Head, you say?' Arthur remarked, pausing briefly to sip from his glass. 'And what would that be, George?'

'It's what I said it was,' George replied, with some irritation.

'Well, if you say it was, then it was. But, if you don't mind, I'd like to see one of these Non-Heads for myself.' Arthur's tone was polite but somewhat slurred.

George left the room, returning moments later with an oil-on-board painting. I instantly recognised the image of a head camouflaged in a stocking mask even though it was somewhat abstract in form. Arthur looked puzzled as he pointed to the work, his index finger wavering slightly.

'And you say that's a Non-Head, George?'

George fixed him with a wicked stare. 'I'd say the Powers Gold Label has gone to yours,' muttered George, holding the painting close to a lamp so we all had a better view of it. 'I suppose you still can't see it, you silly bollocks,' he added, looking directly at Arthur.

Arthur squinted. 'Well, I see the fuzzy outline of a head but what's this Non-Head business about? It's a head or it's not a head, George. Saying it's a Non-Head means even you don't know if it's a head. Am I right?'

'No, you're not fucking right. But then again, in one sense you are. It's not a head because the stocking mask hides the humanity. That's my point, you see.'

George drew his finger along the shape of the head in the painting. Its greyish colour depicted a terrifying image of a human head in a stocking mask with no visible features. Arthur leaned forward, ever so slightly, and stared again at the painting.

'Oh, I see! That's a stocking mask over a head. I thought you said it was a Non-Head, George.'

'If I painted your head that would be a real Non-Head,' snapped George, scooping up the painting and leaving the room.

George died before he could complete his Non-Head series, but his earlier paintings of the Troubles were important reflections of the true nature of political violence. On the day of his funeral in the Wicklow countryside, I remained in the cemetery after mourners filed out of the churchyard to a nearby bar-restaurant to celebrate his passing. I paid the gravediggers to take an early lunch break to allow me time to fill in the grave, which I did with the help of my friend, Colin Lewis. After the grave was filled in, I realised a gold Parker pen I had in my jacket pocket had fallen into the grave while I was shovelling soil. George didn't get the vodka or whiskey he requested, but he had a pen to sketch places and people in his afterlife. I hoped there would be no Non-Heads where he was going.

Now, looking back on the many hours I enjoyed with George after Uncle Gerard's death, I realise we spent most of them talking about my uncle. We were joined on occasions by Tom Caldwell, the Belfast gallery owner, who was at one time a prominent Unionist known for his liberal views. George liked him. His presence often led to spirited political debates about the Troubles. George's wife, Madge, became a staunch Nationalist as events on the streets of Northern Ireland worsened in the early 1970s, and more often than not she used Tom as a political football. He took it all in his stride and rarely felt offended. Tom's contribution to the social life of Belfast at the height of the Troubles was much appreciated, and the same can be said of artists like Brian Ferran and Brian Ballard when they dominated the Northern Ireland Arts Council and organised exhibition openings in the besieged centre of the city. But it was the Caldwell Gallery that stood out because of its salon-like atmosphere. Its openings were held in a cavernous room under the public Caldwell Gallery, which also sold antique furniture. When bombings and killings all but closed down much of the nightlife, a Caldwell opening was not to be missed. Wine and good conversation flowed freely for hours, and it was a wonderful oasis. I often went to these events with my father and met collectors and artists. It was there I first set eyes on the highly gifted sculptor Caroline Mulholland and got to know many of Northern Ireland's serious art collectors. Chief among them were outstanding legal minds like Michael Lavery and Ronald Appleton. There were politicians too, from both sides of the divide, and many notable broadcasters. The wonderful poets, Michael Longley, his wife, Edna, and my BBC colleague, Paul Muldoon, often attended openings. It was not only an opportunity for people to meet, share a few glasses of wine and talk about art, but a place to establish social contacts and discuss political issues.

The Caldwell Gallery wasn't the only art space to enhance life in Belfast in the early 1970s. There was the McClelland Gallery in Chichester Street, run by George McClelland, a former policeman, and his wife Maura. They had a fine taste in art, and their exhibition of the works of Dan O'Neill in 1970 was a milestone for those who loved O'Neill's work. I remember attending the opening with my father, who bought an oil painting of a kitchen scene. There is a follow-up story to George McClelland's role as an artists' agent, which bears mention.

The year before Uncle Gerard died, he was befriended by George McClelland and they both got on well together. For reasons I cannot fully explain, my uncle's Dublin agent, Leo Smith, became very jealous. One reason might have been my uncle's decision to let McClelland buy or sell some of his paintings. Leo might have seen that as complicating his business relations with my uncle. But James White had another take on the episode. He told me Leo behaved like 'a lover spurned'. George Campbell agreed, saying it was somewhat bizarre. Leo Smith had no contract with my uncle that restricted him selling his work to anyone or allowing someone to represent it to collectors. George said it was curious because it could not have been a lover spurned because George McClelland was heterosexual and happily married. I believe Leo was worried McClelland, as a northerner, might manage to steal Gerard as a client by offering him a more lucrative contract. According to George Campbell, always one to inject humour into his renderings of stories, the rift between my uncle and Leo was quickly healed over lunch when they 'agreed they weren't married but could behave like an asexual couple'. Contrary to what has been published in some reports, George McClelland was never Gerard Dillon's agent, but he was nevertheless a trusted agent and gallery owner who loved Gerard's work. He and his wife were respected in the art world.

The Lower Clonard Street Dillons had a profound influence on my life. I inherited their attachment to the arts and a desire to pursue a creative career. But first I would have to pursue the dream my Uncle Joe once had.

FIVE

My Life in a Seminary

I sang Dies Irae, Dies Illa,
accented finely
in its sombre metre.
Gone were beads worn smooth;
indulgences stacked like chips on a poker table.
I longed for November's bleakness,
tiny hands warmed over candles,
flickering before a terrible wrath.
I imagined souls calling to me,
locked in their emptiness.
It was before I learned to sing
Pie Jesu Domine,
dona eis requiem.

A MONTFORT REQUIEM – Martin Dillon

To this day, I am not sure why I chose to study in a seminary run by the Montfort Fathers in historic Romsey in Hampshire, England. Perhaps, I was taken with a brochure someone had given my mother, displaying the college grounds with boys in uniform, football fields and tennis courts. Where the brochure came from remains a mystery, but for me it depicted a magical setting. As a child in the drab streets of the

Lower Falls, Montfort College resembled a wonderland. On the other hand, it would be disingenuous to attribute my priestly enthusiasm just to escapism. I was deeply attached to my religion and, unlike my twin brother, spent a lot of time in the company of my great-aunts whose days were devoted to quietly repeating decades of the rosary. I was also emotionally attached to St Peter's where I was willing to serve as an altar boy whenever the church needed me, even if it meant participating in several Masses a day.

I was eleven years old when I made the decision to become a seminarian, and one might wonder how someone so young could be permitted to make such a life-changing decision without full knowledge of its implications. Of course, seminaries existed throughout history and into modern times. The Catholic Church promoted them on the oft-quoted Jesuitical principle, 'give me the boy and I will give you the man'.

Montfort College was established in 1910 when priests and brothers of the Mission of Montfort Fathers and the Daughters of Wisdom sought asylum in England. Together, they built the seminary in a rural setting, and it quickly became self-sufficient. The new Montfort Mission began farming and made cider from an apple orchard. From the outset, the priests taught pupils, the brothers farmed and performed other jobs, and the sisters cooked and ran the laundry.

The moment I decided on Montfort, I entered a whirlwind of activity since I would be leaving to become a seminarian three months after my twelfth birthday. Family, friends and neighbours were excited, and everyone wanted to help as though I were about to relocate to a far-off land. Like boys going to English public schools, I had to have two uniforms, each with a jacket and short pants. The college provided a list of necessities, and my poor mother and father, with a large family to feed, had to rely on Uncle Joe for financial help. My mother's brother, WJ, offered to make my uniforms and my large bosomed Aunt Vera promised to buy me football boots or a tennis racquet. Years later, I felt guilty I had placed so much pressure on my family, especially when I learned my parents paid a monthly fee to the college.

I also felt I betrayed my twin because we had been inseparable, yet I left him behind. He has never commented on that aspect of my past, but I can only imagine how hard it must have been for him to watch me in the limelight, while he was confined to the shadows. At the time, I had no guilt in my heart as I readied to leave home. I was about to devote my life to the Church, believing I would return to St Peter's someday to preach like the famed missionaries who visited the parish each winter.

Leaving home, on an early September evening in 1961, remains one of the most traumatic moments of my life. I had never been away from my parents, and standing at the rail of the Belfast-Liverpool ferry I was lost and sad when I saw my mother crying and my father consoling her. My twin brother had decided not to see me off and that hurt. As the boat pulled out of the harbour, seagulls rose on air currents in its wake like fans leaving Casement Park after a match. I looked back at the mountains and the Cave Hill and felt a sudden pain in my heart. For the first time, I was being embraced by my native city. I could see where the Falls and Shankill areas intersected, and my thoughts went back to the days spent with my family and friends.

The journey to Liverpool should have been an adventure but rough seas made me sick and depressed. During the night, I wrapped my arms round a metal pillar to steady myself as the boat pitched and rolled. The next morning, I joined several dozen Montfort seminarians on a coach journey to Hampshire. As the coach neared the college gates, an older boy shouted, 'Let's all take a deep breath!' Most did.

On my first night, they gave me a bed in the dormitory reserved for first and second year students, and a cupboard space to store my clothes, which were to be neatly folded at all times. The rules insisted on silence when dormitory lights were switched to night lights. Studying under the bedclothes with torches and wandering around at night, unless one needed to go to the toilets, were forbidden.

Coming as I did from a part of the United Kingdom where the accent had a hard edge, adjusting to Montfort was made tougher because my accent set me apart from English pupils. Fellow students subjected me to the usual questions about whether the Irish kept pigs in their kitchens.

Another troubling experience came with discovering the college possessed the De La Salle Brothers' love of corporal punishment. At the end of my first week, I learned I had been 'written up' by a prefect for talking twice while waiting in line to go to the study/library. I was summoned with other boys, mostly newcomers unfamiliar with the rules, to Fr Mc Keever's personal den. He was a tall, dark, thin man with a five-o'clock shadow, reputed to have a stomach ulcer that made him irritable. When he spoke, I detected a hint of a long-lost Belfast accent. He stood in the centre of his room armed with a leather strap, and his stance reminded me of my days with the De La Salle Brothers. Ready for action, he slapped the strap against one of his hands, anxious to get on with teaching me a lesson. I winced each time the strap made contact with my hands. Fr Clement Marshall, another Belfast priest, assumed Mc Keever's punishment duties a year later. He would sometimes adjust the angle of a student's hands to better meet the downward motion of the strap. I decided the two priests mimicked the punishment techniques they experienced in Belfast primary schools decades earlier. Of the two priests, I liked Fr Marshall because he had a sense of humour, was a fine teacher and took a genuine interest in my well-being.

Sport was a big part of the school curriculum, but I was not a natural footballer or cricketer. I enjoyed cricket but lacked the skills to be a competent bowler or batsman. To my surprise, I excelled at tennis and was happy when the nets went up on the playground at Easter.

Academically, I performed well due to my love of literature and reading. I became the go-to person for the youngest students wishing to know which books to borrow from the library. Some boys often inquired if I knew of any 'risqué' novels, but the priests had cleansed the library of anything unsuitable for young seminarians. I remember a friend fell in love with Botticelli nudes in a book about European art and spent hours upon hours gazing at them. This hardly surprised me since the only time we ever saw the opposite sex, aside from nuns, was when a small number of locals, one of them an attractive young lady, attended our Sunday Mass to hear us singing Plain Chant or visited our small chapel when we sang monthly Compline and Vespers. I joined the choir when Fr O'Haire took charge because he made choir practice entertaining. He was a tall, lively man with a wonderful bass voice and an ability to draw others into his love of religious music. Sadly, he died of kidney failure in 1998.

One of the things I had to overcome was making my weekly confession face-to-face with a priest I might later see in the classroom and playground. I was uncomfortable going to the priest's room. I had only known the confession boxes in St Peter's and Clonard Monastery where wire mesh and darkness separated me from the priests. After some investigation at Montfort, I settled on my literature teacher, Fr Mackrell, who was gentle and eccentric. He spent most of my confessions discussing the literature assignments he set for me. Nevertheless, the days prior to my weekly confession were often laden with inner conflict. Should I confess the sin of masturbation or should I not, I wondered. I didn't doubt my contemporaries faced the same dilemma, but it was something we never discussed. I soon found creative ways to describe my transgressions by admitting I had 'impure thoughts'. This generalization covered a host of venial sins of a sexual nature. Fr Mackrell recognised the deception and saved me embarrassment by never reverting to follow-up questions of the type one might get in St Peter's or Clonard.

During my first year, my grandmother, Margaret Clarke died and so too did Uncle Joe. I was unable to attend their funerals because my parents could not afford to pay my travel costs. Joe died alone of heart failure as he had always feared. Aunt Molly took his little Dachshund, Heine, to live with her and her many cats in London. Uncle Joe's death had a profound impact on his brother, Gerard, who feared he, too, was destined to die young. In memory of Joe, he painted a work entitled, *And the Time Passes* to memorialise their closeness. It depicted two masked Pierrots, one in a striped costume and the other in a ghostly white outfit. The Pierrot in the striped costume was waving goodbye to the one in white departing. He placed both figures on a shoreline with a backdrop of sea and sky. The surrealistic images conveyed sadness and gentleness but were also reminders of the pain of mortality.

I saw Uncle Gerard briefly after his brother died, and we talked about Joe's passing. During our conversation, Uncle Gerard showed an intense interest in my life at Montfort. It amused him to hear about the two Belfast-born priests who dispensed justice. He noted they were definitely admirers of the Irish Catholic teaching method of 'beating into you what you were unwilling to learn'. When he asked if I was happy living in a seminary, I was somewhat baffled because I had never associated becoming a priest with happiness. Seeing confusion in my silence, he patted me on the shoulder and assured me Montfort was a fine academic place for me to learn the classics.

Montfort's rural setting was one of its greatest attractions. It gave me the opportunity to immerse myself in the natural world. As a consequence, I developed a keen interest in birds. Unfortunately, I also pursued the unhealthy hobby of collecting birds' eggs. To justify it, I established a rule that I would only remove one egg from a nest if I could leave at least two to hatch. I persuaded my friend, Michael Casey, to share my egg hobby, and we would often wander casually along the edges of the three football fields, hoping to spot birds entering or leaving their nests in hedgerows. One late spring afternoon I was lying beside Michael on the edge of a football field chatting about egg collecting when a prefect joined us.

'You two should not be here alone,' he noted, motioning to the main building. A priest was at an open window watching us through binoculars.

Until that moment, I had not thought much about being alone with another classmate. But I quickly learned there were unwritten rules, and this appeared to be one of them. The priests preferred to see groups of three or more boys together, the principle being 'two were more likely to get up to mischief'. It denoted an unspoken fear that two boys, who spent a lot of time alone, were more likely to develop a sexual intimacy.

Some boys established the type of emotional relationships one would not have expected from them in the outside world. In other words, they found boys appealing in the way they might have found a schoolgirl pretty or interesting. There was, for example, an obvious flirtatiousness between some seniors aged sixteen and upwards and the newly arrived 12 year olds. A few priests appeared to mimic the behaviour, choosing favourites who were physically attractive, very good at sports or effeminate. In the intense living environment of a seminary, a lack of open discussion about sex created a surreal milieu abundant with secrets. Two students were expelled during my time there for having liaisons in the dormitory toilets late at night. Their expulsion was never discussed or explained by the priests. It was as though they vanished without a trace. In fact, they were held incognito somewhere in the college until their parents arrived to take them home. It was an emotionally upsetting episode. I was close to one of the students, though I never suspected that he had been carrying on a secret relationship.

Aside from bird watching, I devoted my spare time to studying for weekly tests, writing letters home and reading classic novels. During one term, I fell so much in love with Rafael Sabatini's novels *Captain Blood* and *The Sea Hawk* that I spent the remainder of the year reading only novels of that genre by the likes of Alexandre Dumas, Sir Walter Scott, Baroness Orczy and Robert Louis Stevenson.

Fr Liam Cosgrave was a priest I liked and respected at Montfort. A small Irishman with a tanned face and big smile, he was generous, refined and effeminate. He was easily embarrassed and lacked the gregariousness of other Montfort priests. As the college bursar, he handled the finances and raised funds through charitable donations. He travelled widely, flitting in and out of Montfort like the birds on my watch lists. He frequently visited my parents whenever he returned to Ireland and would sit for hours drinking tea and eating my mother's home-baked breads and pastries. He occasionally received gifts of writing paper from companies that made donations. When I revealed to him that I would use the paper for writing poems, he gave it to me.

Everyone liked Father Liam. Generally, he appeared happy-go-lucky, though I sensed he did not share any closeness to the other priests, even the two from Belfast. Like others at Montfort he, too, had his secrets.

Years after I left Montfort, he continued to visit my parents. They always gave him gifts of money for his personal use. Three decades later, it shocked my family when they found his photo splashed across the front page of Ireland's *Sunday World* newspaper. I was living in France at the time, and by sheer chance saw a copy of the paper. After reading the headline about Fr Liam, I tossed the paper aside in disbelief and took a solitary walk in my garden. Fr Liam had been found dead during an undercover police raid on a seedy, male massage club in Dublin. The newspaper confirmed he was a regular customer and probably died of a heart attack before the raid. Police speculated patrons had not known what to do with his body and left it lying in a hallway of the premises. I immediately phoned my father in Belfast and he admitted, on the basis of all the news coverage, the story was true and it was 'our Father Liam'. He asked me not to discuss it with my mother.

'Your mother has convinced herself he was working undercover for the Vatican in order to expose paedophile priests who frequented such clubs. She believes he had a heart attack because the secret job put him under terrible stress. It's her contention the Vatican can't admit he was working for them because it functions like an intelligence agency, and protects the identity of its spies at all costs. God help her foolish wit, but it's better for her to cherish a theory that softens the reality. What Liam was, he was, and we have to accept it. None of us has the right to judge him. His life could not have been an easy one if he spent most of it hiding his true self.'

My father was a realist and humanist, whereas my mother, who by then had been a stroke patient for ten years, did not always see the world as it was. The fiction she spun to explain Father Liam's death in a seedy establishment came as natural to her as her stories about my gay uncles, Gerard and Joe, never marrying because of their dedication to the arts. I wondered how many years Fr Liam had lived a double life.

It may well be that his bursar role permitted him to have secret sexual liaisons as he travelled across the British Isles. I will always remember him with fondness.

Most of us at Montfort undoubtedly had secrets. I had some, too, buried in memories of my past. I had been one of four boyhood friends abused by a Belfast paedophile. Another was my cousin, Don O'Rawe, who later followed me to Montfort and became a Montfort Father. The third was Brian Mulholland, my best friend, who would die a decade later from leukaemia. The fourth boy I will not mention for personal reasons. We were an innocent, lively bunch of kids who regularly played together, but we all lived with a secret we never discussed. We treated the abuse as if it never happened. We fell into the clutches of a middle-aged man who was a friend of Don's parents. He would take us to the cinema and for trips in his car so he could fondle us. My memory of that time is incomplete. Perhaps I blocked out most of what transpired. However, I can still recall how each of us hated being the one chosen to ride alongside our abuser while he was driving. The front seat was a long, high-backed leather bench, and the kids in the rear could not see into the front. Nevertheless, each of us knew what would happen when one of us was told to sit in front.

Why I never shared this horror with my parents remains a mystery to me. Being a child, I must have been frightened and confused. Perhaps, I found it difficult to explain. Then Don saved all of us by telling his mother. He was two years older than the rest of us and more articulate. I discovered decades later that Don's parents banished the paedophile from the neighbourhood. My parents must surely have learned about it, but they never raised the matter with me. After Don went to Montfort in the late 1960s, two decades passed until we saw each other again. One evening in the mid-1980s, I saw him drinking alone in the Linenhall Bar next to my BBC office in Belfast and joined him. He was dressed casually, without a clerical collar, and seemed a little embarrassed when I greeted him. We struck up a conversation, and I said I heard he was having problems in his ministry. He had been threatened by Provisional IRA sympathisers after he used his pulpit to denounce IRA violence and implore young men to reject a life of terror. When I questioned him about the risks his pronouncements posed to his life, he replied he was not frightened. Nevertheless, his demeanour suggested he was a man on the edge with a drinking problem.

We swapped stories about our childhood, but when I tried to engage him about the sexual abuse we suffered as kids, he made it clear he had no wish to revisit that part of our past. His said his memory of it was vague anyway. I saw him one more time before his death of a heart attack in November 1999. My father and I visited the Sacred Heart Church in North Belfast where Don was celebrating Mass. When he finished he greeted us with a brief handshake and left in a rush. I thought this rude, but my father said he was not the sociable type. He subsequently visited my parents, bringing my mother communion and staying for lunch. They concluded he was a lonely, unhappy person. When I heard of my cousin's passing, I was reminded of my unpublished book of poems, *The Witnesses of Time*. The following verse is about the secret Don and my other boyhood friends buried for so long:

ABUSED

It was a time of leather car seats, cinema visits and chocolate bars.
His hands roughened found me in the stench of stale pipe tobacco.
I tore his image like paper but it repaired itself,
arriving without warning in the mind's eye
where gentler thoughts fought for space.
I put a knife into it, feeling only pain.
The loss was real but now
I only see it on the page.

During my time in Montfort, aside from trips home for summer break and Christmas, I attended college without television, radio, newspapers or phone calls. The outside world was a place of mystery. I truly lived in a bubble, unaware of the life young people of my generation were experiencing. The assassination of President John F. Kennedy shocked them, yet it had no impact on me. I was told little about it. Still, it was the year I discovered the Beatles, thanks mostly to my father. My siblings serenaded me with 'I Wanna Hold Your Hand', which blasted from the gramophone when I arrived home for the Christmas holidays. I couldn't believe my ears that my conservative father liked the Beatles since I had only ever seen him play classical recordings. Soon he bought himself a Joan Baez LP and gave my mother a gift of a compilation album by country and western balladeer, Marty Robbins. The endless playing of the Beatles that Christmas reminded me of the world beyond the confines of Montfort.

Returning home biannually was never easy for me. My English accent and the refined ways I'd acquired did not find favour with my twin brother and his friends. They mimicked my new accent the way students and priests at Montfort had once made fun of the downward inflections of my Belfast dialect. I felt uncomfortable wearing my school uniform in the streets of the Lower Falls because people stared at me, puzzled by the badges on my jacket and cap. My boyhood friends didn't wear school uniforms, but my mother insisted I dressed like a seminarian when she walked out with me.

When I went back to Montfort, I shared with my friend, Paul Scarlett, my newfound love of the Beatles. He told me his 16-year-old cousin was a big Beatles fan, and she had given him a copy of the lyrics to 'She Loves You'. He suggested I write to her and tell her how much I enjoyed the Beatles, and she might send me copies of the lyrics of their songs. I wrote to his cousin and a week later Fr Owen Cannon, who handled student mail, told me he had intercepted my letter. I was not to write to the young lady again. Fr Canon was one of the most intellectually gifted men I have ever met. He taught me Greek and Latin and played the role of classical DJ on Sunday mornings when he piped music into the study for an hour or two. He always seemed to have the opera arias I requested, though not necessarily the artists I preferred, such as Beniamino Gigli and John McCormack. Once, he asked me how I amassed my knowledge of opera, and I explained that my father and Uncle Joe had sizeable collections.

In 1964, while thinking about my vocation, I was shocked to discover I liked girls too much to be a priest. I reached the conclusion after meeting a very pretty girl on a train from Liverpool to Southampton. She was seventeen, attending a school on the Isle of Wight. A two-year age difference between us hardly mattered, and we talked for hours about literature, music and the Beatles. Before we parted, she gave me her address, and I promised to write to her. We did not even exchange a kiss, but I was in love. In the days that followed, I thought about little else but her. I wrote her a romantic letter, hid it in my desk and considered ways to mail it to her. The girl wrote back, but I never saw her letter. Instead, I received a vague reprimand from Fr Cannon for writing to a young lady without informing the college.

A month later, I came across Ian Fleming's novel, *From Russia with Love*, abandoned on a park bench in Romsey. I told no one I had it, suspecting the staff would regard it as lurid and expel me. For three weeks, I waited each night until students around me fell asleep before opening the novel and reading it furtively by torchlight under the bed covers. Like James Bond, I, too, fell madly in love with the Russian Corporal, Tatiana Romanova. I had never come across a book with such intrigue and sexual content, and I felt excited.

I found myself breaking many of the basic rules of my seminary life, and after some introspection I knew it would be immoral to remain at Montfort while my parents continued to pay a monthly stipend. However, the prospect of telling my parents I had become disenchanted with my vocation terrified me.

SIX

Fathers and Sons

By 1964, my family had invested a lot, both emotionally and financially, in my decision to be a priest. And what about my siblings who had watched my preferential treatment at their expense? In retrospect, I find it remarkable my little sisters never complained when our parents couldn't buy them new clothes and they had to wear hand-me-downs from older siblings. Frances, the eldest girl, who was two years younger than me, helped with the housework and ran errands to the extent she missed school too often. My mother kept a balance book in which she entered every penny she spent in order to manage her small weekly budget. She bought broken biscuits and damaged fruit for a fraction of their true cost, and dinner often consisted of bread with bowls of boiled Marrowfat peas topped with butter and a dash of vinegar. My sister, Attracta, remembers how she and Bernadette, the youngest of the girls, often went hungry to school because our parents were too proud to accept state charity in the form of free school lunches. Eventually, a woman working at the school spirited my sisters into the canteen after everyone else had eaten and fed them leftovers every day.

My father was a man with a short fuse, quick to use a strap and cane. That ensured life in 7 Ross Place was never easy when I was at Montfort. He dispensed corporal punishment with an abandon unthinkable in today's world, though this was common in most homes and schools in Ireland. My father was unemployed for two years and, while his lack of a full-time job bred frustration, I suspect he was deeply unhappy and confused. He was saddled with the responsibility of caring for an ever-increasing family when many of his contemporaries were, in their words, 'free and easy'. Catholicism's sexual rules, insisting marriage and sex were about procreation rather than pleasure, trapped him and persuaded him that only an intense devotion to God and the Church could offer meaning and provide serenity in his life.

He never left me with the impression he desperately wanted a large family, whereas my mother loved having lots of children. Did she know intuitively by having a child every twelve months she was weaving her web round him? It is a possibility I have toyed with over the years, one that might contain an element of truth. After all, when he entered the bosom of the Clarke family, with his mother-in-law and her sisters living yards from his front door and St Peter's his backdrop, Catholicism would inevitably have a major role in his daily existence. No doubt, the dynamics of his marriage also played a significant part in shaping his life. In retrospect, two forces dominated him − a deep faith in God and a wife with a forceful personality. My mother made all the critical decisions for the family and joked about how much she spoiled him. She suffered the pain of childbirth over and over, did all the housework and managed the budget while raising ten children. Only when it came to enforcing the family rules was he the prime mover. 'Wait until your father comes home,' was a serious threat from Mum when one of us transgressed.

Not long after his marriage, my father found himself with no close friends and only the Church to provide guidance. During the many hours he spent with Fr Armstrong in the confessional, he was probably advised to stay in his marriage, pray about it and make the best of his lot. Irrespective of some of his failings, I admired his special attachment to the arts and his intellectual sophistication, which my mother lacked. She was bright and extremely capable, but she did not possess his natural intelligence. Nevertheless, her adoration and energy made her a more formidable character, enabling her to keep him corralled within her small social circle. She effectively detached him from people outside his family, including his father and siblings.

He had grown up as 'the darling' of the artistic Dillon set in 26 Lower Clonard Street. As a boy, he spent a lot of time with Uncle

Gerard, who was nine years older than him. He accompanied Gerard on sketching trips to Colin Glen and Black Mountain. When Uncle Joe returned to Belfast from London, he held nightly soirees in his tiny house for male friends, which my father frequently attended. They used to listen to Joe's extensive classical music collection, evaluating the merits of one singer against another, drink copious cups of tea and coffee, and smoke a lot. My father was never a smoker but liked tea. He kept attending the soirees after his marriage, but my mother soon insisted on joining him. This displeased Joe and his companions, and they made their feelings known. My mother was hurt by their rejection of her and eventually persuaded my father to stop going to Joe's. It was another example of how she denied him a life beyond their marriage, yet I fear it was also about something else. It was one thing keeping him apart from his younger siblings, but the senior Dillon clan represented a greater challenge to her dominance. In her eyes, they were artistic, bohemian and self-opinionated. They inhabited a world she knew little about. She may have feared they would entice her husband into their world, excluding her forever.

She always insisted Gerard and Joe Dillon never married because of their intense commitment to the arts. She claimed, however, that Joe fell in love with a rich woman in London, who paid for his singing lessons. The woman later jilted him when she met his brother, Gerard. The woman in question was Madge Connolly, who was gay and a friend of Molly, his sister. Madge established a deep friendship with Gerard after Joe left London. It is unclear if Madge became Molly's lover for a period. They remained close for the remainder of their lives. The presence of a rich female on the edge of Joe's life, and later Gerard's, allowed my mother to create the fiction that both brothers were ladies' men. I was never convinced my mother seriously believed her stories about 'those Dillons', even though she weaved them for decades. It is conceivable Uncle Joe and his siblings intimidated her because she could not easily define them as she did everyone else. Years later, she grew close to Gerard and Joe but still refused to accept any of the Dillons were gay. Yet, in a curious way, she loved it when Gerard, and his Dublin agent, Leo Smith, who was also gay, camped it up when they were with her.

I realised, in 1964, the biggest issue facing me was choosing how to frame my desire to end my 'vocation to the priesthood', a phrase my mother used fondly and often. She loaded these words with her expectation to have a priest for a son and her desire to convince me the calling came from God. I was very attached to her, so I reckoned I could convince her it was better for me to abandon my vocation if I could not give it the true and total commitment it deserved. I was not so confident I could have such a conversation with my father. He had never been the kind of man I could talk to freely and expect affection and understanding in return. He was rigid and demanding. His mantra was, 'It is not enough to be as good as the next guy, you must be better.' When anyone praised his knowledge of the arts or admired his art collection, he would reply, 'I'm just an ordinary man.' The fact he was a skilled watchmaker, later a telephone engineer and serious art collector did not improve his self-esteem. Knowing him well, as I did, I decided to say nothing to him about my personal drama and hope time would provide an answer on dealing with my problem.

That year stands out for the many changes occurring in my life, as well as in the world around me. While I was distancing myself from the priesthood, my grandfather, Patrick Dillon, was dying of cancer. Before he died, I was fortunate to spend five days with him and my father in Bundoran in the north-west of Ireland. He was too weak to fish, but he went with me to the Bundrowse River on the edge of town. We strolled along its banks, and he pointed out the spots where he had once fly-fished for salmon and sea trout. According to him, the river often gave up Ireland's first salmon of the season at the start of January. As he talked, his slight frame bent into the wind off the Atlantic Ocean, and there was a delay in his voice, as if he were choosing words carefully, knowing he would never speak them again. I could see he was savouring the opportunity to revisit his past, using the river to conjure up images of early spring and summer mornings when his fly drifted into the edge of a ripple that seconds earlier had betrayed the presence of a fish fresh from the sea. We talked about his Second World War experiences, which had been, until then, a closed topic. He said it was a period he had tried to forget. He did not like recalling the horror of watching his fellow soldiers being slaughtered on the beach at Dunkirk. He had been sure he, too, would die a lingering death from a German bullet. But luck had saved him. Before the end of the war, he returned to France armed with his Thompson submachine gun and a fly-rod. Prior to the Normandy Landings in 1944, he read that Northern France had fine trout rivers. He expected the Allies to defeat 'the Krauts', and he was determined to catch fish to celebrate the victory.

In the months before he died, he fought a different war, this time against the terrifying pain of cancer, refusing painkillers the way his late wife Francie did. Like her, he saw suffering as a form of redemption. In the final weeks before his passing, the pain became so unbearable he agreed to manage it with morphine. On the morning he died, I was at his bedside with my father and his brothers. We said prayers over him before my father and his brothers lifted his naked body, ravaged and browned as it was by cancer, and placed it on a bed sheet on the floor. While the adults left to make funeral arrangements, I remained behind.

Sitting on the floor next to my grandfather, I was a confused and bewildered 15-year-old boy, asking myself how life could recede so quickly, leaving behind an uncomfortable silence. I wanted to say something to him, but I couldn't find the right words. I reached out and touched his hand, as much to say a final goodbye as to receive the affirmation he was dead. His flesh was clammy and soft, and his fingers were as thin as those of a skeleton. I sat there, almost in a trance, until elderly Mrs Mc Court from next door arrived to wash his corpse.

In Ireland, we often respond to death with the sentimentality we associate with people leaving to settle abroad or with the wild beauty of our native land and its troubled history. People's reactions to death and their mortality can be so varied. Uncle Gerard's fear of an early death greatly influenced his artistic output and gave his life a sense of urgency. Gerard was only 45 years old, but he confided to my father that he felt he was 'on his way out'.

Growing up in Belfast, children of my generation were familiar with death, since we were often asked to pay our respects at wakes for relatives or neighbours. It was not uncommon to be in a house when someone died, or to stand over an open coffin saying the rosary. Woven into the fabric of life in Protestant and Catholic communities was a genuine closeness among friends and neighbours when it came to the tradition of waking. They shared a measured reverence for death.

SEVEN

Coming of Age

In late 1965, having made the break from Montfort, I found the end of my priestly vocation was not as traumatic as I imagined. Thankfully, my parents supported my decision to move on, even after several Montfort priests had travelled to Belfast to persuade me to return. It was not, however, all clear sailing. Leaving Montfort coincided with a transformative event in the life of my family related to my late uncle Joe. He left most of his worldly possessions to my parents, and in handling his last will and testament, they became personal friends of his legal advisers, Jim and Peter Fitzpatrick, who owned a reputable law firm in Belfast. Jim Fitzpatrick, a devout Catholic, was so impressed by my parent's devotion to the Church that he guided them through the purchase of a large family home in Chestnut Gardens, off Cliftonville Road in North Belfast.

For my mother, who had battled with raising a large family in a tiny two-bedroom house in Ross Place, a posh terrace house with three floors and five bedrooms was a gift from God. I was the first of my siblings to see it when I went with her to measure windows for curtains. It was in a neat, majority Protestant, middle-class area and had a garden at the rear. A cricket club sat opposite Chestnut Gardens, and on that first day I stopped to watch men 'in whites' play the game. Adjoining the cricket ground was the walled convent of the Poor Clares, an order of nuns who lived secluded from the world. Realising we would be the only Catholic family in Chestnut Gardens, my mother self-consciously remarked, 'We'll have to be on our best behaviour when we move in. We'll have to show a good example.' It was a philosophy she would follow in the years to come.

Damien was the only one in the family reluctant to leave our old stomping ground of the Lower Falls. His friends were in St Peter's parish, and in my years at Montfort those friendships had deepened. Just before the house move, he left St Gabriel's Secondary School and began working on construction sites before becoming a barman. After we settled in Chestnut, he chose to spend his spare time in the streets of our old neighbourhood. He liked drinking alcohol, a fact that caused a lot of friction with my parents. Damien was a free spirit and more in step with contemporary life than me. For example, he wore Levis jeans and bleached them white. He knew about Bob Dylan and some of the great blues singers before I had ever heard of them. His modern outlook, however, did not sit well with my mother's philosophy that we 'had to set a good example' for our Protestant neighbours.

She felt Damien compromised the image of a respectable Catholic family by strolling up and down Chestnut Gardens in his whitened jeans and laced-up leather boots. His growing rebelliousness related to our parents' decision to shut out the life we had once lived in Ross Place. He felt hurt when Mum told him he was an embarrassment. Sadly, he and I had grown apart during my Montfort years, and this left him with no one to share his feelings, especially his unhappiness with our new place. Meanwhile, I was coming to terms with life beyond the seminary, and a smaller rebellion was taking shape within me. I left St Malachy's College, which had been my first stop after Montfort. It reminded me too much of the seminary. The final straw came when a priest at St Malachy's beat me cruelly on the hands with a leather strap on a cold winter morning when I arrived at school two minutes after the bell rang.

On the advice of a friend, I transferred to St Patrick's Barnageeha School on Belfast's Antrim Road. An unusual academic institution, it offered a relaxed atmosphere. It was open to boys and young men of any religion, and when I enrolled there were students in their early twenties who had left jobs to return to study. The principal, Jimmy Steele, was undoubtedly one of the most freethinking school leaders of his generation. They used no physical discipline, and the staff comprised young, creative instructors. My literature teacher, Tony McAuley was a great example of Steele's educational strategy. Tony brought a fine intellect and an easy, contemporary manner into the classroom. In his spare time, he was a folk singer touring clubs throughout Ireland. We subsequently worked together as BBC producers, he in Schools Broadcasting and I in Arts. In some ways, I saw my new school as an ideal environment, allowing me the freedom to sample a life I felt had passed me by at Montfort. But it equally presented me with freedoms I did not know how to handle. I was like a victim released from captivity. I was anxious to enjoy every moment, minus the focus I had applied to my studies while I was a seminarian.

I was a late entrant to the Swinging Sixties era of psychedelic music and pot, so I felt I had to make up for lost time. Damien found my sudden interest in current music and my fascination with pot more than a little amusing. He had smoked pot, did not like it and advised me that alcohol, particularly Guinness, was a better option. One evening, after ranting about how fed up he was with our parents' strict guidelines, he packed some clothes in a rucksack and asked me to accompany him to Belfast Docks. He was bound for Birmingham where he believed lots of money could be earned in labouring on construction sites. He expected me to convey the news of his departure to our parents and only made that clear to me an hour before he left. Ironically, he departed Belfast on the same boat that once took me to Liverpool on my way to Montfort College. This time I was on the dockside to wave him off.

Our parents got upset when I told them he was gone, but they quickly tracked him down with the help of one of his buddies. Dad went to Birmingham and brought him home. But within a year, Damien was off again, this time for good. For the next fifteen years, Mum hoped every day he would contact her. But he never did. I tried unsuccessfully to trace him through the Salvation Army's International Investigation Branch, an organisation for which I have a special admiration. Damien's absence took an emotional toll on our mother. She had fears of him falling into bad company and being murdered. When Damien wrote a letter home, fifteen years later, it came with a Newcastle-Upon-Tyne address. I drove to England to see him, and when we met he pretended not to recognise me at first. I spent several days with him and met him again briefly when he paid several visits to our parents.

The detachment he exhibited towards his family was surely born from the isolation he felt before he left home. Perhaps, he believed he was unloved, although he has never spoken of it. In the few times we have been together, I have tried to discuss my feelings with him, but he has been reluctant to revisit the past in a serious way.

Instilling order in my life proved elusive for several years after leaving the seminary. I lacked responsibility, and that became self-evident when I left home in 1967 without as much as a goodbye to my parents and siblings. I took the ferry to Liverpool and hitch-hiked to London, arriving at Uncle Gerard's flat in Hampstead the following evening. He was shocked when he came home at midnight with a boyfriend and found me sitting on my rucksack at his front door. Nevertheless, he was pleased to see me and I was thrilled to be with him. His flat was just as I had imagined it. The walls were covered with works of art, not all of them his, and he had painted his bathroom door and bed board with figures and abstract images. He made tea and insisted on knowing why I left home so unexpectedly. I told him I wanted to escape the narrow confines of Belfast for the summer. I planned to travel to King's Lynn as soon as possible to earn money working on the North Sea gas pipeline or in factories canning strawberries and peas. I intended to meet a friend from Belfast, Paul 'Stevie' Stewart, in King's Lynn, but we would later go to France and work there too. Uncle Gerard found my plans 'more than a little unstructured' and suggested it might be better to work several months in England and return to Belfast. Since I had once confided in him my desire to become a journalist, he conceded my experience away from home would be valuable, but it should not be an end in itself. I remained with him for three weeks and then took to the train to King's Lynn to meet my friend Paul 'Stevie' Stewart. Stevie chose the nickname to honour his idol, the famed guitarist and singer-songwriter, Stevie Winwood.

Our trip to England had been bankrolled by an ingenious, if not criminal enterprise to raise the money. From experience, we had learned that the majority of young people who boasted about smoking grass had never smoked the real thing, much less rolled a joint. Such ignorance offered us a wonderful opportunity to provide an alternative to weed. We had discovered how a combination of parsley, thyme and oregano could be marketed to naïve thrill seekers. We once bought the herb mixture and purchased small brown packages of the type we had seen drug dealers use. We marked the packets as £5, £10 and £20 deals and filled them with the herb concoction. We then sold approximately £100 worth of the stuff in well-known Belfast bars like The Hercules and Kelly's Cellars. However, one of the unpleasant aspects of the scam involved having to smoke our herb and tobacco concoction, to convince prospective buyers to hand over their money. When we arranged meetings with 'buyers' we staged little performances, cupping a joint between our hands and sucking loudly to enhance the overall effect. Sometimes, we would remark how strong it was and pretend we had just taken a powerful hit that sent us to another dimension. Not wishing to appear naïve, our customers were always anxious to demonstrate their coolness and never questioned the quality of the 'weed'. There must have been a placebo effect because we saw people puffing our product and behaving as though they were on LSD.

By the time Stevie got to King's Lynn, I had begun working on the North Sea gas pipeline. But when I couldn't get him a job, I joined him in a factory canning strawberries but earning less money. At that stage, we lived in a friend's flat in the centre of King's Lynn where we hung out in the Whisky-A-Go-Go café and acted like hippies, much too late to the party. It seemed like a good time to leave England, so we hitch-hiked through France in early autumn, sleeping in barns and in cemeteries. One morning in Nice, on the French Riviera, we decided to make a pilgrimage to Kathmandu in the Himalayas where it was said people smoked a lot of weed and achieved enlightenment. In order to bankroll the trip, Stevie proposed phoning his brother, a bank manager in Northern Ireland. However, he did not have his phone number, so we had to ask the British Consulate to help. When Consulate staff could not locate his brother, I asked them to contact my father, believing he would show us generosity. I was wrong. He insisted on speaking to the consul and told him to send me packing to England. The consul seized our passports but provided us with boat and train tickets to England. The British government returned my passport the following year when I reimbursed them for my transport costs. The whole incident was embarrassing, though it proved to be a salutary warning that I had to get my life in order.

When we reached England, I told Stevie I was heading home, and he accompanied me as far as Blackpool. From there, I hitch-hiked to Stranraer and took the ferry to Carrickfergus. It depressed me to part ways with Stevie, given all we had shared. We shook hands on a patch of waste ground near railway tracks after I told him my days of being a hippie had ended. His had just begun, he declared, because he planned to travel a lot. I can still see him waving goodbye, his long hair tied in a ponytail, a guitar slung over his shoulder. I only met him one more time when he paid a brief visit to Belfast years later. I heard from a mutual friend he lived on the Channel Islands before settling in Australia. I often wonder if he still calls himself Stevie. It always seemed an appropriate name for him.

I was returning to a Northern Ireland where the past was returning with a vengeance. Angry people were constructing the elements for a bonfire of tribal prejudices, and before long they would light it. Little did I know that life would soon change in ways I could not have imagined.

PART TWO

EIGHT

The Troubles and Journalism Beckon

On my arrival home, my sisters greeted me like the prodigal son, but my mother took a little longer to accept I was ready to change my life for the better. She looked at my hair, the long sideburns, the John Lennon spectacles and bleached jeans, and she ordered me to leave. Like Damien often did, I hurried through the rear garden and was halfway down the back lane when all my sisters ran from the house and caught up with me. They surrounded me, some of them in tears, and pleaded with me to return. Grabbing my arms, they led me indoors. Seeing their determination, my mother's mood softened. When I unloaded my rucksack, she was shocked to find it full of poetry anthologies, a critical work on TS Eliot and novels by Andre Gide and Stendhal.

'Did you carry all those books through England and France?' she asked, in disbelief.

'They were with me everywhere I went,' I said.

'Well, let's hope you learned something from reading them,' she said. Smiling, she picked up a scrapbook in which I had written poems and journal entries about my travels. 'There's someone I must talk to about you because your Uncle Gerard seems to think you have talent. God knows where he got that idea,' she added.

The 'someone' was Jim Fitzpatrick, the solicitor, who had made it possible for my parents to buy the house in Chestnut. Jim and his brother, Peter, owned a sizeable share of the *Irish News*, and Jim was on the Board of Directors.

I had often shared my journalistic ambitions with friends like Stevie, Elise Blake, Kieran Halligan, Deirdre Brady and her sister, Ann. Kieran went on to become a highly successful international entrepreneur. For once, I sensed I was on the right road, having purged my brain of the nonsense I filled my head with after leaving Montfort. Now, I was ready to focus on a writing career. Jim Fitzpatrick read some of my poetry and asked me if I wanted to work for the *Irish News*. He persuaded the Mc Sparrans, the majority owners of the paper, to take me on as a trainee journalist. I was fortunate to be mentored by veteran journalist, Joe Devlin, editor of the *Irish Weekly*, a title owned by the *Irish News*. He was responsible for selecting and editing news stories and features. Also a wonderful teacher, he involved me in everything he did, including putting the paper to bed each week. I happily worked as many hours as he required and was thankful when he enlisted me in a journalism course. It provided me with a shorthand speed of 160 words per minute, a useful tool for a budding reporter. While I enjoyed working with Joe, my ambition was to be a full-fledged reporter. With his help, I undertook late shifts on the *Irish News* sub-editorial staff to learn how to re-write copy and identify flaws in stories written by my colleagues.

At that time, I had not paid much heed to the politics of my native city, even though I was familiar with the social, political and historical complexities of Ireland. My entry into journalism changed all that because it also coincided with major political upheavals in Northern Ireland. These disturbances began towards the end of the failed 1956– 62 IRA campaign, when a new generation of young, better-educated Nationalists burst on the scene. Their appearance coincided with the dynamic rise of the Reverend Ian Paisley. He preached a brand of fundamentalist Presbyterianism riddled with anti-Catholic rhetoric and downright hostility. Paisley quickly became a larger-than-life figure towering over Northern Ireland in the mid to late 1960s. His influence undoubtedly led to the re-emergence of the cult of the gunman in both communities. He also presented a threat to the Unionist political monolith, much like Tea Party candidates within Republicanism in the

United States in 2010. On the sidelines, the IRA was licking its wounds, uncertain about its future. Its leaders had begun to accept that violence would not bring a United Ireland any closer. The realisation constituted a political metamorphosis with roots in the political education process among IRA members incarcerated during the organisation's disastrous 1956–62 Border Campaign. They left prison disillusioned and shunned by Catholic Nationalists. In their desire to come to terms with the new reality, they fell back on the attachment they formed in prison to the teachings of James Connolly, the prominent socialist of the 1916 Rising. In Connolly's writings they saw the genesis of a solution to their own faded political philosophy and toyed with the prospect of marrying Connolly socialism with Marxism to create a political agenda for a new era. Their desire to concentrate on politics and forsake the cult of the gunman should have convinced the majority ruling Unionists to be magnanimous and recognise Catholics were entitled to the same basic rights as people throughout the British Isles.

According to Eamonn McCann, a fine writer and commentator, who was a prominent figure in the politics of the mid- to late 1960s, there was a general perception in 1962 among Catholics in Derry's Bogside that the IRA was finished as a mechanism for advancing the community because its Border Campaign had been its 'last throw of the dice'. Unionists, especially the Rev. Ian Paisley, did not see it that way, and McCann asserts that was due in part to them lacking 'lines of communication into the Catholic community'. McCann stated, 'With all the benefit of hindsight, I think they must have known that the IRA was a dead duck in places like the Bogside. And I think one of the reasons, therefore, they kept on about the IRA and warned the Protestant people it was lurking in the shadows, waiting to emerge at any moment, was precisely to frighten their own people and keep them corralled within Unionism.'

The late 1960s, as I recall, was the era of a presidential-type Unionist leadership. Prime Minister, Capt. Terence O'Neill, a product of Eton and the landed gentry, talked about reform but lacked a fine political intelligence. After becoming Northern Ireland's fourth prime minister, he presented himself as a liberal, but the reality was different. His real aim was to ensure the survival of the Unionist political machine rather than rid the society of its many ills, in particular gerrymandering and discrimination against Catholics in jobs and housing. He offered Catholics the prospect of change, but it was an offer lacking commitment, direction and assertiveness. He showed little appetite for a loyal opposition in the Northern Ireland's Stormont Parliament and believed the Northern Ireland Labour Party of 1963 was a greater threat to Unionism than the Catholic Nationalist Party. In his defence, from the outset of his premiership, he faced a formidable challenge to reform from Paisleyism and more significantly from the political hard men in his own party, who had no desire to alter the status quo. By 1967, he also had to deal with a more vocal Catholic community after the Northern Ireland Civil Rights Association took to the streets. He and his cohorts in the Unionist Party's ruling class saw NICRA as a tool of the IRA even though it was not advocating dismantling the State. At its formation, it was a broad church without mass appeal and with modest aims, which included the granting of one man, one vote and the ending of discrimination in housing. Young Republicans, as well as students and reformers impressed by US civil rights marches, joined its ranks. In some respects, the fact NICRA was never a mass movement led to individual interests believing they could manipulate it.

Some in the Protestant community genuinely feared an imminent threat to the State. It flowed from the rise of a more demanding Catholic minority and traditional fearmongering by Unionist leaders, plotting in the shadows to overthrow their own prime minister. They feared his reforming zeal would weaken Unionism's grip on the society. They didn't have to fear O'Neill because he was not a true reformer. They could not see that. Political narrow-mindedness and a lack of vision persuaded them any concession to Catholics was dangerous. Some of the plotters had connections to extreme elements within Loyalism, including the Ulster Volunteer Force and members of Paisley's Free Presbyterian Church. Due in part to Paisleyism, a bonfire of prejudice and bitterness had been building since the early years of the decade, and by 1968 it became a real danger, needing only an event or a person to ignite it.

Towards the close of the 1960s, a great deal of blame could be shared for the fragile state of Northern Ireland and the basic flaws in its body politic. In my opinion, the majority of it lay with Westminster because Britain was the sovereign power. It had turned a blind eye to the problems of the Northern Ireland State from its creation. It pursued a principle of non-interference as long as Unionists kept a lid on the Ireland problem. It did not matter how Unionists did it as long as it worked. It was a morally bankrupt philosophy by successive British leaders, which resulted in Northern Ireland being logged in a dusty file in the British Home Office as though it held no political significance to the parliament's business in London. As a consequence, the Westminster political elites had zero intelligence on how the Unionist ruling machine functioned or how it employed prejudice, fear and discrimination as political tools. Catholic and Protestants were betrayed by successive British governments whose hands-off principle contributed enormously to the eventual breakdown of civil order and the emergence of a new and reinvigorated IRA built for a long war. An event that symbolised for me the developing chaos of the late 1960s was the police violence against civil rights marchers, including several prominent Catholic political leaders, on the afternoon of 5 October 1968, on Duke Street in Derry.

The violence of 5 October shocked people internationally and encouraged leaders in both communities to step back from the brink. NICRA declared a moratorium on marches and the N. Ireland Prime Minister, Terence O'Neill, responded with a broadcast speech to the people of N. Ireland, which became known as the 'Crossroads Speech'. In it, he reminded Catholics and Protestants they were all 'Ulstermen' and appealed for communal unity and sanity. I suspected Kenneth Percy Bloomfield, his Cabinet Secretary, crafted the speech in part or in full. Bloomfield was later knighted and became Head of the N. Ireland Civil Service. In retirement, the British Broadcasting Corporation appointed him as their Northern Ireland Governor. In that post, he succeeded Lady Lucy Faulkner, widow of Brian Faulkner, who was a major figure in a plot to overthrow Capt. Terence O'Neill in the late 1960s. The BBC had a penchant for appointing mostly Unionist figures to the role of Governor and also to its Broadcasting Council, which oversaw the Corporation's radio and television output in N. Ireland. Unlike Lady Faulkner, Bloomfield set up a personal office in BBC Broadcasting House, Belfast. I always felt the BBC did itself a disservice by appointing heavily politicised figures from one community to the role of overseeing broadcasting in N. Ireland. Bloomfield, however, had a deep knowledge of broadcasting and was helpful when I met him in 1991 while producing a documentary series on the Troubles for BBC Television's *Timewatch* department. I was keen to interview him for the programme, but an opportunity never arose.

At this time, I was trying to locate, and if possible retrieve, BBC archive film of Brian Faulkner marching through the predominantly Catholic Longstone Road area of County Down in the mid-1950s. I believed the footage of Faulkner provided a singularly potent image of how Unionist and Orange Order triumphalism of the period asserted itself. I told Bloomfield someone had reliably informed me a senior BBC executive had gifted the archive film to Lady Faulkner when she retired as National Governor. I also informed Lady Faulkner I needed to locate the film. She was not helpful. At the same time, I discovered that most of BBC N. Ireland's archive film footage of past political events, including the early days of the Troubles, had been destroyed in the 1970s, or perhaps early in the 1980s. I did not ask Bloomfield to legislate the matter. He was not involved with the BBC during that period. I did, nevertheless, mention it to others, who hinted the archive was destroyed 'by mistake'. They said 'somebody' had given permission to get rid of unnecessary archive files, and the person charged with the task destroyed a large number of files representing a vitally important record.

Capt. O'Neill's 'Crossroads' speech was seen by some as a genuine attempt to encourage both communities to unite in a common cause for peace, but others felt it was too little too late. Michael Farrell, a young left-wing socialist, deemed it 'a sham' and, in its wake, embarked on an enterprise that would provide the spark to light what the historian, Paul Bew, called 'the prairie'. Farrell was part of a political student group, Peoples Democracy, also known as the PD, within the civil rights movement. According to PD members, the moratorium on marches was capitulation to a prime minister who could not be trusted. They decided to march from Belfast to Derry, beginning on New Year's Day, 1969. It went into history as the 'Burntollet March', named after a place along its route where marchers were set upon and badly beaten by extreme Protestant elements and members of the B-Specials out of uniform. The RUC stood by idly at various points along the route where attacks took place, but it was at Burntollet where the most savage assaults happened.

After the events in Duke Street, the prospect of such a march had worried many civil rights leaders, while others remained ambivalent. Some commentators subsequently categorised the Burntollet March as a 'nakedly sectarian enterprise'. Eamonn McCann said he thought at the time it was 'explicitly devised to challenge O'Neill and say to people in civil rights they shouldn't trust him'. He added, 'Those who trusted O'Neill said logically enough, "well let's get off the streets and let's give the man a chance". We said no, no more chances, he's had his chance. Unionism's had its chance.'

The Burntollet March began on the morning of 1 January 1969, and I can still recall watching it from a window of the *Irish News*, with my mentor, Joe Devlin, at my side. A ragtag group of thirty-five to forty student activists, some carrying placards, shouted slogans while marching up Donegall Street as if they were going to a football game. Joe thought it was comical and commented they were in for 'a real drenching and frostbite' on their way across the Sperrin Mountains to Derry. Neither of us felt we were witnessing the genesis of an event that would radically change the dynamics of protest in general and set the tone for an inter-communal war.

Soon I began hearing daily reports of the marchers being attacked, especially when more people joined the march as it traversed the outskirts of predominantly Protestant districts. Policemen were supposedly on hand to form a protective shield around the demonstrators. But as Eamonn McCann later pointed out, the police had melted away near Burntollet, leaving marchers exposed to a carefully planned ambush. They were pelted by a barrage of stones and other objects thrown from a hillside. Attackers whooped and hollered, descending in groups on the main body of the march. As marchers scattered onto the banks of the nearby River Faughan and into fields, McCann recalls them being 'hunted down' by men with clubs studded with nails. Some police mingled with the assailants, and that was something McCann later concluded could not be explained by the State.

Over two decades later, Michael Farrell shared with me that the march was modelled on the famous Selma to Montgomery civil rights march in the United States. He also linked it to the events in May 1968 in Paris. In my opinion, he missed an important element in trying to establish those connections. The radicalism in Europe and the protest movement in America lacked the political variables in Ireland. In the wider Northern Ireland civil rights movement, people held varying political perspectives and objectives, including the Romantic Republicans, who saw the rising political unity of the Catholic community as an asset to be nurtured. Historians sometimes overstate that particular element, but it was nevertheless present within the civil rights movement. The radical Left, with its eyes on Europe, also wanted a piece of the action, as did the failed IRA leaders of the 1956–62 campaign, who saw the social issues of the civil rights movement dovetailing with their developing critique of Connolly socialism and Marxist-Leninism. In the mix, too, were those who ardently wanted democracy to work and some who hoped the British government would finally exercise its moral and sovereign responsibility for governing Northern Ireland in a meaningful, British, democratic manner.

NINE

Setting the Record Straight

On 2 June 1969, I turned twenty and officially became a reporter with the *Irish News*. I also began dating an attractive, intelligent girl, Mildred, who was two years my junior. She would later be a better wife than I would be a husband. Having a girlfriend and a job impressed my mother who praised me for showing 'signs of maturing'.

In June and July 1969, the rhetoric on the streets was shrill and threatening. Adults of my parents' generation began warning of a return of 'The Pogroms', which blighted the 1920s, but I felt they were being alarmist. Within three years, however, I would find myself trying desperately to avoid the pitfalls of reflex journalism in order to investigate the conflict in depth. For example, as the society descended into a ghastly sectarian war I had to fight to make sense of macabre assassinations. Reporting them as facts without examining the underlying causes did a disservice to readers and to my profession. Over time, this approach would even place me at odds with several of my bosses in print and broadcast media. I would eventually go to great lengths to try to present the truth even when it meant professional conflict with editors and threats from terrorists.

For those of us who lived through the Troubles, four days of August 1969 symbolised much of what was wrong with our society. In that short time span, sectarianism opened up festering wounds, vigilantism became the norm, paranoia spread like a virus, and British troops marched into the Lower Falls, somewhat bemused and bewildered. Most of them had probably no understanding of the Ireland issue, and some might have thought Northern Ireland was a far-flung colony of the United Kingdom. That was understandable. Northern Ireland had always been a place apart for the British Army and British diplomats as some of them later confessed. Therefore, it was hardly surprising in August 1969 the tribal geography of Belfast and Derry confused the British Army.

Violence erupted in Derry on 12 August, proving once again the walled citadel was a lightning rod for all the historical grievances of Catholics. It was also the cradle for a Protestant community burdened with a siege mentality. This had been driven by real fears their cherished traditions were being trampled on by Irish Republicans. Trouble began, as it always did, in the traditional way when thousands of Apprentice Boys arrived from across the Province to commemorate the defence of the city against the forces of the Catholic English King James in 1689. Tension was already high after sectarian clashes in early summer, and in any other society the march would have been banned in the interests of public order. Such a move, however, was unthinkable for a Unionist Establishment built on decades of triumphalist Orange parades. In many instances, organisers routed Orange parades directly through Catholic districts, or skirted the edges of them. Bands, some of them day visitors from Glasgow in Scotland, played 'Kick-the-Pope tunes' while their followers sang anti-Catholic songs. It was a manifestation of a majority population saying to the minority we can march where we wish because this is our land.

To suggest, as some have, the Orange parades I witnessed as a youngster were Mardi Gras events is simply blind revisionism. Had the Orange Order of the time cared about the sensitivities of the other community, it would have excised the bitterness in its ranks and stamped out the anti-Catholic nature of its parades. It would also have exercised discretion in the routing of its marches, given the sectarian geography of the Province. In that way, the parades might have taken on a more generally acceptable character. In fact, the Orangemen in my circle of friends when I was older did not regard the summer marching season as an opportunity to offend Catholics. I respected their attachment to their tradition and their right to celebrate it but not in the way the Orange Order and the Unionist political establishment saw fit.

The real problem lay with the State as constituted, in that both sides lacked the ability to respect or understand each other's inherited cultural and political values. Most significantly, the mechanisms of the State were shaped to guarantee a majority rule, which was constructed round the manipulation of electoral boundaries and a determination to ensure Catholics remained second-class citizens void of British civil rights. Ironically, Catholic and Protestant working-class families were much alike in many ways. They lived in substandard housing, had high levels of unemployment and worked in the same linen mills as their forebears. When my old friend Mary Mc Kenna told me, 'even the cats in the Shankill and Falls were like the people in those districts' it struck a chord with me.

On 12 August 1969, Derry embodied every element of separateness dating back longer than any of its citizens could remember. Nevertheless, most of them knew their respective community's history well enough, even if they had never read it on the page. That was the crux of the problem. No one needed to read it on the page because emblems, slogans, poems and songs had given Ireland its shape and voice. The same applied in the Middle East and the Balkans where a word or a flag can, even today, lead to mass protest and conflict. In Derry, the oral history tradition kept everyone abreast of what was presumed to have happened hundreds of years earlier. Now, following the controversy and anger generated by the 5 October march of the previous year, and the Burntollet March seven months before, the smallest offence was likely to give way to violence. Community leaders on both sides should have realised calmer heads were needed that August day and holding a parade might invite a riot.

Trouble erupted when Apprentice Boys on the ramparts began hurling coins into the Bogside. A short time later, the main Apprentice Boys' parade snaked towards Waterloo Place on the edge of the Bogside where a large Catholic crowd, hemmed in by lines of policemen, met it. Leading Catholic Nationalist figures like John Hume tried to calm the Catholics, but most had little appetite for sanity, including the police.

Eamonn McCann was there in the Bogside and felt people were not sure if they were 'preparing for war or preparing to prevent it'. In Waterloo Place, insults exchanged between the two camps failed to increase the tempo. It appeared the situation might be contained until someone on the Catholic side threw a handful of nails at the police lines. It was enough for all hell to break loose. Acting on orders, the police cleared Waterloo Place and charged the Catholics. Apprentice Boys joined the police in what would quickly become known as the 'Battle of the Bogside'.

Back in the *Irish News* in Belfast, I was dealing with stories about the Bogside rioting phoned in by a wide range of people in Derry. Most of the callers expected Belfast to erupt, too, and wild rumours circulated that the Irish Army was moving to the border. In Derry, some people claimed Irish troops had already arrived. By the morning of 13 August, the police in Derry had been fought to a standstill, their lines severely weakened by scores of injured. Nevertheless, Bogsiders called to Catholics elsewhere in Northern Ireland to open up fronts to take the heat off them. They responded with impromptu rioting. In Belfast, Catholic mobs attacked police stations in the Falls area and shots rang out. The Irish prime minister, Jack Lynch, warned his government would 'not stand idly by'. It was an incendiary threat, which led many Protestants to fear an invasion from the South was imminent. When James Callaghan, the British prime minister, heard Lynch's warning, he told his advisers the Irish premier 'had lost his mind'.

On the evening of 14 August, Protestants unleashed a backlash in response to many factors, including fear and anger at the attacks on the police by Catholic mobs. Historically, the two communities settled their differences with violence. Not surprisingly, the thrust of the counterattack came in the area where I was born but no longer lived: the Lower Falls. It was vicious and well-orchestrated, involving extreme Loyalists, as well as members of the RUC and B-Specials, some of whom were out of uniform. Protestant mobs swept towards the Falls, systematically setting alight Catholic homes in Cupar Street, Dover Street, Percy Street and Conway Street. Catholics in those streets piled what belongings they could on carts and fled. In the Clonard area, fire claimed houses alongside Clonard Monastery, and there was a real fear the monastery would be overrun and its priests slaughtered. Cathal Goulding's IRA was unprepared since there were probably only six or seven weapons in the hands of the Falls area IRA. Strolling through the Falls on the afternoon of 15 August, I was shocked at the scale of the devastation. Rows of homes were still smouldering, and people wandered aimlessly, as if in a daze. Clonard Monastery had not been damaged, but homes in several streets close to it were on fire or were fiery ruins.

At the corner of Clonard and Bombay Streets, a young man with a shotgun brushed past me. I recognised him from my primary schooldays in St Finian's. Within minutes, he vanished into an alleyway, accompanied by a second gunman carrying a Winchester rifle. Bombay Street was a burning wasteland, the air heavy with the acrid smell of charred wood and slate. I backed against a wall when gunfire erupted from the interface of Bombay Street and the Protestant streets adjoining it. RUC documents later presented to the Scarman Tribunal, which investigated the events of August 1969, claimed twenty-one Protestants in the area behind the monastery were treated for non-life threatening gunshot wounds from two weapons – a shotgun and a rifle.

A small number of British troops arrived on the streets of Belfast and Derry by the afternoon of 15 August, but they were in such small numbers they were unable to change the dynamics of the situation, especially in Belfast, where the geographical borders of the two communities were blurred. As a young reporter, eager to be close to the action, I watched soldiers marching up Divis Street, bayonets fixed like they were on a parade ground. Catholics welcomed them, offering them tea and biscuits. The veteran reporter, Jim Campbell, who also observed the troops, said they looked thrilled, if not somewhat confused by the warmth of their welcome. He heard locals singing the Irish national anthem, 'The Soldier's Song', and judged by the response from the troops they thought it was sung in their honour.

I was also on the scene with my notebook when locals in Clonard Street pleaded with Lieutenant Colonel Napier of the Prince of Wales' Own Regiment to deploy troops to protect the monastery. He told them he lacked the resources to do the job. The opinion of the local IRA, always ready to exploit a situation, was that it was typical of the British Army to stand by while Catholics faced danger. But Catholics themselves didn't see it that way. They hailed British soldiers as heroes and showed hostility to Republicans. Within days, slogans reading 'IRA = I Ran Away' appeared on walls throughout West Belfast.

I visited my family to discover my parents, sisters and little brother were terrified Protestant mobs would selectively burn out Catholic homes in the Cliftonville area. To the credit of three of our Protestant neighbours, one of them a leading member of the Orange Order, they visited my family to offer their protection. That night, and for several subsequent nights, the three men stood for hours at the corner of Chestnut Gardens and the Cliftonville Road, prepared to confront intruders, even though they lacked weapons. My parents and siblings never forgot the gesture. It epitomised what was good about people on both sides.

In the aftermath of the attacks in the Falls and Bogside, barricades appeared in Catholic and Protestant districts and vigilantism took hold of Belfast and Derry. I was on the streets of Belfast chasing down stories every day, unconcerned about the dangers I might encounter. I was young, full of enthusiasm and naïve. I believed my press card guaranteed me immunity, and to some extent it did. It was a time when the press was respected. The fact I worked for a Catholic Nationalist newspaper rarely generated antagonism when I visited Protestant areas. On the contrary, people were determined to tell me their side of the story, and they were pleased if they thought I would truthfully reflect it. In the Shankill, locals complained Protestants had got a bad press since the start of the civil rights marches. However, they blamed the international media, rather than local reporters like me, for believing the Catholics' version of events.

There was some truth in that. The international media had tended to focus more on the plight of Catholics, and foreign correspondents had received a warmer welcome in the Falls and other Catholic districts than in Protestant ones. Protestants often had themselves to blame because they were instinctively antagonistic when faced with foreign television news crews.

Catholics, on the other hand, craved the limelight like stage performers. They were more public relations savvy than their Protestant counterparts, having learned from the mid-1960s how embracing the media brought their story to a wider audience, thereby placing greater pressure on British political leaders in London. There was also a young, educated Catholic generation anxious to face the cameras and have their voices heard. In particular, I would single out Eamonn McCann, Bernadette Devlin, John Hume, Seamus Mallon and Austin Currie. In contrast, Unionists like Brian Faulkner and William Craig were dour figures, and international reporters often perceived Paisley as the leader of a religious, lunatic fringe.

Since those violent days of August 1969, several commentators have attempted to re-write the history of what occurred, seeking to blame one side or the other. For example, I read where a local scribe tried to make the point that Catholics had refused to accept they were responsible for the backlash that left the Falls burning that August. That is simply a crude rendering of the events of the time, which ignores a complex historical backdrop. It speaks to how a few writers, prompted by a desire to make a name for themselves, refused to embrace the truth, fearing they might be tainted by it. Over the years, honest reflections of the Troubles have attracted critics on both sides because people often choose to see the past through the prism of their deep sense of hurt or by way of learned untruths, oral or written. In my opinion, it is foolish to try to weigh and attribute blame to one or other community. History created fault lines throughout the island of Ireland, and people are slowly trying to repair them. If blame is to be directed at a source, it should be placed squarely at the door of those successive British governments who had constitutional authority over Northern Ireland. I have no objection to contemporary writers investigating and writing about the Troubles as a way of explaining why they happened. My worry is that some of them might feel it is time to create a scorecard. The dead and the families of the victims on both sides deserve a gentler and more exact accounting of the reality. To boldly state Catholics invited the horrors of those August days, or Protestants alone were to blame for the environment in which those events occurred, is to miss the nature of our history, namely the recurring tribal trends of the period. After the communal horrors of August, a new phase of the conflict took shape, exposing even deeper sectarian tensions. It began with the rise of vigilantism.

TEN

A Surreal, Violent Landscape

Belfast was quickly transformed into a surreal and dangerous place. Parts of the Falls and Shankill were all but sealed off from the outside world, and young men manning the blockades were members of hastily formed citizens' defence committees or new paramilitary recruits. They tended to be unpredictable and therefore dangerous and unpleasant. For many of them, protecting their own people was considered a badge of honour. So they often displayed arrogance and swaggered through the streets like they were in a Wild West show.

Scores of pubs across Belfast were looted and razed to the ground during the August mayhem. They were replaced by illegal drinking clubs, known on the Catholic side as 'sheebeens'. They became the focus of the social life of each community, providing cheap booze and in many instances live music. Before long, they fell under the control of paramilitaries, who used their profits to pay their staff salaries and to buy weapons. Criminal elements also ran some clubs and shared their profits with gunmen. Those profits were considerable because the alcohol sold in the clubs was looted from existing pubs deliberately selected for destruction or from hijacked brewery trucks. The club phenomenon mirrored life in the speakeasies of 1920s Prohibition America. Behind the revelry and entertainment, terror and criminal scams arose from smoke-filled backrooms.

I believe the clubs played a significant role in furthering divisions and promoting dangerous political agendas. In Catholic neighbourhoods, people exchanged rumours, talked politics, listened to revolutionary tunes and drank excessively in them. The violence had suddenly created an alternative universe in which everyone seemed to be drinking heavily or popping pills to stop hyperventilating. As time passed, a National Health centre, which treated aggressive psychopaths, closed for lack of patients. Society was dysfunctional at its core, lacking a mental health focus, which would traditionally have been applied to those with dangerous personality traits. Prior to the Troubles, men with very violent tendencies were shunned or filtered out of society and placed into restricted care. The explosion of naked anger and tribalism had the opposite effect. The sadistic Shankill Butchers and others like them were often glorified because they directed their sadism at 'the enemy'. It should be noted, though, that psychopaths of this kind were feared by the people they lived among. Neither community was spared the phenomenon, but Loyalist paramilitaries carried out most of the grisly murders involving torture. It could be argued their crimes reflected a religious, tribal war, but they were also part of the inhumanity that found expression in an atmosphere of lawlessness. In a society in conflict, humanity and many social norms frequently do not apply. People can find it difficult to distinguish between true ideologues and individuals living out bizarre fantasies.

A factor rarely mentioned, which may help explain why Loyalist killers carried out more horrific murders, was the lack of discipline within Loyalist paramilitary ranks. In contrast, the IRA had a tighter organisational structure, which permitted better control over rank-and-file members. While some within the Provisional IRA embraced criminality, as a rule, it tried to root out people with a criminal history from its ranks, and thieves and drug dealers were either executed or publicly punished. It also worked hard on promoting itself as the policing body in Nationalist areas. The fact it also had an ideological focus meant it was not shaped simply for tribal warfare or for the furtherance of a sectarian agenda. I met several prominent IRA leaders, both Officials and Provisionals, who fought sectarianism in their own ranks. I did not see a parallel effort within the command structures of Loyalist groups, especially the UDA, which was responsible for most of the sadistic murders of the 1970s. The UDA not only lacked ideological focus but fostered sectarianism and criminality. The organisation was fixated with the numbers of men it could put on the streets in masks and combat jackets and paid little heed to whether they were criminals or aggressive psychopaths. From its inception, the UDA nurtured a reflex desire for vengeance, and racketeers crammed its higher ranks. The UDA inevitably encouraged extreme violence, vengeance and organised crime.

In contrast, the UVF portrayed itself as a body modelled along military lines like the IRA. It effectively presented itself as an organisation with a military mystique. But like the UDA, it, too, played to a bloodthirsty element in its ranks. For example, the Shankill Butchers were members of the UVF, though the organisation's leadership pretended it never knew what the Butchers were up to or if they were truly UVF personnel. That was a deliberate fiction since the gang operated in the Shankill area, which was not merely the heartland of Loyalism but an area where the UVF held sway and where many of its rank-and-file officers lived. Drawing parallels between paramilitary groups on both sides, I would be inclined to say the UVF and the Provisionals had a lot in common. They both had politically astute leaders, and they understood the value of depicting themselves as inheritors and defenders of their respective traditions. They also recognised the importance of symbolism and were keen to proclaim they were ideologically pure and opposed to criminality. In many respects, the UVF mimicked the IRA and learned a great deal from its dual strategy of the ballot box and the Armalite. It never managed, however, to forge the relationship with its community that the Provisionals developed with theirs. It simply lacked the political imagination the Provisionals displayed by making Sinn Féin part of the cutting edge of their overall campaign. It could be argued the UVF was hampered by its closeness to its bigger brother organisation, the UDA, which helped give Loyalist paramilitaries the reputation for being sadistic killers and thugs. High levels of drug running within Loyalist groups by the mid-1980s and feuds between the UVF, UDA and other Loyalist paramilitary offshoots tainted the UVF and made it too difficult for it to become part of mainstream Unionist politics. That being said, there were many men I knew well in Loyalist ranks, who would just as likely have been prominent Provisionals or Officials had they been born Catholic. Equally, there were Provisionals I met, who would have become sadistic UDA killers had they been born Protestant. The Official IRA, through its creation of the Workers Party, set itself apart from all the other paramilitaries by arguing for greater dialogue between parties to the conflict and calling for an end to sectarianism.

As widespread sectarian violence engulfed the society in the early 1970s, Loyalist paramilitaries, including the Shankill Butchers, used some of the illegal drinking clubs in the Shankill and in East Belfast as killing sites. It was not uncommon for gangs to abduct Catholics off the streets late at night and take them to clubs to be beaten and tortured in front of revellers. Some of the most notorious murders I documented in *The Shankill Butchers* and *Political Murder in N. Ireland* happened in clubs. My friend, James Nesbitt, the detective who eventually brought most of the Shankill Butchers to justice, once shared with me the story of how he raided a club in the Shankill on a Saturday morning. He concluded from the blood-spattered walls and ceiling someone had been beaten and killed there the previous evening, more likely than not in front of a drunken, cheering audience. He was stunned by the fact no one had felt compelled to clean up the blood.

There was an unusual camaraderie behind the barricades, which I felt derived from a 'we're-all-in-it-together' philosophy. I saw young men strutting through clubs, pretending they were seasoned gunmen when they were simply loosely affiliated to local defence committees. In some instances, teenagers told me what was happening in their areas, but all they were doing was circulating gossip. The emotional intensity created by walled-in communities was fascinating, though frightening to observe. It produced dysfunctionality, enabling men with defined political objectives to impose their ideological templates on the majority.

In the days following 15 August, I was elated to be on the streets reporting for twelve hours and more each day. I got a call from Uncle

Gerard in Dublin, who was very upset by the televised images of streets ablaze in the Clonard area. He wrote to my father that it was fortunate his brother Joe was dead and no longer living with his little Dachshund in Lower Clonard Street. In an open letter to the *Irish Times* on 20 August, he announced he was withdrawing his work from an Irish Exhibition of Living Art scheduled for viewing in Belfast. His actions, he wrote, represented a public protest against the persecution of the Irish people in the North by the Unionist government. In particular, he singled out the Rev. Ian Paisley for special criticism. His *Irish Times'* letter displayed his anger and underlying compassion for the Lower Falls and its people. The tone, however, was ill-advised, a product of his impetuous nature. He also prepared a press statement, hoping his fellow artists and prominent people in the art world in Dublin would sign. Twenty-five Living Art Exhibitors signed the petition, as did 108 others, three of whom later withdrew their names. Gerard felt betrayed by artists he knew well, especially his friend, George Campbell, who refused to sign. My uncle seemed to have forgotten George was from a northern Protestant tradition and couldn't have been expected to align himself with a statement, which read as follows:

> We, the undersigned, propose that the Exhibition of Living Art should make a protest against the persecution of the Irish People by the present Stormont government by withholding this year's exhibition from the Arts Council of Northern Ireland, which had planned to show it in Belfast after it leaves Cork. And that the Living Art should give a lead in this and encourage all cultural bodies in Ireland to protest in every way and any form against the horror that the Stormont government has inflicted on the Irish People. Anything that will make the Stormont appear respectable should be denied them.

An *Irish Times* editorial subsequently took issue with my uncle, pointing out 'art should be above the battle'. It was a peculiar assertion. One cannot cushion art from life or expect artists to be apolitical or indifferent to politics. On the other hand, the *Irish Times* was justified in feeling Gerard had overstepped some boundaries. For example, he wrapped his protest in rhetoric that was unhelpful and hurtful to many Unionists who did not have an affinity with bigotry. One of the valid criticisms levelled by the *Irish Times* was the way Uncle Gerard's protest placed certain artists in a difficult position. In my opinion, my uncle should not have felt betrayed because some fellow artists would not withdraw their works from the exhibition. George Campbell, in the years following my uncle's death, regretted he had not signed, but that may have been due to the fact George and his wife, Madge, had by then become vocal in their opposition to British policymaking in Northern Ireland. By 1970, any ill feelings between my uncle and friends in the art world were forgotten. George Campbell later shared with me that he felt Gerard got caught up in the awful turmoil in 1969, and emotions were 'ragged' because he felt helpless watching events tearing at his attachment to his birthplace and its people.

In January 1970, the IRA, which had fractured after the events of the previous August, gave way to two movements – the Provisionals and the Officials. The latter were men of the Cathal Goulding variety, who had moved away from armed struggle into social action in the 1960s. In the aftermath of the August 1969 burning of hundreds of Catholic homes, followers reproached Goulding for leaving Catholics defenceless. His response was that he kept the IRA's guns in dumps south of the border during the mid to late 1960s to prevent them being used against Protestants, thereby creating a bloodbath in the North. The Provisionals were primarily anti-Goulding elements from the 1950s, who wanted the IRA to cast aside its Marxist ideals and return to orthodox Republicanism. At the core of the new Provisional IRA was a familiar romanticism driven by the 1916 Pearse tradition of the cult of the gunman. It promised action for a new generation of young men who had been on the streets battling the RUC and B-Specials with stones and petrol bombs. With its creation, the Provisional IRA was primarily focused on defence, but anyone with knowledge of Republicanism knew it was only a matter of time before it advocated rebellion as the means of 'cleansing Ireland of the British'. Before long, the new organisation would label British soldiers as members of an army of occupation. Real political energy and an underlying atmosphere of revenge defined January and February 1970. Young people on duty at the barricades in Catholic areas of West Belfast flowed into the ranks of the Provisionals. Among them were pupils from my old primary school, St Finian's, including Gerry Adams. By then he was already well schooled in Irish Republicanism, having come up through the ranks of the IRA's youth section, Fianna na hÉireann, commonly known as The Fianna.

A more defined agenda existed behind the Provisionals' public rhetoric of defending the Catholic Nationalist community. They wanted to build an arsenal of weapons, and the Republicanism they promoted required adherence to the principal objective of creating a United Ireland. The leadership cleverly realised from the outset the organisation was not militarily ready for a direct confrontation with the heavily armed British Army. It therefore told members to avoid, at all costs, gun play with British soldiers. The strategy helped the fledgling movement to grow unhindered and encouraged British political and military leaders to believe, naïvely as it turned out, it served no threat to the status quo.

One of the striking failures of British policymaking in 1969 was the unwillingness of the British Labour government to impose direct rule from London once troops were deployed to Belfast and Derry. Instead, Labour left the Unionist government at Stormont in control, thereby enabling it to influence the manner in which the British Army operated. An Army cannot function without an enemy, and it was only a matter of time before it found one. As far as Unionist leaders were concerned, the enemy was a Catholic population riddled with Republican insurgents, and the Army needed to deal decisively with them. In the heady days of August 1969, and for several months following, the British Army believed its role was to protect Catholics and restore order by placing itself between the warring factions. Some commentators have since referred to it as 'the honeymoon period', claiming it lasted from August 1969 until December 1969. I am not sure it lasted that long.

If anything, it lasted no more than six weeks because of two factors. First, the British Army Commander of Land Forces began attending twice-weekly security conferences at Stormont where rabble rousers blamed everything on the Catholic population, or as police chiefs and Special Branch might have put it, 'the enemy within'. Second, but equally as relevant, army officers argued they could only operate efficiently until a definable enemy faced them. They were the guys in the middle and knew it would be a dangerous place to be if a big religious shooting war began. At least that was the argument of senior army figures, though a disingenuous one, I contend. After all, it was a professional army trained to deal with a shooting war.

The Army's natural tendency to be heavy-handed quickly alienated Catholics in Belfast and played well for the emerging Provisionals. In Derry, as in Belfast, I witnessed small incidents involving soldiers and youths multiply. As a consequence, Catholics in the Bogside and Creggan areas of Derry became less congenial to the Army. I saw the same pattern play itself out on the streets of West Belfast and in the Ardoyne and New Lodge areas in the north of the city. I became increasingly aware of a growing antagonism towards the troops among Catholics who were not IRA supporters. They disliked the soldiers' rude and physically aggressive treatment of 'youngsters'. I recall being spreadeagled against a wall in the Lower Falls by a British Army foot patrol. They frisked me before I could reach into my pocket for my press card. When I asked an officer why I had been stopped and searched, he replied his men were doing their duty.

What I could not have anticipated was the chaos that would ensue after the British Labour government was replaced in June 1970 by a Conservative government led by Edward Heath. The worst sectarian violence in Belfast since the previous August erupted ahead of Heath's first visit to Northern Ireland. Orange marches and clashes in the Ardoyne area ensued, spilling over into a small Catholic enclave beside St Matthew's church in East Belfast. In the course of gun battles, five

Protestants and one Catholic were shot dead. The gunmen on the Catholic side were Provisionals, and in East Belfast, Billy McKee, one of the organisation's founders, led them. His perceived defence of St Matthews Catholic Church quickly entered Republican folklore. The gunmen opposing him were UVF members, as well as British soldiers and RUC personnel. I met a senior police officer, within weeks of the St Matthew's episode, who told me off the record he had had been on the roof of a factory in East Belfast from where police and soldiers fired on Provisionals operating from the grounds of the church. After McKee was shot, compatriots spirited him across the border for medical treatment.

Edward Heath and his Home Secretary, Reginald Maudling, had a British Army on their hands that was itching to impose its solutions on the growing conflict. Among its commanders were men with experience in colonial outposts, such as Kenya, Aden and more recently Cyprus. With Heath's approval, the Army was told it could get on with the job as it saw fit, and there would be no interference in its business. The Stormont government, too, told the generals it was time to take off the gloves. For reasons I can only conclude related to ignorance and a willingness to rely on Special Branch for intelligence, the military brass authorised a major weapons search in the Lower Falls. Anyone with a basic knowledge of the district knew it served as a predominantly Official IRA stronghold, and the Officials had played no part in recent gun battles. They also had made it clear they had no desire to kill soldiers. Nevertheless, on the afternoon of 3 July 1970, a search began, which yielded nineteen guns.

I was in the newsroom when word of serious rioting in the Lower Falls reached me. I grabbed a notebook and ran straight to Divis Street in time to see a mob stoning soldiers. Locals were angry that a military vehicle had run over a Catholic man, who died hours later. I didn't stay long. My goal was to get to Albert Street where most of the action was taking place. On my way, I heard explosions, which I took to be nail bombs – sticks of gelignite wrapped with nails. By the time I got to my childhood enclave of Ross Place, rioters had erected barricades in nearby streets. The area was a wasteland of burning cars, broken paving stones and other debris. The Provisionals drove the violence to show the locals they were gearing up to take on the Army. In reality, it was a boast they had no intention of fulfilling. They had no desire to start a minor war that might leak outside the Lower Falls into areas where they had their arms dumps.

Some Official IRA activists later admitted to me the Provisionals suckered them into a confrontation with the soldiers by throwing nail bombs and forcing the Army to commit more troops to the area. The Provisionals 'objective', so the theory went, was to deal a fatal blow to its Republican rival, the Officials, by dragging them into a big shootout that they would surely lose. I never found evidence to support the claim. On the contrary, what developed that evening reeked of inevitability. Yes, the Provisionals engineered a great deal of the street violence that night, but the British Army had already decided to bare its teeth.

I believe the Officials were reluctant to break out their guns until the Army forced their hand. A significant factor that motivated their transition from a non-offensive to an offensive posture was the residue of embarrassment they felt failing to protect the Lower Falls from Loyalist mobs the previous August. They had been demonised as cowards by Catholics in Belfast, and memory of the humiliation was still raw on that July evening in 1970.

The British Army leadership responded to the mayhem by deploying 3,000 soldiers. In the hours following, they fired 1,600 canisters of CS gas into the tiny streets of the Lower Falls. In many instances the gas was propelled from catapults over the roofs of houses in the most indiscriminate fashion. The operation quickly resembled ones used by the British military in 'colonial emergencies', most recently in Cyprus.

Clouds of CS gas rose from the ground as gas canisters exploded and were sometimes kicked like small footballs by young rioters. My eyes and throat burned, but much to my astonishment, many teenagers seemed immune to the gas. Elderly people and children were the real victims, and I heard many of them cry out in pain. I kept moving, fearing if I got too close to the action I could end up injured or dead.

When I was trapped by the rioters moving from one street to another, I used my local knowledge to find shelter. The air became so laden with gas, I sprinted to the nearby Royal Victoria Hospital and persuaded a nurse to give me a surgical mask. I soaked it in water and made my way back through the barricades to Raglan Street. At the corner of Panton Street, I saw several Official IRA officers taking rifles from a car. Minutes later, I heard the sharp crack of a rifle and realised guns would quickly make the areas insecure for everyone, including reporters like me. My friend, Michael Wright, an independent photographer and native of West Belfast, had spent part of the evening with me. But we lost touch when whole streets were blanketed by CS gas. He later told me he had made a sensible decision to retreat to the fringes of the area when the first shot was fired.

As darkness descended, I found myself back in Ross Place under St Peter's twin spires, overwhelmed with memories of Mary Mc Kenna and my great-aunts, their faces staring at me from the shadows of my childhood. I wondered how they would have felt to see their streets strewn with rubble and burned-out vehicles and hear the screams of anger and confusion. A man in a balaclava mask, armed with a sub-machinegun, brushed past me and hurried into an 'entry' next to No 7. Across the street, No 4 seemed to be empty, but in its narrow doorway a small, black cat was sheltering. He stared nervously at me before zig-zagging down the street into the church grounds. Above, the dark outline of the spires reminded me of the hawk that used to visit them in my boyhood.

At 10 o'clock that July evening, a British general announced from a helicopter everyone was to go indoors or face arrest. With the imposition of a curfew, I sensibly left the area, though some journalists remained and were arrested. During the night, a gun battle broke out between the Official IRA and the Army, and when the gunfire subsided, members of a Scots regiment ran amok in the area, ransacking homes and smashing and defiling religious ornaments. By dawn, scores of people had been dragged from their homes and placed in military custody. A large number of men and women, who had taken shelter in a school on Raglan Street, were also placed under arrest. The Army seized hundreds of pounds of gelignite and one hundred weapons, allowing them to claim the operation was an overwhelming success. The Stormont government said the weapons' seizures proved Catholic areas were in rebellion. Ironically, the Provisionals lost no men or guns and benefited significantly from the Catholic anger that followed. The Lower Falls Curfew, as it quickly became known, was a turning point for the whole society, politically and militarily.

Field Marshall Lord Michael Carver, whom I greatly respected, later shared with me in an interview that he felt the Army's Lower Falls strategy was 'a crude operation' because of an excessive use of force. He admitted it alienated the entire Catholic population, convincing moderate Catholic leaders the Provos were right when they claimed the Stormont government controlled the British Army. In the weeks following, the Provisional IRA's ranks swelled with young men ready to take on the soldiers. The IRA, however, persuaded its new members the time was not yet right for a direct challenge to the military. At the root of the Provisionals' standoff policy was the recognition that moderate Catholic leaders were not ready to countenance the killing of soldiers, who had arrived the previous year to protect Catholics. Nevertheless, that did not stop the Provisionals bombing businesses throughout Northern Ireland.

One can justifiably blame British Army generals for the Lower Falls Curfew debacle because it spoke not only to an excessive use of force but a desire to teach the Catholic population a lesson. The same generals and their political masters in the Heath Cabinet in 10 Downing Street were equally irresponsible in the indiscriminate use of internment without trial thirteen months later. As for the torture of several detainees at the start of the internment process, the guilty party was a special unit of British Military Intelligence, with close links to MI6. Some people will question my use of 'torture', but no other word adequately defines the techniques employed by that intelligence unit. The legal phrase subsequently used to describe what the detainees suffered was 'inhuman and degrading treatment'. I have never believed the phrase properly met the definition of what took place.

Field Marshall Carver told me that advisers misled him about the treatment of detainees and the special interrogation techniques used on them. He pointed an accusing finger at Sir Dick White, Heath's Chief Coordinator of Intelligence, whose job was to brief the PM and his cabinet on all intelligence matters. According to Field Marshall Carver, White may also have deceived Heath, Maudling and the Defence Secretary, Lord Carrington. Two decades later, when doing research for my book *The Enemy Within*, Michael Carver told me he regretted not asking enough questions when the intelligence unit's activities first came to his attention. While his honesty implied he and the British Cabinet might not have been operating with full knowledge of military intelligence strategies, it did not explain why Heath and his cabinet compromised the British Army by permitting it unfettered control over events on the ground in Northern Ireland.

Of all the British politicians I met, Sir Edward Heath was the most arrogant and obnoxious. His Home Secretary, Reginald Maudling, was so bored by his first visit to Northern Ireland that the only advice he gave the Army's top brass before leaving was to 'deal with these bloody people'. On his way back to London, he ordered an aide: 'Pour me a large Scotch! What a bloody awful country.'

In 1994, when I interviewed Heath in his wonderful home in Salisbury, I found him to be a most unpleasant man. Like his Home Secretary, Reginald Maudling, he regarded Northern Ireland as a troublesome place the Army knew best how to handle. My interview with him would later form part of a television documentary for Channel 4 entitled *The Last Colony*, examining the origins of the Troubles. Heath agreed to the interview after he was promised a fee of £1,000. I would have persuaded the producer, Ian Kennedy, to pay twice or three times that amount had Heath demanded it since I was sitting on explosive information about statements he made during a secret cabinet meeting in 1972.

Months before the arranged interview with Heath, I spent considerable time talking to Michael Carver. He expressed distaste for Heath and assured me other generals felt the same way. In talking to other generals, I found he was right. He let me into the secret of how he used to enter 10 Downing Street from a secret passageway linking the prime minister's residence with Whitehall. The passageway led to the garden of Number 10, and Carver normally used it to enter the residence. Once inside, he retrieved a key from a hook inside the door, and it granted him access to an upstairs room where a secret Committee, GEN 42, met to discuss Northern Ireland issues.

During a GEN 42 meeting in May 1972, Heath horrified Carver when he told him it was legal for soldiers to shoot protesters on the streets of Northern Ireland if they 'obstructed the Armed Forces of the Queen'. Protesters, by doing so, were 'the Queens' enemy'. Soldiers did not have to be fired on before opening fire. This is how Carver recalled Heath's bizarre pronouncement:

> He said this was being put forward by a legal luminary in the Cabinet. I said to the prime minister I could not, under any circumstances permit or allow a soldier to do that because it would be unlawful. I think he did say that his legal advisers said to him it was all right, and I said you are not bound by what they say. What I am bound by is my own judgment of whether the act by the soldier would be legal, because it is the courts that decide in the end, not your Attorney General or Lord Chancellor.

Carver explained that the legal luminary giving the prime minister advice was his Lord Chancellor, Lord Hailsham.

The Sunday morning of Heath's interview, I was armed with Carver's explosive secrets. I travelled to Salisbury with my producer, Ian Kennedy, the director and a camera crew. We planned to use two cameras. One would be devoted exclusively to Heath and the other to capture me if I had to pose the same question several times, something I anticipated would occur. Heath's home, 'Arundells', was an exquisite building inside Salisbury Cathedral Close. He had spent a lot of money refurbishing it when he moved there in 1985. Expensive antiques and a fine art collection completed the furnishings. On our arrival, we were informed he was at church and would return within the hour. We were given a room off the entrance to set up our cameras, and while that was happening, I examined some of the paintings hanging in the library and the hall, including works by John Piper, a twentieth-century English artist. I was admiring some of them when Sir Edward Heath arrived. Silvery-haired and portly, he looked just like he did on television. I held out my hand in greeting, but he brushed past me, announcing he would be back in five minutes. He sounded impolite, just as some of his contemporaries warned me. When he returned, I tried to break the ice by complimenting him on his art collection to which he bluntly replied, 'What would you know about art?'

That was my introduction to Sir Edward Heath, but during the course of the interview things would get much worse. It was clear from the outset he was doing it simply for the money. Everything about his demeanour suggested boredom. He behaved like he expected to knock off the interview quickly, in time for lunchtime aperitifs. He knew nothing about my journalistic background and had no reason to be concerned I might ask him inconvenient questions. I deliberately started with simple ones to put him at ease and then presented him with my rendering of Carver's recollections of GEN 42 meetings. In particular, I focused on the one in which Carver said Heath advocated shooting protesters. Heath glared at me, realising I knew more than I should. He denied Carver's account of the meeting as I outlined, so I essentially challenged him to call the Field Marshall a liar. He looked like a deer in a car's headlights as I continued with my questions, constantly quoting from what Carver had told me. Finally, Heath couldn't take it anymore. He rose angrily from his fine upholstered chair, declaring I had no right to be in possession of classified information. He then ordered me and the crew to leave his home and threatened to call Sir Charles Curran, Director General of Channel 4, right away. As a parting gesture, he said we had to leave in a hurry as he was hosting lunch for the Japanese ambassador.

'I am also expecting Lord Carver to join us for lunch,' he added, thinking this news would shock me. I phoned Carver a short time later and told him Heath was expecting him for lunch.

'He's the last person I would ever have lunch with, but I wouldn't mind a bottle or two of fine claret from his cellar,' he joked.

True to his word, Heath complained to Sir Charles Curran. Word then came from the top brass in Channel 4 that I had to re-interview Heath. This time, I would have to provide him in advance with the questions I intended to ask. Second, I would not be allowed to use Carver's evidence identifying Lord Hailsham as the 'legal luminary' who advised Heath it was legal to shoot protesters. The ruling disappointed me, though I knew it was likely Hailsham would launch an expensive defamation suit against Channel 4 were he to be named as the source of such advice. Channel 4 editors were unsure they could depend on Field Marshall Carver to restate what he told me in the event of such a legal suit. I felt differently, pointing out Carver was a principled man who would not only defend what he had told me but would be a powerful witness for us in any court action. Channel 4's legal advisers didn't buy my assurances.

I prepared a list of more than thirty questions for Heath. I told my producer I was now happy to re-interview the former prime minister because I was better prepared, having studied his inadequate responses to the questions I put to him first time round. If Heath felt that had been a torrid experience, he would emerge worse off this time. I spoke again to Michael Carver, who provided me with additional information to challenge Heath's recollections of the period. I was meticulous in my preparations. Some questions, I peppered with traps, suspecting Heath would be evasive. Before I could mail the list to him, he pulled out of the interview, declaring he was withdrawing our right to use anything he said at our first meeting. He warned he would launch a legal action against Channel 4 if it broadcast my interview in whole or in part. Unfortunately, for Heath, in his eagerness to get paid quickly, he had signed a contract with my producer and had cashed the payment we sent him. Legally, he was in no position to claim copyright without appearing foolish.

Channel 4 decided to 'publish' the interview but ruled out my references to Hailsham in the subsequent television documentary.

In 1994, Channel 4 and the Irish network, RTÉ, broadcast *The Last Colony* a total of four times, and Heath did not follow through on his threat to mount a legal challenge. My interviews with Heath and Michael Carver later constituted part of a submission I made to the Bloody Sunday Tribunal investigating the deadly shooting by British paratroopers of thirteen unarmed civilians on the streets of the Bogside in Derry on 30 January 1972.

My encounter with Heath made me realise how unpleasant and dismissive he must have been while in office. I had heard stories about his enormous ego and notorious arrogance from several generals, but I had dismissed them. Seeing Heath in the flesh convinced me he must have been a dreadfully conceited prime minister during one of Northern Ireland's most difficult and violent periods. Under his watch, the Army spun out of control, and events like the Lower Falls Curfew, Internment without trial, Bloody Sunday, the torture of detainees and talks with the Provos took place. His premiership saw the genesis of the Provisional IRA's 'Long War' and a sectarian campaign, which terrified both communities.

My friend, the esteemed journalist and author, Tim Pat Coogan, sought an interview with Heath when writing his book, *The Troubles*. I had supplied Tim Pat with transcripts of my interviews with Heath, Carver and several generals. He was anxious to follow up on the Carver material and on other stories he had unearthed about Heath's time in office. According to Tim Pat, Heath's secretary told him the former prime minister would not be doing any more interviews about the Ireland issue. It appeared I had opened up an unwanted line of questioning, one which Heath knew he would be asked to revisit anytime he agreed to talk about his premiership in the early 1970s.

In 2003, the Bloody Sunday Tribunal summoned Heath to give evidence, and my interview with him was brought to light, in particular the parts involving him telling Carver it was legal for the soldiers under his command to shoot Northern Ireland protesters because they were enemies of the Crown. Heath shifted blame to his Chancellor, Lord Hailsham, but Carver had been adamant that Heath only named

Hailsham when challenged to cite his legal authority for making the statement on the legality of shooting protesters. The ever wily Heath threw Hailsham under the bus by characterising him to the tribunal as a hothead who was prone to offering him outrageous legal advice. Heath declared the shooting of protesters was really Hailsham's idea. By then, of course, Hailsham was dead two years and in no position to challenge Heath's rendering of the past. Nevertheless, Heath was humiliated before the tribunal. He died in 2005 and, as far as I know, he never granted an interview about the Troubles following my questioning of him in 1994.

Heath presided over a dark period during which I would witness the horrors of the conflict and the senseless waste of human life. Grisly murders would shock even the most hardened journalists and detectives.

ELEVEN

Balaclavas, Breadcrumbs and Romper Rooms

I was clutching a notebook and pen when the crack of an automatic rifle shattered the stillness of the street. Tracer bullets zipped through the air, and I hit the ground, my face flush with the pavement. I lay there as a gunman returned fire from a position so close to me I could hear him breathing as he squeezed the trigger of his Mark 1 carbine. I crawled towards a doorway like a dog begging for food, only to be turned away by a burly man whose wife pushed him inside and slammed their door in my face. Ever so cautiously, my knees aching, I moved along the street to find all the doors shut. Slowly, I began retracing my steps to the gunman with the carbine. In the semi-darkness, I realised he was a young man in his twenties. Unseen hands dragged me to my feet and pulled me behind the security of an entry wall.

'What the fuck do you think you're doin'?' said a man, jamming a pistol into my ribs.

He was stocky and much older than his buddy with the carbine. He shoved the gun in his waistband and backed me against a wall.

'We were about t' shoot you, you silly bastard. We almost took you for a Prod,' he hissed. 'Get t' fuck outa here, if y' know what's good for you,' he added as he and his companion melted into the darkness of an entry.

I slowly edged my way from door to door, at one point running at breakneck speed to cross a street. There is always a moment in life when a sound conveys its own reality. I had just found shelter in a doorway, trying to get my eyes better accustomed to the darkness, when a sharp crack from a high-powered rifle shattered my concentration. Minutes later, several men rushed past me carrying James Saunders, a young IRA officer, who had just been shot by a British Army sniper. A 7.62 calibre bullet had entered his chest and exited his back leaving a torn, gaping hole from which his life's blood was oozing onto the pavement. I would learn later Saunders had fired at gunmen in a nearby Loyalist area, unaware it was being protected by British soldiers. It was 21 February 1971. I was in The Bone, a tiny Catholic enclave in the Oldpark area of North Belfast, a mere five-minute walk from my home in Chestnut Gardens. The violence from the Falls had followed me here, too.

On that evening, however, my editor had sent me to The Bone following reports of serious rioting. When I got there, darkness was closing in. The violence had begun after a Protestant mob from Louisa Street attacked Catholics on the Oldpark Road, the main thoroughfare that served both communities. When shooting replaced stone throwing, people in The Bone hurried indoors and shut their blinds or curtains, leaving the area bathed in an eerie darkness. By the time the dying James Saunders was carried past me, I realised I had waited too long to get out of the area without risking life and limb. I cautiously began edging my way from door to door, hoping to reach the Oldpark Road. I planned to sprint across it into Oldpark Avenue. From there, I would be able to make it to my home in Chestnut Gardens and phone a story to my news desk. Suddenly, a strange man grabbed my arm. In a reassuring voice he told me to follow him, and I would be safe. He guided me along a street and into the cramped living room of a house. As my eyes adjusted to light streaming from a bare light bulb suspended from the ceiling, the man's hand propelled me gently downwards into the deep folds of a chair.

'Take it easy, son. Just make yerself at home. It looks like y' might be here a while.'

He was wiry and wore a shirt unbuttoned to his waist as though he had just finished a hard day's work.

'You reporters are gluttons for punishment,' he noted with a wry smile.

The author and his family, 1963, when he was home for the summer from Montfort College Seminary. Back row (L to R): Damien, the author's twin; their father and mother; and the author. Second row (L to R): Frances; Patrick, the baby of the family; and Bernadette. Third row (L to R): Imelda and Mary. Front row (L to R), Ursula, Attracta and Monica.

Ross Place, Lower Falls, Belfast, 1957. From left: the author; his cousin, Gerard Clarke; and his sister Ursula.

Centre: the author's mother and father at a dance in Belfast in the 1940s.

An early photo of the author's mother, Mary Theresa Clarke, known as Maureen.

The author's great-uncle, Joe Dillon, walking his dog, Heine, on Belfast's Royal Avenue in the late 1950s.

The author's great-uncle, Gerard Dillon, one of Ireland's most celebrated twentieth-century artists.

The author outside his home at Le Rapt in the Charente, France, 1995.

The author and his siblings in 2006, on the occasion of their mother's death. It was the only time since 1963 that the siblings were photographed together. Back row (L to R): Imelda, Bernadette, Attracta, Patrick, the author and his twin, Damien. Front row (L to R): Frances, Mary, Monica and Ursula.

The author's parents in Donegal in the 1990s.

The author with his wife, Bulgarian journalist and translator Violeta Kumurdjieva, in Greece, 2016.

The author's daughter, Nadia, with the author's father in the author's Buckinghamshire home, 1991.

I glanced into the tiny kitchen where a woman was making sandwiches, her hair swept back in a bun, a red apron covering her expansive waist. She had the look of a gentle grandmother who enjoyed catering for others. She was lashing huge amounts of butter onto thick slices of bread. I lurched into survival mode when a noise to my right captured my attention. Four IRA men wearing balaclava masks were elbow to elbow on a large shabby couch, one of them perched on the arm of it. Through narrow slits in their masks they were peering at me.

'What the fuck is he doing here?' asked one of them, easing himself off the arm of the couch onto a tea chest.

My head was spinning, and I was wondering how to graciously get out of this predicament.

'Leave the lad alone,' shouted the woman in the kitchen. 'He's not doin' any of y's any harm. Y' can be hungry without being angry. The lad needs shelter and a rest like yous all do. He was wanderin' around like a lost soul out on them streets. The Brits could have shot him if he'd stayed there like an eejit.'

I had been grateful her husband found me, but now I was beginning to think I should have turned down his help.

'If he writes about what he's seen here, he's a dead man,' said one of the men on the couch.

I wanted to look inconspicuous, or at the very least humble and inoffensive. Fortunately, the atmosphere lightened when the woman presented the IRA foursome with a dinner plate piled high with double-decker sandwiches. As each man grabbed a sandwich, the stack leaned to one side like the Tower of Pisa. She hastily placed the plate on a chair and pushed it in front of them.

'You'll get yours later,' she said, smiling at me.

'These lads have work to do, and they need a full stomach for their kinda business,' she added and sauntered back to the kitchen.

Eating sandwiches through mouth slits was no easy feat and required brute force to finish quickly. The task was made more challenging by the sheer depth and width of each sandwich, comprised of large slices of cheese, potato crisps and ham. The foursome soon resembled dogs trying to clamp their jaws on bones too large for their mouths.

'What the fuck are you looking at?' asked the one whose balaclava wasn't large enough to reach his neckline.

He was manoeuvring a sandwich sideways into his mouth by widening the mouth slit of his balaclava with one hand and shoving the sandwich into his mouth with the other. Breadcrumbs had accumulated like a mini snowstorm on the wool of his mask.

The feast ended after they devoured steaming mugs of tea and a second plate of sandwiches. The woman emerged again from the kitchen, this time carrying an assortment of weapons, including a 9 mm Browning pistol. The gunmen got to their feet, their black balaclavas spotted with breadcrumbs, and left without glancing at me.

My eyes strayed to the far corner of the room, and my pulse quickened. A bomb made from sticks of gelignite with nails wrapped round it was lying under the television. The husband noticed my nervousness.

'Sure the lads will be back for it when the time's right,' he grinned.

'I'd better go,' I said, getting to my feet.

'Not until you've been fed!' shouted his wife from the kitchen. 'Nobody leaves my house on an empty stomach.'

Seconds later, the door to the street flung open, and a man armed with a Thompson submachine gun, his face hidden by a balaclava, strode past me and picked up the bomb.

'I see you're still here,' he said, pausing momentarily to stare at me. He juggled the bomb in one hand, inches above my head and laughed. 'Be careful what you write! We know who you are,' he added and disappeared into the darkness of the street.

'Don't worry about him, he's got an ulcer, and it makes him mean when he eats too much,' said the husband as he turned on the television. It had no picture because he had tuned it to pick up local British Army and police radio communications.

'The lads are psyched up, if you get my drift,' he added.

'Hey, let's give the lad a stiffener, he's not on active service,' he shouted to his wife, who arrived in her own time with a glass of whiskey.

'This'll stiffen you,' she assured me. 'It's Jameson. The best of the best. It's against the rules for the boys to drink the hard stuff when they're on active service. It dulls the brain you see. But it's all right after an operation when they want t' relax.'

I was enjoying the whiskey when an explosion rattled the windows and jolted me upright.

'That's the boys!' exclaimed her husband gleefully. 'That'll be a few less Prods and Brits to worry about tonight.'

'He doesn't really mean that,' said his wife, jabbing a finger in his chest. 'We've nothing against the Prods. It's just that they have the Brits on their side and that makes them the enemy, too, you see. The Brits let the Prods fire into our area and then back them up when we fight back. If it was just the Prods and us, I'd say it would be a standoff. The Brits just can't keep their noses out of other people's affairs.'

She retreated to the kitchen to make more sandwiches while a gun battle raged outside. In a while, there was a lull, and whether it was the whiskey she gave me, or self-preservation, I got up to leave. It was time to escape the madness, and besides I had a story to file.

'Would you care for another sandwich?' I heard the wife shouting as I was leaving.

'No thanks,' I replied and stepped gingerly into the street.

'Hey you!'

I recognised the voice of one of the four gunmen.

'The Brits have laser night sights,' he whispered, patting the notebook in my pocket. 'Say a few prayers because that book won't stop a bullet.'

Six months after my trip to The Bone, I stumbled across a document widely circulated around the River Streets next to The Bone. I would later refer to it as the birth certificate of the Ulster Defence Association, which would become the largest paramilitary organisation in Northern Ireland. Unlike the Provisional IRA, it would be permitted to remain a legal body while it ran a vicious sectarian assassination campaign in the early to mid-1970s.

The document read as follows:

> Being convinced that the enemies of the Faith and Freedom are
> determined to destroy the State of Northern Ireland and thereby
> enslave the people of God, we therefore call on all members of our
> Loyalist institutions, and other responsible citizens, to organise
> themselves immediately into platoons of twenty under the command
> of someone capable of acting as a sergeant. Every effort must be
> made to arm these platoons, with whatever weapons are available.
> The first duty of each platoon will be to formulate a plan for the
> defence of its own streets or road in cooperation with platoons in
> adjoining areas. A structure of command is already in existence and
> the various platoons will eventually be linked in a coordinated effort.

The document was born three days before Brian Faulkner and
the Stormont Unionist government imposed internment. Its language
fell into a now familiar pattern. The reference to the 'people of God'
signified Protestants were God's chosen ones while Catholics were
not. For many Protestants, Catholicism and Irish Nationalism were
synonymous with Republicanism, and the reckless use of internment
confirmed this belief because it was directed solely at the Catholic
population. The other notable aspect of Loyalist-inspired writings was
the depiction of Catholics as 'animals' or 'vermin'. For example, in a
Loyalist news-sheet from 1972, a writer sought to remind Protestants,
'these animals are crawling into Ulster, hitting vital points like RUC
stations etc. The ugly thing is that the bastards are getting away with it.'

When internment was introduced I reported nightly on rioting
in Catholic neighbourhoods. The fact that military arrest operations
focused solely on Catholics convinced them that the Unionist
government, and not the sovereign parliament in London, was in
control of the British Army. Internment was a crude, widespread and
destructive strategy. It contributed more to the rise of the Provisionals
than the Lower Falls Curfew did. Files used by the British military
to select men for internment were provided by Special Branch, and in

most instances were outdated. They often contained the names of men involved with Republicanism in the 1950s, as well as trades unionists and left-wing students. The perceived introduction of a Third World military policy, such as forced imprisonment, in the early hours of 9 August, shocked Catholics throughout Ireland and the United States. Its use heralded a return to the bad old days when the Special Powers Act was used exclusively against Catholics. In London, Prime Minister Edward Heath and his cabinet ministers considered it a wonderful strategy. Little did they know the Provisional IRA, with lots of new recruits in its ranks, remained untouched by it.

The Official IRA, which was no threat to the State at the time, was hit hard by the internment arrests because its members, especially its leaders, were prominent in Special Branch files dating to the IRA's Border Campaign of the 1950s. They were prime arrest targets. In contrast, many prominent Provisionals were young men like Gerry Adams who had not been in the IRA during the previous decade. As a consequence, the Provos were left with an intact leadership, making them the dominant paramilitary force on the streets of Catholic areas. The avalanche of criticism of internment fed into the new IRA's ability to sell its political and military aims abroad, especially in America. In the United States, prominent Provo supporters promoted the message that the British were helping the Unionists to brutalise Catholic Nationalists. In the Irish Republic, anger translated into financial and moral support for both wings of the IRA, especially the Provos. Most of the guns at the time came from American sympathisers, some of them aided by members of New York's Finest, its Police Department. Supporters smuggled guns through the port of New York into Southampton Docks on the south coast of England or on planes out of Kennedy airport into Heathrow.

The FBI was aware of pro-IRA elements within the NYPD and made determined efforts to recruit informants within the force, often with little success. The NYPD was a tightly knit body, and anyone snitching to the 'Feds' would have been ostracised by colleagues. I was told by an FBI source that surveillance was directed at NYPD uniformed cops and detectives known to have Irish Republican sympathies. The Bureau was convinced the NYPD had been instrumental in IRA gunrunning.

The British Army transferred the majority of detainees to corrugated iron huts in compounds on a disused aerodrome, ringed with barbed wire and machinegun posts. It became known as 'Long Kesh' and evoked twentieth-century images of British colonial internment without trial in Kenya, Aden, and more recently, Cyprus. According to Field Marshal Michael Carver, internment was a disastrous policy. If there had been any hope of the society surviving the violent maelstrom of August 1969, internment washed it away with the bitterness it generated throughout Catholic Ireland. By the end of that year, the IRA had fired more than 20,000 bullets, and at least 1,500 nail bombs had been thrown at British troops and their armoured vehicles.

Political rhetoric on the Catholic side was incendiary. Nationalist politicians made public pronouncements without concern for the impact they would have on hotheads. One such politician was Paddy Devlin, a fiery leader of the moderate Social Democratic Labour Party, which was led by the likes of John Hume and Gerry Fitt. Devlin had a short fuse. Even his SDLP colleagues were wary of his temper. His background was Republicanism though he had emerged from the 1950s convinced the IRA and its reliance on the gun was a political anachronism. After internment was introduced, he claimed British military interrogation centres used a 'torture rack apparatus'. It wasn't true, but it nevertheless linked the British Army with medieval torture methods. Devlin had no love for the emerging Provisionals, yet they spoke the same language. Before long, Catholic Nationalist Ireland was united against the Northern Ireland State and the Heath government in London. Effectively, the Provisional IRA was able to claim it was now aligned with all the moderate elements of Irish Nationalism in common opposition to British policy making in Ireland.

It was a period when leaders in both communities, as well as the military top brass and Heath government figures, might have benefited from taking the political temperature on the streets. In doing so, they would have been alerted in the first six months of 1972 that their society was descending into a vicious sectarian war.

Much of my time in 1972–73 was devoted to writing about some of the most ghastly killings of the Troubles. Many mornings, my news editor dispatched me to alleyways where bodies had been dumped – bodies mostly of innocent people who had been abducted on their way home from social clubs or bars. In too many instances, the victims were oblivious to the dangers posed by the sectarian geography of their town or city. In Belfast, the borderlines between Catholic and Protestant communities often criss-crossed and were not obvious to everyone. Men who drank heavily were less aware of the dangers lurking in the shadows. The bitterness infecting the politics of the time leaked into paramilitary activities and was quickly transformed into barbarity. A lack of discipline infected Loyalist ranks, and, unlike the IRA, these men had no clear political objective. As a consequence, violence sometimes took on an element of revenge, which translated into gory killings. They abducted innocent Catholics off the streets and subjected them to torture before killing them. In one instance, an elderly man was carved up the way a sculptor would carve a block of wood. Though he had over 145 knife wounds on his body, none was deep enough to kill him. Some paramilitaries derived pleasure from torture, claiming they used it to extract intelligence on the IRA. It was a bogus argument since the vast majority of tortured victims had no IRA links.

Brutality of the most horrific kind sent the society into a spiral, and I believe it touched everyone. Many began to fear they could be the victims if they found themselves in the wrong place at the wrong time. As a result, people drank heavily to cope with stress or sorrow. That led in turn to a cavalier approach to basic moral values. Rules people had lived by were forgotten or neglected because of a heightened sense of mortality. Some who lived on the edge of dangerous districts developed an acute awareness of death, especially as more innocents died in back alleys or in IRA bombings and shootings. Society was victimizing itself. Journalists, myself included, tended to be blasé when asked about life on the streets. But underneath our bravado, we all feared for our lives at some stage during the Troubles. While we scavenged for stories, we were conscious of the risks when travelling through troubled districts. Some journalists were more effective working from the office and others were better equipped to work outside. Those who stayed behind often made our stories more meaningful through fine editing or chased up stories from phone tips from members of the public or the security forces.

In retrospect, it was easy for me to ignore the fact that my parents and sisters worried about me. I was so consumed with my job that I was oblivious to their fears. I was still living in the family home in the Cliftonville area, often returning late at night from assignments to see the panic etched on my mother's face. I was anxious about Mildred, too. In 1971, she and her family rented a house in North Belfast. I recall being unable to leave her place one evening because armed members of the UDA were looting and firebombing a furniture store across the street. After the tortured bodies of several murder victims were found in the same locality, I persuaded Mildred and her family to move out. By then sectarianism was redefining parts of the city, carving them into tribal zones.

By June of 1972, I was reporting for the *Belfast Telegraph*, Northern Ireland's evening paper. It had one of the largest circulations in Ireland and was highly regarded for its journalism. Traditionally, it had been a Unionist Establishment paper, but by the time I joined, its output was taking on a mainstream feel. By then, I had cut my teeth on all aspects of news reporting thanks to my years with the *Irish News*. From a purely personal perspective, the *Belfast Telegraph* not only offered me more money but it brought my work to a larger audience. I was one of very few Catholics employed on the paper's editorial staff, but I was never made to feel uncomfortable because of my religion. As a rule, the staff remained professional and objective.

As I began reporting on an increasing number of sectarian murders, I wanted to know why they were becoming so prevalent, but editors had no desire to devote resources to in-depth investigations.

The ongoing warfare on the streets demanded the use of all staff, leaving no spare capacity. In my view, print and broadcast journalism was becoming reflexive, with little space or time being set aside for investigative journalism. I felt frustrated at not being able to rise above instantaneous, minute-to-minute coverage of a fast developing conflict. When I sensed a pattern emerging in sectarian assassinations, I wanted to know what was shaping it. Slowly, I began building a personal file, noting the victims' abduction locations, their age, religious persuasion and the likely allegiances of the killers. The copious notes I took when reporting sectarian murders for the *Irish News* aided me in this task.

During my research, I discovered several victims had been patients of a prominent psychiatrist, Dr Jack Nabney, who worked in Purdysburn Mental Hospital where my uncle, John Clarke, had once been examined and selected for a lobotomy. At a later time, my mother claimed Dr Nabney had been one of my uncle's doctors. When I met him to seek his opinions about the mindset of sectarian killers, he willingly briefed me about some of his murdered patients. He felt their mental illnesses had made them more vulnerable to death squads because they lacked an acute awareness of the dangers surrounding them. In difficult situations, he argued, they were less likely to be tight-lipped about their political opinions and would have been unable to detect danger lurking in the places they frequented. But not all his patients who lost their lives were mentally unbalanced. One was William Pavis, a 32-year-old Protestant with a very high IQ. In February 1971, authorities charged Pavis with possessing a Luger pistol, and a witness at his trial testified he was fascinated with guns and ready to sell them to anyone. The Pavis case had a curious aspect to it. He had struck up a friendship with a priest. As a result of their common fascination with weapons, they went on hunting trips. Their unusual relationship attracted the attention of Special Branch after it was alleged, though unproven, that the priest asked Pavis to get him guns. They were both arrested, and the priest was subsequently fined for having an unlicensed shotgun. In contrast, Pavis got three years for possessing illegal weapons and ammunition. Before he was murdered, Pavis told a magistrate someone was out to kill him, but the magistrate thought he was delusional and sent him to Dr Nabney for evaluation. At Nabney's request, police guards were assigned to Purdysburn Mental Hospital to protect Pavis and prevent his escape while he underwent psychiatric tests. According to Dr Nabney, he liked Pavis and was impressed by his intellect. He judged him mentally fit to serve a prison sentence and returned him to the court. The magistrate placed him on parole, and he was shot dead at his home shortly after. One of his killers was Lenny Murphy, the notorious leader of the Shankill Butchers gang. It is thought the revelation in court that Pavis was linked to a priest signed his death warrant.

I also established excellent contacts with some Belfast detectives, and they helped me recognise familiar patterns in many of the sectarian killings, as well as the suspected loyalties of the likely culprits. An incident, however, encouraged me to think I was not getting to the heart of the killing phenomenon. One morning when I got to the *Telegraph* newsroom, I received an assignment to report on the discovery of a body in an 'entry' in East Belfast. I arrived around eight o'clock and because I was dressed in a raincoat and carrying a notepad, a policeman assumed I was a member of a forensic team and allowed me into the entry. The sight before me was horrifying: the tortured body of 23-year-old Patrick Benstead, a Catholic from the Short Strand area. He had been missing since the previous afternoon when his mother sent him on a shopping errand. He was known to behave immaturely, and people said his speech confirmed his low intelligence. His killers had subjected him to the most terrible torture. A bullet to the head had ended his life, but the palms of his hands and feet were burned, and a cross was branded into his back with the number four. The killing occurred in a part of the city where several Protestants were subjected to similar treatment by the IRA. In those cases, as in the case of Benstead, authorities denied the victims had been tortured.

When I saw the torture marks on Patrick Benstead's body, I rushed to a nearby funeral parlour – the only place I was likely to find a phone. Right away, I dictated my story to the news desk only to be told an hour later it could not be published as written. The RUC press office had denied my torture claims. With this rejection, I suspected they might have created a policy to withhold information from the public. Even now, I know of no reports of killings at the time in which the RUC confirmed torture, yet it was a prominent feature of many of them.

For example, in July 1972, two Protestant men in their early thirties, David Fisher and Hugh Clawson, were abducted by Catholic vigilantes as they walked past The Bone area. They were returning to the River Streets late at night after drinking heavily in an illegal drinking club run by the UDA in the Alliance district, a ten-minute walk from The Bone. They were abducted as they strolled home along the Oldpark Road. Vigilantes guarding The Bone knew the two men were strangers. When they learned they were also Protestants, this sealed their fate. They were beaten, interrogated and at least one, if not both, was burned with cigarettes. In the early hours of the following day, the vigilantes led the victims to the grounds of Cliftonville Cricket Club opposite Chestnut Gardens and shot each man in the head and neck at close range with an automatic rifle. Fisher took three bullets and Clawson five, a number that suggested overkill. The torture wounds confirmed the high levels of revenge and anger in the minds of those who carried out the double killing. In that case, as in others, the RUC made no mention of the manner in which the victims were brutalised.

By July 1972, the grounds of Cliftonville Cricket Club, where I had often watched teams in their 'whites' play the game I played in my Montfort summers, was a wasteland. The clubhouse had been burned down, and the cricket field suffered from overgrowth and refuse. Gone was the quiet middle-class atmosphere of the mid-1960s. It had become the favoured zone for killers cruising for victims after dark. For my parents, the closure of the cricket club was a depressing signal of decline. My mother prayed constantly my father would not be abducted and murdered as he went to and from his job or when he attended early morning Mass in the nearby Poor Clares' Convent chapel. She was no different than other mothers, Catholic and Protestant, who knew terror lurked close in areas like Oldpark, Shankill, New Lodge and Ardoyne.

Had denial of torture in the Benstead murder been an uncommon occurrence, I might have dismissed it as an example of someone in the police press office not doing his job. But I detected a pattern in the way the RUC responded to requests for detailed information about a growing number of grisly murders. I suspected then, as I do now, that the authorities were genuinely concerned that making public the precise nature of many of the murders would further inflame sectarian passions. It must be noted, however, a fledgling relationship existed between the RUC information service and the British Army, which regarded the manipulation of news as part of the war against the IRA. A British military disinformation unit, known as the Information Policy Unit, routinely fed bogus stories to selected journalists, including me. Whether withholding torture details fed into information policy strategy is not clear.

As for the media, investigative journalism was in its fledgling phase. It neglected to examine patterns of violence, relying too much on official sources such as the RUC and British Army press outlets. I grew highly sceptical of the dissemination of information from official sources from 1972 onwards, especially when it originated from British Army HQ and its press operations. Some of it was filtered through people with a keen interest in psychological operations and the distortion of news. If anything, I placed more reliance on the RUC press staff because I knew some of its personnel and regarded these individuals as honest professionals. My general instinct, however, was to personally undertake detailed background work on certain stories, particularly on the increasing numbers of political assassinations. I spoke to detectives, paramilitaries and their contacts, and to ordinary people in Republican and Loyalist districts. By researching in that fashion, I learned about 'Romper Rooms,' which were essentially killing rooms used by murder gangs.

However, I feel it is important at this stage to clarify what I believe the police and military knew about sectarian murders at the time. Throughout the Troubles, British Military Intelligence and RUC

Special Branch ran agents within Loyalist paramilitary groups. In fact, highly classified British Intelligence outfits recruited Loyalist and Republican terrorists to assassinate Republicans. That was true of the MRF – Military Reconnaissance Force – in the early 1970s that had Loyalist and a few Republican gunmen in its ranks. Therefore, there was little the Intelligence community did not know about the workings of the paramilitaries, especially the UDA, UVF and similar Loyalist groupings. Much of that insider British military knowledge remained classified and did not find its way to hardworking RUC uniformed staff and detectives from the Criminal Investigation Branch. They tirelessly investigated hundreds of unsolved murders without cooperation from other parts of the security apparatus.

I have been asked many times, in the context of collusion that existed between Loyalist paramilitaries and British Intelligence and the RUC Special Branch, if RUC criminal investigators knew the identities of murderous gangs like the Shankill Butchers. The Butchers were a tight crew, and no evidence suggested they were ever recruited as informers by the security forces. I also came across nothing to confirm the UVF leadership betrayed the Butchers to Special Branch or to British Military Intelligence at any time during their vicious killing spree. However, the Shankill Butchers' leader, Lenny Murphy, was eventually set up for assassination by the UDA leader, James Pratt Craig, who was not only a CID informant but had links to Special Branch and the British military. It has often been speculated that the policing authorities knew the identities of gangs like the Butchers and allowed them to kill at will because they were exterminating Catholics. Such a theory is dangerous and has no basis in fact. Even so, British Military Intelligence and Special Branch hid critical information from CID and engaged in a dirty war in which they used Loyalist gunmen to target Republicans for assassination. In many instances, they targeted people who were not IRA members. In fact, the British Intelligence apparatus, including the British Army, expended little effort or resources investigating Loyalist gangs murdering ordinary Catholics. Instead, British Military Intelligence focused on monitoring Loyalist paramilitaries for the purpose of recruiting agents from within them, and to ensure they did not pose a threat to the British Army. They used the agents they recruited in a proxy war in which they eliminated Republicans and blamed the murders on Loyalists. The major thrust of the British Intel system was directed at Republican organisations, especially the Provisional IRA. It was a misguided policy, and in many respects led to a large number of extrajudicial killings.

Many innocent Catholics, however, perished in 'Romper Rooms'. These were basically Loyalist paramilitary drinking dens where victims, randomly snatched off the streets, were beaten and tortured in front of revellers and paramilitary members. The 'Romper Rooms' came into being in 1972 and were bizarrely named after a local children's television programme hosted by Helen Madden, whom I later worked with in the BBC. As 'Miss Helen' on 'Romper Room', she entertained young children with songs, poems and toys. Loyalist killers subsequently adopted the term 'rompering' to denote the savagery meted out in their illegal clubs. Ironically, Loyalist paramilitaries caught up in feuds or judged to have been informers were also 'rompered' by their own people. In order to give the reader a sense of what happened during a 'rompering', the following is a description of some of the events that took place when Lenny Murphy, the leader of the Shankill Butchers, decided to 'romper' Nogi Shaw, a member of a rival UDA 'team' with whom he was feuding. He chose the Lawnbrook Social Club, a UVF hangout, as the venue for the 'rompering'. Murphy sent some of his murderous buddies to fetch Shaw, and they brought him to the club where Murphy and twenty others were drinking. The following passage is from my book, *The Shankill Butchers*:

As Shaw was dragged into the club, drinks were abandoned and he was set upon, kicked and beaten by those who fought to get closest to him. After several minutes, Murphy and Mr A (name withheld for legal reasons) intervened and requested Shaw be carried to the front of a small wooden stage normally reserved for musicians. Murphy placed a chair on the stage and Shaw was strapped to it. The stage overlooked the whole of the club and its drinking environs and while Shaw was being tied to the chair Murphy summoned his men to leave the bar and move closer to the stage. Most of the twenty or so men did so, taking their drinks with them. Murphy left the stage for several minutes and returning brandishing a Browning pistol. While the others waited in anticipation, he walked to the front of the stage and to within a few feet of Shaw. Murphy said it was time to interrogate Shaw and began striking him several times across the head and face with the pistol butt. He continued beating Shaw to a background chorus of 'kill the bastard'.

Murphy told eighteen-year-old Shaw he was going to die and the young man cried out in fear and pain. Murphy then discussed with Mr A, in front of the victim, whether they should draw straws to find out who should have the honour of killing him. Straws were drawn but the young man selected to undertake the killing refused to do it. Murphy decided to do it himself. He first shot Shaw through the wrist and then several times through the head. When Shaw's dead body fell to the floor Murphy turned to his men and said, 'Clean up the fuckin' mess!'

The killing was an illustration of what happened during 'romperings', but sometimes more than twenty men were present and women too in some instances. Victims were not only beaten but tortured while the bar staff served drinks. When rumours first reached me of the phenomenon, I spoke to some detectives who confirmed they had heard of the existence of 'Romper Rooms' in Loyalist areas of East and West Belfast.

My intense interest in the subject drew me into a professional relationship with Denis Lehane, a colleague in the *Belfast Telegraph* newsroom. He was a journalist in training in the Thomson Organisation, which owned the *Telegraph*. He arrived in the newsroom with no experience in covering the conflict and no contacts. I befriended him, as did my family and friends, and shared with him my interest in investigating sectarian murders. I showed him my research. It included lists of victims, where they were found and the likely terror affiliations of the killers. I had also noted the fact that the assassins were increasingly torturing their victims. Many of the killings I had personally reported on for the *Irish News*, and the *Belfast Telegraph*. We began working in our spare time on a series of articles exposing the truth behind the murders. When we presented our findings to Eugene Wasson, the *Belfast Telegraph*'s editor, he rejected them. In fact, he appeared to doubt our claims about 'Romper Rooms' and suggested we hand over the research to his features staff. We refused and undertook further research, which led us to write *Political Murder in Northern Ireland*. It was published by Penguin as a Penguin Special Edition in 1973. It was one of the first books to examine a major aspect of the Troubles. In retrospect, my work as a reporter on the streets provided me with the material and the motivation to write future works like *The Shankill Butchers* and *The Dirty War*.

I have often been asked if I left the *Belfast Telegraph* in 1973 because its editor-in-chief, Eugene Wasson, rejected the research material leading to the publication of *Political Murder*. The answer is no. The editor's decision perplexed me and that was made clear in the book's foreword. However, the *Belfast Telegraph* praised the book. The failure to publish our research was solely the editor's decision, and I believe newsroom editors at the time, in particular Martin Lindsay and Jim Gray, would have acted differently had they been responsible for the feature content of the newspaper. I had great respect for my fellow journalists on the paper. I continue to hold them in high regard. The same can be said of the *Irish News* staff and the majority of print journalists I worked with in the British Isles. On reflection, I believe the print journalists I worked alongside, with a very few exceptions, were consummate professionals.

TWELVE

The BBC Years

I cannot fully explain my decision to move to the BBC. Perhaps meeting television and radio journalists such as Don Anderson at news events drew me to broadcasting. I began my BBC career as a news assistant, working mostly on the radio news desk, which shared space with television news. My boss was news veteran, Cecil Deeney, who reminded me of my print mentor, Joe Devlin. Deeney was one of a small number of Catholics working in BBC NI programming. Another was Terry Sharkey, who once joked with the BBC Director General he was the 'Corporation's token Catholic'. There was some truth in the joke. People from a Protestant Unionist heritage dominated the BBC from its inception. As the British Broadcasting Corporation, it reflected the Britishness of Northern Ireland, paying scant attention to Nationalist culture or social injustice. One could argue it ignored the arts in general. In my first year at the BBC, I was amazed when executives held their yearly drinks party in Broadcasting House to celebrate the 12 July Orange Parade marching by the building. Unionist politicians and dignitaries, who gathered in a sixth-floor room with BBC staff, attended it.

When I joined the newsroom, I was surprised to learn that my colleagues relied almost exclusively on information supplied by RUC and British Army press outlets. In contrast, print journalists I had worked with had developed many contacts while covering events on the streets. BBC news staff tended to be desk bound. One editorial figure was well known for refusing to interview a priest because it would not have sat well with his friends in the Orange Order. Others saw Catholics as the source of the violence. These views had the cumulative effect of ensuring BBC news personnel had no lines of communication into the Catholic community. I began to regret leaving the *Belfast Telegraph* but decided to be patient, telling myself to stay focused and give broadcast journalism a chance.

After the publication of *Political Murder*, Denis Lehane remained for a time at the *Telegraph*. Denis and I discussed writing a second book to expose the undercover war between British Intelligence and the IRA. I was familiar with many aspects of the war taking place in the shadows and would later write *The Dirty War*. But in late 1973, I decided before co-authoring a book on the topic, the correct thing to do was to present an outline of it to the senior BBC programme executive, Dick Francis, whose title was Controller. He scheduled a meeting with me and Head of Programmes, Ronald Mason. They insisted the BBC could not be associated with such a controversial project. They were worried it might conflict with the Corporation's independent editorial policy and make me appear less objective to a BBC audience. Their joint reaction reminded me of the *Belfast Telegraph* editor's rejection of the 'Romper Room' material, but it troubled me much more. I had naïvely assumed the BBC was a much more open and forward-thinking organisation. I would later consider their argument against my future book specious at best. They were, I believe, manipulative. They were concerned they would not be able to control what I planned to publish. As for their reference to the BBC's objectivity, I would discover the BBC's obsession with the topic was not always matched by an understanding or dedication to fairness or balance. I suspected they couldn't comprehend the prospect of me writing controversial things about the British Army. The book outline promised revelations about extrajudicial murders by secret military units. I accepted the BBC management's ruling and walked away from the project. Denis Lehane was unable to proceed. It would take another two decades before I could write my own book, *The Dirty War*. The hiatus with the BBC over the project turned out to be the best course since I learned a lot more about the war in the shadows in the decade that followed.

After this experience with Dick Francis and Ronald Mason, I discovered that the BBC's concept of objectivity sprang from a flawed interpretation of the BBC Charter and the inherited prejudice of some of its editorial figures. They had the tendency to believe, somewhat naïvely, they were above the conflict and the prejudices underpinning it. In Belfast, senior programming figures seemed unable to understand that when staff entered Broadcasting House, they did not always leave their inherited social, political and religious values at the door. Not long after I joined, I learned a journalist closely linked to an institution with a history of anti-Catholic rhetoric refused to interview a Catholic priest. He was not reprimanded. Some local BBC news staff made no secret of the fact they saw the Catholic community as the sole driving force of the conflict. That reflex judgment contrasted sharply with the views of trainee journalists from London such as Jeremy Paxman, whom I and my family befriended. He developed a genuinely thoughtful understanding of the conflict and its origins. The same could be said of all BBC reporters from network programmes like 'Panorama', who visited Northern Ireland from time to time to make documentaries. A few England-based reporters, however, drained local journalists' information sources, and then made revealing reports without crediting any of the local help they received.

A year into my BBC career, Loyalist paramilitaries took control of Northern Ireland in what became known as the 'Ulster Workers Council Strike'. The term 'strike' was misleading because strong-arm tactics by the UDA, UVF and other Protestant paramilitary bodies ensured people could not get to work even if they wanted to. Power plants, factories and most workplaces shut down due to widespread intimidation. Men in balaclavas, many of them with guns, barricaded and guarded major roads. The event had all the hallmarks of a modern rebellion, and one British government minister described it as an 'an outbreak of Ulster Nationalism'. The British Army and RUC had orders not to interfere with the activities of the Ulster Workers Council and the paramilitaries controlling the streets. The 'strike' objective was to wreck an Assembly and Executive in which Unionists and Nationalists shared power for the first time in the history of the State. As the 'strike' took hold, rumours of a civil war and pogroms circulated. Privately, British generals feared their soldiers would be caught in crossfire between Loyalists and Republicans, especially if they moved against the 'Ulster Workers'. In that scenario, generals suspected the IRA would launch attacks on the British Army, placing it in the middle of a shooting war.

In my opinion, there was an important issue related to editorial freedom during the UWC shutdown, and Dick Francis did not adequately address it. It was how the BBC responded to the constant flow of information being pumped out by the UWC and its paramilitary bedfellows, especially the UDA. The BBC relied heavily on the UWC as an information source. At times, they succumbed to pressure from the UWC to carry its statements in full, fearful they would deprive the Corporation of access to its news assembly line. By controlling public broadcasting, the UWC and UDA cleverly hardened the impact of the shutdown.

In retrospect, it is easy to blame the Corporation, but one has to recognise the awful dilemma it found itself in. It operated in an atmosphere of high intimidation, and the British government failed miserably to limit the power of the Loyalist paramilitaries. The BBC was aware if it invited confrontation with the UWC, its staff, especially news crews, would be placed at greater risk. I was asked by Dick Francis and Ronald Mason to use my paramilitary contacts to acquire UDA passes to get BBC executives through paramilitary road blocks. The journalist, Robert Fisk, whom I greatly admired, wrote an exceptional book about the UWC 'Strike' entitled, *The Point of No Return: The Strike Which Broke the British in Ulster*. He was *The Times* correspondent in Northern Ireland back then. Nowadays, he writes for the *Independent*, lives in Beirut and is one of the foremost commentators on Middle East events.

Dick Francis and Ronald Mason were angry when his book was published. It was made clear, not in any official memos, but by way of private conversations, which was a customary in-house tactic, that its author was *persona non grata*. The reaction was unjustified. Robert

Fisk was an objective reporter, and what he had to say about the BBC's failures during the strike represented a reasonable and accurate commentary. The BBC had bowed to pressure from the UWC to carry many of its press statement verbatim. Robert Fisk also damned the British government for its 'shambolic response' and was just as scathing about the British government's Northern Ireland Office. Dick Francis and Ronald Mason were stung by his criticism and privately vowed not to be caught napping should there be a repeat of the 'strike'. In 1977, Ronald Mason became the newly appointed head of Radio Three Drama based in London, but Francis still held the position of Controller in Belfast. Suddenly, he had his chance at redemption when the Rev. Ian Paisley announced plans to repeat the success of the 1974 'strike'. Paisley miscalculated because the British government, now led by Prime Minister James Callaghan, had learned from their mistakes of four years earlier. And so, too, had the BBC.

The British government was determined second time round to control the flow of information to the media in order to win the propaganda war. To do it, they needed the BBC on board because it provided more broadcast hours daily than any other outlet. I was in Dick Francis's company when he outlined how the BBC would not be caught napping again in the information processing game and would not be intimidated or restricted in its broadcasting freedoms. He said he had met with British government figures in its Northern Ireland office at Stormont and learned there would be a coordinated flow of information once Paisley's 'strike' got under way. According to him, 'everyone had agreed they needed to be on the same page'. He meant that the BBC, along with the British government's political and information machinery at Stormont, as well as the police and military press functions, would all be singing from the same hymn sheet. He admitted he had been assured during the Stormont discussions that 'the dynamics' would be different this time round. He meant information about events on the streets would be tightly controlled, with the BBC a major cog in the process. I was concerned the BBC was willing to be part of such an overt political strategy. But the company could not leave itself vulnerable to the pressures it experienced in 1974 when it relied on the UWC as its main news source.

I had no reason to doubt that Francis took whatever steps he considered necessary in 1977, even if they meant getting into bed editorially with the British government's information mandarins to avoid falling into the trap he found himself in four years earlier. The Paisley strike turned out to be a disaster because Paisley failed to match the support the UWC attracted in 1974. He also lacked the same paramilitary backing and did not control the flow of information, which had been one of the decisive paramilitary elements in the UWC's 1974 success in bringing about the collapse of power sharing.

When he later became Director of News and Current Affairs in London, he was asked to preside over an inquiry into one of the most controversial BBC episodes of the 1970s. It involved my friend, Jeremy Paxman, who filmed an armed IRA unit marching through the town of Carrickmore to set up a roadblock. News of the filming was leaked to some British government sources and found its way to Prime Minister, Margaret Thatcher's desk. She seized the opportunity to accuse the BBC of giving the IRA the oxygen of publicity. When news of the Carrickmore episode later made headlines in the United Kingdom, some BBC London executives scrambled to cover their butts. The BBC's Director General would surely have told Dick Francis, who by then was editor of News and Current Affairs Television, that Margaret Thatcher wanted heads to roll and wanted stricter editorial rules imposed throughout the news and current affairs division. In the final analysis, no heads rolled, but the BBC went through a tortuous public and private debate about its editorial referral process. As a consequence, anything to do with Northern Ireland that was deemed controversial had to be shunted through a complex editorial chain, which stretched from Belfast to Dick Francis and on to the office of the Director General. If programme chiefs worried about putting their imprimatur on a controversial news item or current affairs documentary, they deferred to the Board of Governors. Everyone in a position of power in the BBC was conscious of what I once termed 'The Thatcher effect', evidenced by her frenzied response to Jeremy Paxman's Carrickmore footage.

During the in-house inquiry, Dick Francis sat with a note taker and interviewed many of the people directly connected to the Carrickmore broadcast. One BBC figure, who found himself across the table from Francis, realised Francis was pretending he had no prior knowledge of the Carrickmore filming. Frustrated by Francis's approach, the interviewee told him, 'But you knew about it Dick!' In the blink of an eye, Dick Francis turned to his note taker and said, 'Scrub that from the record!'

Dick Francis subsequently served with the British Council and was later knighted, becoming Sir Richard Francis. In Northern Ireland he remained known to some as 'Inter Dick', a nickname that had arisen from his frequent references to covering the Apollo Mission early in his career, and the tiny replica of an Apollo rocket he kept on his desk as a memento of that period of his life. In keeping with Northern Ireland humour, 'Inter Dick' was shorthand for Inter Stellar Dick. He was a flamboyant character with a fine intellect and was generally well respected by those of us who knew him.

My BBC news career was not what I had anticipated. I had hoped for more investigative work, but I was rarely given an opportunity to make use of the contacts I had built up through my newspaper reporting. There were, however, several occasions when news editors allowed me to follow a good story, and one in particular occurred during Robin Walsh's reign. I shared with him that I had unearthed material about members of a local football team who had fallen victim to sectarian assassins. He encouraged me to compile a report for television and radio.

A flamboyant editor, Walsh had many admirers among BBC news staff in London and Belfast. I was not one of them, despite the green light he'd given me on the football story. Before I joined the BBC, I met him once socially while he was playing poker in the Midland Hotel with Bob Lennon, a Belfast Telegraph colleague. We did not speak much, and I was left with the impression we had little in common.

At the time, he worked for Ulster Television. Formerly, he had been a *Belfast Telegraph* reporter like me. He was tall, slim, dark-haired, and had a slightly pinched expression. He was notable for wearing suits decorated with breast pocket handkerchiefs of varying colours. One of his distinctive characteristics was his use of an expletive ending in 'ie' in the company of fellow journalists. A decade later, when he disliked a programme proposal I put to him in the presence of my colleague, Colin Lewis, he turned to me and said: 'You can shoot me in the fucking foot, but not in the fucking head.' It was classic Walsh. By then he was Controller, BBC Northern Ireland.

    I never played poker with him in the 1970s, or sought his company in the BBC club. Some news staff walked the walk to impress him, taking on some of his characteristics. I did not. Instead, I resigned from the newsroom and became an arts producer shortly after his appointment to News Editor. However, I did not leave the News division because I disapproved of his leadership. He was an experienced newsman, and unlike some of the more pretentious BBC 'suits', he was approachable. He also had a keen knowledge of political issues and was decisive. Sometimes, he could be very blunt to the point of being offensive. Our parting at that stage of my career would not, however, end my dealings with him.

    I was fortunate to meet Graham Mc Kenzie when I joined BBC Radio News in 1973. He possessed a dry sense of humour, and after one or two drinks he would dispense advice about his craft. I learned a lot from him, especially the need for precise phrasing in the compilation of news reports. He had a reservoir of amusing stories about his time as a print journalist with Express Newspapers in London. He was once tasked by Lord Beaverbrook, owner of the *Daily Express*, to dig up dirty on Lord Louis Mountbatten, godfather to Prince Charles. Beaverbrook and Mountbatten became bitter rivals after Beaverbrook portrayed him as a narcissistic liar who ordered a botched military raid against the Germans in 1942. It cost the lives of hundreds of British soldiers and sailors. Beaverbrook lambasted Mountbatten for handing the intelligence components of that raid to a buddy of Cuban origin who was a racing driver. Decades after the raid, Beaverbrook was still trying to amass and print scandal about his rival. He dispatched Graham and a photographer to stake out a rural hideaway he had been told was being used by Mountbatten for extra-marital trysts. For days, Graham and his photographer hid in a ditch recording Mountbatten's comings and goings, but they uncovered no evidence that he had lovers.

'If we'd only focused on Lady Mountbatten, we would have picked up lots of scandal because she bedded a lot of famous men,' Graham explained.

In the Radio Arts department, I worked alongside the exceptionally gifted poet, Paul Muldoon, and Brian Barfield, the senior producer in charge who guided us both through the rigours of learning radio production. Our boss was Ronald Mason. He was happy for us to call him Ronnie, but anyone else who took such a liberty without his approval risked his sharp tongue. Politically, he was conservative and like most Unionists he called Northern Ireland 'Ulster'. In 1975, he played an instrumental role in creating BBC Radio Ulster, giving it that title. The move hardly endeared him to Nationalists, who regarded Ulster as one of the nine historic provinces of Ireland. In contrast, Northern Ireland had six counties resulting from partition of the island whereas the historic Province of Ulster comprised nine. Protestants nevertheless continued to refer to Northern Ireland as Ulster, illustrating the divisiveness in the way both communities used the name. I felt Mason should have taken those historical differences into account when naming Northern Ireland's new BBC Radio station, but he did not. While his aim was not to be offensive, I nevertheless felt he inappropriately responded to his inherited political bias. Given his fine intellect, Mason's lack of partisan finesse disappointed me, but it did not surprise me, given the prejudices I had seen during my tenure at the BBC.

He had a reputation as a highly talented radio drama producer in his early BBC career. When I showed him a play I had written called 'The Squad', he liked it so much he decided to personally produce it. He also sent it to Martin Esslin, the BBC's esteemed head of Radio

Three Drama and a renowned figure in the drama world. He coined the phrase the 'Theatre of the Absurd', and his book of that name, published first in 1961, remains a classic. He brought the works of Beckett, Edward Albee, Harold Pinter and many other great writers to Radio Three. Mason took me to meet Esslin, and I was thrilled when he told me how much he liked my play and had already commissioned it for Radio Three. I remember Esslin having a warm smile and sharp, piercing eyes. I said to Mason he reminded me of someone who carried a terrible burden. Mason found my observation interesting. Born a Hungarian Jew, Esslin fled Austria in 1939. He subsequently lost family and many friends to the Holocaust.

The storyline of my play focused on paramilitary murder squad members meeting before a hit. It was influenced mostly by my research for *Political Murder* and by killers I had interviewed. Mason produced it on Radio Three and also on television. In 1976, Ronald Mason succeeded Martin Esslin as Head of BBC Radio Three Drama. BBC Northern Ireland lost Mason's intelligence and creative thinking when he died on 16 January 1997.

THIRTEEN

Irish Literary Giants and a Stray

Shortly after I began working in Arts, Ronald Mason suggested it might serve me well to spend a month in London, taking part in a BBC radio production course. The Corporation regularly ran workshops in The Langham, a large Edwardian building opposite Broadcasting House. They focused on radio production techniques and brought together producers from across the United Kingdom. I arranged to stay in a BBC colleague's apartment near Golders Green, commuting every day by bus to and from Central London. My evening routine included a 10-minute walk from Broadcasting House to a bus stop on Oxford Street and a half-hour ride to my friend's place on the Finchley Road.

One evening as I strolled along Oxford Street, a scrawny, black-and-white cat emerged from a subway entrance and sidled up to me. It remained still and just purred while I ran my hand down its back and scratched under its chin. It was a young tomcat, probably a stray used to prowling the Underground for rats. Realising I could miss my bus, I stroked him one last time. He then ran ahead, stopped, and looked at me. I waved at him, hoping to send him back to his subway haunts, but my gesture had no effect. He followed me to the bus stop. Seeing he was much too close to the roadway, I picked him up as the bus pulled alongside us. The conductor pointed to the cat, shaking his head as he did so. He explained in clipped Cockney slang pets were not permitted on public transport unless they were 'boxed'. It had never been my intention to take the cat with me, but on the spur of the moment I decided I had to. I couldn't leave him in the middle of the street to be run over. I pleaded with the conductor until he relented, stipulating I had to sit on the upper deck, keeping the cat concealed inside my coat at all times. My furry friend was quiet on the ride home, but I anxiously wondered what to do with him. When I got off at my regular stop, I pulled my jacket tighter to keep him secure, and as I did so my feet knocked against something. I looked down at the pavement and to my amazement saw a wicker cat basket in pristine condition.

'This can't be true,' I told myself, and I looked around to make sure no one was pranking me. It didn't make sense for someone to discard a perfectly good cat basket at a bus stop late at night. I put the cat in it and named him 'Oxford' because we had met on Oxford Street. By the time I reached my friend's place, panic set in. Chris Scofield was a nice, generous colleague, but he was no cat lover. The sight of a flea-ridden moggie was sure to send him into a rage. I put the basket in my bedroom and found Chris in his bedroom. He angrily reminded me he had a cat allergy; Oxford would have to go. However, he wouldn't object if I gave the cat the run of the back garden until I found him a proper home. He was also gracious enough to let Oxford have a tin of salmon from his pantry. I thanked him and left to examine the garden. To my dismay, I found a walled garden with no shelter suitable for a cat. I put Oxford back in the basket and placed it in a secluded part of the garden, with a heavy plastic sheet draped over it. Before going to sleep, I set my alarm for half past six, determined to get up and feed him. I even toyed with the idea of flying him back to Belfast to live with my other cats.

At seven o'clock the following morning, I entered the garden but there was no sign of Oxford. Upset by his departure, I spent hours searching for him. I knocked on doors and posted notes with his description, as well as my address and phone number. I felt guilty I had taken him from his familiar environment to an upmarket area where rats and mice probably fasted all year. Every night when I got home, I expected to find a message that someone had found or spotted him. Finally, I confided my despair to a pretty, dark-haired BBC secretary who hailed from Sibford Gower in Oxfordshire. She said if anyone found Oxford, she would keep him until I was ready to go back to Belfast. Chris felt sorry for me, too, but held out little hope for my cat's return. Nevertheless, he promised to phone me in Ireland if the rascal returned.

On my last morning in London, I made my customary trip to the garden. The empty basket was still there with its door wide open. Fifteen minutes later, when loading my luggage into a taxi, Chris leaned out his bedroom window and pointed frantically to the low wall at the front of his house. To my utter disbelief, Oxford was walking towards me, his tail in the air. He was scrawnier than before, but his loud meow told me he was okay.

'Chris! Get the basket,' I shouted, as I took a firm hold on Oxford, determined not to let him vanish a second time.

'That cat looks like he's full of fleas,' hissed the taxi driver as I held Oxford tight to my chest. I stared down the driver, whose stubble was dense enough to contain an army of fleas.

Within a half hour the driver dropped me off outside The Langham. Like most official London buildings, it had tight security because the capital was a prime target for IRA bombs. When I walked to the front door, laden down with suitcases and a cat basket, I became the focus of two big security guys. They didn't know if they should smile or frown at the sight of me. The rule was clear – no animals allowed in the building unless they were guide dogs. Perhaps it was Oxford's charming grin, or my plea that I was leaving for war-torn Belfast later that day, but they waived the rules for once.

My secretary friend gave Oxford the run of her office while I phoned British Airways and managed to get Oxford booked on my flight to Belfast that evening. I then went off to say goodbye to colleagues. In Broadcasting House, I ran into the legendary BBC radio producer, Reginald Donald Smith, known to the world as Reggie. He was a big, distressed-looking man, married to the famous novelist, Olivia Manning. Detractors accused the pair of promoting communist ideals, but Reggie always dismissed the accusations. He once joked that British Intelligence services had spent a small fortune watching them.

It would have been enough to have provided him with a pampered existence. He always seemed to be in a hurry to get somewhere. But if you slowed him down for half an hour, he was highly entertaining. Reggie was renowned for his close relationships with literary greats like Dylan Thomas and Louis MacNeice. He was also a confidante of the poet, Bertie Rodgers, a close friend of my Uncle Gerard. His most celebrated programmes with famous personalities were made in the 1940s and 1950s for the BBC's *The Third Programme*, later to be called Radio Three. One afternoon in The George, a bar near the BBC, he whispered in my ear, 'You are sitting at the table where Dylan Tomas once got drunk and misplaced *Under Milkwood*. He thought he'd lost it until he sobered up and realised the only place he could've left it was at this table.' Whether the story was true or not, Reggie had a way of making you believe what he said. He was the kind of man you could not dislike because he was a reservoir of knowledge and a larger-than-life personality.

When I returned to The Langham I found Oxford asleep in a shoebox under the secretary's desk. I phoned British Airways to confirm our reservations and, to my utter astonishment, I was informed there was no record of me making a reservation for a cat. Worse still, it was too late to get Oxford on my flight. Left with little choice, I booked him a flight to Belfast the following week. My secretary friend assured me the cat could stay at her place and she would personally take him by taxi to Heathrow Airport.

When I called her early the following day from Belfast, she told me Oxford was gone. She had taken him home as promised, but when she awoke the following morning he was missing. She wasn't sure how he managed to get out of her apartment because she had locked all the doors and windows before retiring to bed. I knew Oxford excelled at vanishing, but he was hardly the Houdini of the cat world.

'I'll call you later,' she said curtly and hung up.

A week passed without a call from her, so I phoned, hoping she might have news. She assured me she had searched her neighbourhood without success. Something in her tone convinced me she was being insincere, and this prompted me to phone several times a week for almost a month. She eventually stopped answering the phone. I resigned myself to the sad inevitability I would never see Oxford again. Nevertheless, I kept him in my thoughts when I visited London that same year and found myself on the same stretch of Oxford Street where we first met. No matter how incredible it seemed, I hoped to catch a glimpse of him.

I had all but forgotten about him until five years later when I visited the home of the famed Irish literary figure, Denis Johnston, in Dalkey outside Dublin. He loved cats and found my story of Oxford amusing. A playwright by trade, Denis had spent part of his life working as a play-doctor and university professor in the United States. Weeks after my visit, Oxford's name surfaced again when I was sharing Martinis with Denis and Sean O'Faolain, one of Ireland's greatest twentieth-century short story writers. Both men were in their mid-seventies, and they had been estranged for decades until I had used my friendship with them to arrange a reunion.

Sean O'Faolain lived in a small, modest house in Dun Laoghaire on the outskirts of Dublin, whereas Denis Johnston had a fabulous home at Sorrento Terrace, a row of beautiful Georgian properties overlooking the sea, less than an hour's drive from Dublin. At the time, Denis Johnston's literary star was fading, but Sean O'Faolain was still the majestic short story writer held in admiration by young, aspiring writers.

Sean agreed to stage the reunion in his house, and when I arrived with Denis, he greeted us with Martinis. It was Sean's way of reminding Denis of a shared memory of time spent in America. Sean had relocated to the US early in his career and was a senior Harvard Fellow from 1928 to 1929. When he returned to Ireland in the 1930s, the Catholic Church's censors banned his work and prevented him from teaching in Catholic colleges.

Denis Johnston was born a year later than O'Faolain, in 1901, and by the 1920s he had established himself as a distinguished lawyer and playwright. Described at the time as a protégé of GB Shaw and the poet,

WB Yeats, he held prominence in the Dublin literary scene dominated by Lady Gregory at the Abbey Theatre. The playwright, Sean O'Casey, with whom Denis had many acrimonious exchanges, was one of his prominent contemporaries. Later, Denis became a celebrated BBC war correspondent and played a central role in the development of British television. By 1959 he had published a memorable biography of Dean Swift – *In Search of Swift* – and had moved to the United States. When I first met him in the mid-1970s, he truly believed he had been denied the literary accolades he deserved. His lamentations may have been justified, at least in part, though he was not the great Irish playwright he had aspired to be in his early twenties. He called one of his plays *The Old Lady Says No* as a reproach to the Abbey Theatre founder, Lady Gregory, for refusing to stage it. The play told the story of the Irish revolutionary, Robert Emmet, and was staged instead at Dublin's Gate Theatre, founded by Micháel Mac Liammóir and his partner, Hilton Edwards.

Denis Johnston raised the question of a reunion when I casually mentioned I had produced an interview with Sean O'Faolain about his collection of short stories entitled *Foreign Affairs*. Denis said he would love to meet him and wondered if I could make it happen. I suspected they had been critical of each other at some time in the distant past, an occurrence not unusual in the world of writers. Whatever made Denis Johnston feel slighted, he now wanted to put the past behind him.

Before I could fulfil Denis's request, I had to make sure Sean O'Faolain was prepared to meet him. I phoned Sean and he said he felt there had to be a pretext to bring them together – some pretext to smooth the transition from long silences to dialogue. I came up with the idea of producing a radio programme in which both of them could discuss their respective childhoods. They warmed to the idea, with Sean insisting I record the programme in his house. I chose my late friend, Barry Cowan, to host it.

After the first round of Martinis, Sean refilled our glasses, and the two great writers affectionately reminisced about the America they had once called home. An hour later, I managed to record a 30-minute radio programme that had the simple title, *Talking of Childhood*. It turned out to be a wonderful testimony to their creative grasp of the past, as a well as to the genuine admiration they had for each other.

Denis Johnston died less than a decade later, and Sean O'Faolain passed away on 20 April 1991. Every time I look back on that day in Sean's place, I do so with endearment, especially when I recall what happened after they recorded the programme and I was alone with them. With a mischievous glint in his eye, Denis asked me, 'Have you told Sean the story of your Oxford?'

I shook my head.

'Well, I'd like to hear it again and I've no doubt Sean would enjoy it, too,' he added, smiling at me over the rims of his half spectacles.

With a little reluctance, I threw myself into a lengthy description of my first meeting with Oxford, the basket at the bus stop on the Finchley Road and the pretty secretary who lost him. Both men grinned a lot when I recounted Oxford's disappearance, followed by his sudden resurrection and his final vanishing act. When I finished the story, Denis turned to Sean.

'What do you make of that, Sean?' he asked, nudging him playfully.

Sean feigned seriousness. 'Well,' he said quietly, pausing for effect, 'there's only one rational explanation. This was a cat fascinated by Martin's nightly routine. One evening, the cat dragged the basket to the bus stop on Finchley Road and returned to Oxford Street to await his new Master. You should never underestimate the determination and cunning of a cat.'

He paused again, a smile creasing the edges of his mouth. 'As for the pretty secretary, one might consider the possibility she still has Oxford as her pet. After all, a cat with genius and personality is a treasure. On the other hand, we should not lose sight of the most important character in this whole drama – Oxford himself. I prefer to think he had the measure of the secretary and took off in search of a better mistress. I suspect Martin was not the last person who found a cat basket at that bus stop on Finchley Road.'

The three of us burst out laughing, amused by Sean's theory. As I was leaving his home, he took my arm.

'Have you ever asked yourself why Oxford chose you?' he whispered.
I shrugged and smiled awkwardly.

'He chose you because he knew you would tell his story. That's my kind of cat!'

I admired the writings of O'Faolain and Johnston, and I liked both men even though they had very different personalities. Denis was a very tall, distinguished man with silvery hair who dressed like an Oxford Don. His speech was refined, with just the hint of an American accent. In contrast, Sean was neat, yet ordinary in appearance, with a disarming manner. When he spoke, he beautifully crafted his language to suit his temperament. He reminisced about Joyce and Beckett's Paris as though he were there. He was always happy to discuss his writings and to dispense advice to younger writers.

'A short story is like a kite,' he told me one day. 'You have to work hard to keep it moving, knowing it will not be in the air for very long. On the other hand, a novel is like an airplane. You can be confident it will be in the air long enough for you to build a story around its passengers.'

During my frequent stays in George Campbell's home in Dublin, I was fortunate to get to know Benedict Kiely, a great writer and one of the most gifted storytellers I have ever met. Ben lived next door to Madigan's pub in Donnybrook, which was one of George's favourites. He had a deep love for his native Omagh, even though he lived most of his life in Dublin. We shared something special, namely we had both been seminarians who eventually decided against the priesthood. As a student, he was hospitalised with back problems and during his recuperation decided 'the road of the collar' was not for him. Instead, he became a journalist, broadcaster and writer admired by his peers.

One evening, George Campbell chided me for not making enough BBC radio programmes about creative Northerners living in the Irish Republic. He especially mentioned Ben Kiely, who happened to be my father's favourite broadcaster. Two years passed, however, before I followed George's advice and organised a series of interviews with writers living in the Republic. Ben Kiely agreed to be on our programme, and the person I selected to interview him was a Scot, Gavin Essler. He was a BBC colleague who worked in the News and Current Affairs department and had been, like me, a *Belfast Telegraph* reporter. I regarded him as an excellent journalist with a refined love of the arts.

Since we would be interviewing Ben in Dublin, I added the Irish-American writer, JP Donleavy, to our programme schedule. I had not met Donleavy, but like many people of my generation I had read his book, *The Ginger Man*. One of the lines from it became a popular mantra in Dublin pubs: 'When I die I want to decompose in a barrel of porter and have it served in all the pubs in Ireland.' Not that Donleavy spent much of his life in Dublin pubs by the time I arranged to visit him. In 1979, his bolthole was Levington Park – a 200-acre estate close to Mullingar. His large Georgian house was one of the finest in the region and resembled the residence of a Lord rather than a writer of the Beat generation.

While writing this book, I contacted Gavin Essler, whom I had not spoken to for almost two decades. He had become an international reporter and had published five novels and a non-fiction work entitled, *The United States of Anger*. I asked him if he remembered our 1979 project, and he replied he had never forgotten it. He said he had just finished reading *Proxopera*, a Ben Kiely novel. He recalled Ben praising his interviewing style.

Upon arriving at Donleavy's gentrified Georgian mansion, a snooty female assistant led us into a large drawing room and offered tea. When Gavin asked him about his writing techniques, he waved his hands imperiously and said he dictated his books to his secretary. I sensed he wanted us to leave his fine surroundings as quickly as possible. He was not overtly rude but he was overbearing.

Gavin was struck by his detachment, which contrasted sharply with world famous people he interviewed in the years following. In Gavin's opinion, Donleavy's odd behaviour could be best summed up as, 'Have a coffee; I'm going to feck off!' It was a different story with Ben, however. 'Kiely I loved – he was a genius,' Gavin recalled.

Ben Kiely and I shared a unique attachment to the northern part of our island. One particular trip I made to Omagh with him, in the mid-1980s, has a special place in my heart. He was due to open the Omagh Festival one Saturday and wondered if I could pick him up from his place early in the morning. We could have a long chat on the leisurely drive north and sit down for the interview on the Sunday morning.

I drove from Belfast to Dublin, arriving at his place around 10 a.m. He appeared at the door unshaven, wearing slippers and an untied, woollen bathrobe. He walked off, leaving me to close the door. I found him minutes later lounging in a chair in his front room, his bathrobe still untied. Sitting opposite him was a young, slim, dark-haired American lady taking notes. The drapes were drawn, reminding me of being in a cinema waiting for the opening reel. Although Ben looked like he had spent a hard night on the tiles, he was responding lucidly to her questions and was soon his entertaining self. She displayed an unusual calm, keeping her eyes locked on his or on her notebook. On her way out, she shot me a glance, which seemed to indicate her relief. I had provided a distraction of sorts. I never learned her reason for conducting the interview, though I suspected she was a visiting academic. When I told Ben how he had unwittingly exposed himself to the young lady, he nonchalantly remarked, 'I'm sure her mind was on more wondrous things than my anatomy.'

I soon realised Ben was in no fit state to travel right away to Omagh, so I made him a light breakfast to cure his hangover and steady his nerves. He then disappeared into the bathroom for a wet shave and discovered he posed a serious danger to himself with a razor in hand. After two bloody nicks to his chin, he asked me to shave him. I had never shaved anyone in my life so I approached the task with considerable caution, and it seemed to take forever. Ben talked incessantly, and I had to ask him to be quiet when I was shaving his chin and upper lip. After the shave, he joking said he would not ask me to brush his teeth. I helped him get dressed, but the drama was only unfolding.

It was close to midday when he looked in a mirror, praised his own appearance and announced that Omagh awaited us. Unfortunately, Omagh would have to wait much longer than either of us anticipated. By the time I negotiated Dublin City traffic and reached the outskirts, Ben suggested visiting 'a fine establishment' to prepare ourselves for the journey. We headed straight to the pub, where I ordered a mineral water and he had a double Bloody Mary, which he sipped like it was nectar. Not surprisingly, Ben was a recognisable celebrity. He took it in his stride when strangers insisted on shaking his hand and telling him how much they enjoyed his broadcasts on Raidió Éireann.

After two more 'refreshment stops' along the road, the prospect of us making it to Omagh in time for him to open the festival looked far from realistic. We got to Omagh early evening after someone declared the festival open. At least, that is what I understood happened. I drove Ben to his hotel and went to mine. When I returned to his hotel forty minutes later, he was surrounded by a throng of admirers, many of whom had travelled from Dublin to hear him speak. He agreed to meet me the next morning at 10 a.m. I planned to stroll with him along the Strule River and visit his parents' grave in the local cemetery, recording memories of his childhood.

When I got up the next day, I found the centre of Omagh empty like a ghost town. Ben's hotel was very quiet, given the majority of guests were still sleeping off the effects of late-night partying. I asked the desk clerk if he had seen Mr Kiely. He shot me a disapproving stare.

'Jesus, didn't he have me bring him up a boiled egg and a large Bloody Mary an hour ago,' the clerk complained.

I found Ben sitting up in bed reading the Bible. On seeing me he extolled its virtues, explaining it was 'a wonderful read when one's senses are finely tuned to the nuances of language'. In his opinion, it was not just beautifully written, it contained some of the classic stories of all time. He reminded me the Sabbath was a time for leisure and relaxation, and a Bloody Mary would 'do the trick'. At the very least, it would revitalise him sufficiently to meet the 'challenges ahead'.

I agreed to get him the drink if he promised to be in the lobby within an hour.

'I shall be there,' he grinned and returned to his reading.

He rose within the hour and by midday we were strolling along the banks of the Strule River. He pointed to some houses with backyards hanging over the river's edge, saying the yards once had toilets that effused into the river, leaving the trout blind drunk from one end of the Strule to the other.

In the nineteenth century, a certain Baroness Von Molke, travelling through the town in a carriage, was so taken with the 'hanging lavatories' that she declared them the Eighth Wonder of the World. He never explained who the Baroness was or her reasons for being in Omagh. One rarely challenged Ben's claims or his sincerity because he delivered his stories with style and conviction. An hour later, we visited his parents' grave and I recorded him talking about their influence on his life.

In 2007, a phone call to my New York apartment brought the sad news my friend, Ben, had died. This saddened me, but I rejoiced in having shared a few adventures with him.

FOURTEEN

Challenging the BBC's Ethics

By the end of the 1970s, I had transitioned from Radio Arts to General Programmes Radio, becoming editor in charge of a wide range of programme disciplines, including light entertainment, consumer affairs, documentaries and a weekly Friday morning programme I created to discuss the most contentious political issues driving the Troubles. Initially, it was called *On Friday It's Peter Martin*, after its presenter's name. Peter was a young lawyer with a sharp intellect and, though he was new to broadcasting, I felt he had the potential to be an accomplished interviewer. From the outset, I assigned Colin Lewis, a senior producer, to work closely with him, but I was always involved in choosing the content and shaping it editorially.

In the BBC, as in many corporations, there are turf wars between competing interests. So by creating this programme, I stepped on the toes of some colleagues in News and Current Affairs, who believed they alone were qualified to work in the hallowed halls of news coverage and analysis. The fact I might have had more journalism experience than many of them didn't matter. They were determined to ambush me by questioning the integrity of the Peter Martin show during Programme Board Meetings attended by radio and television producers. The meetings were colourful events when Ronald Mason presided over them, but when Cecil Taylor replaced him as Head of Programmes – HPNI – I found them dull affairs. People used them so often for settling scores that producers made sure to attend when their programmes were listed for review. Non-attendance meant leaving the 'battlefield' to one's enemies. Minutes of meetings were circulated and were necessarily limited in what they reflected of the discussions that took place.

In 1978, the dynamics of the BBC power structure in Belfast changed to include a new Controller, James Hawthorne, and a new Head of Radio Ulster, Don Anderson, who had a superb reputation as a national television news reporter. All the staff respected Anderson. Hawthorne, a tall, thin, bearded figure, who had lately been head of a television station in Hong Kong, was best remembered in BBC Belfast as having been a Radio Schools Programmes producer in 1960. Most of his contemporaries would have agreed his abilities as a producer never matched theirs, but he possessed a driving ambition. He was cunning and had acquired a professorial persona, which impressed BBC mandarins and politicians alike. As Controller, he established a reputation for defending news and current affairs freedoms in the face of political pressure from the British government, but some of that was offset by his private editorial decisions. I found him supportive and easier to communicate with than his deputy, Cecil Taylor, whose nickname was 'The Bald Eagle'. Taylor tended to be the blunt newsman, whereas Hawthorne exuded a sugary sophistication and innate skill for diplomacy. From my experience, Taylor was more familiar with the minutiae of news and current affairs programming and was not timid when it came to asserting his knowledge. Over time, their relationship would suffer from discord. There was a seedy side to Hawthorne's character, reflecting a warped personality, but that would only become apparent to a few of us before his BBC tenure ended.

On Friday, 13 October 1978, vitriol towards the Peter Martin programme reached a crescendo during a programme review meeting that I was unable to attend. Cecil Taylor, HPNI, presided over it. The outspoken critic was Simon Berthon, a producer with the television current affairs programme, *Spotlight*. I still have copies of the minutes of that meeting. The Peter Martin programme up for review had dealt with the alleged ill-treatment of Republican prisoners under interrogation in police custody. It had come to the attention of Colin Lewis, the programme's producer, that a prominent Unionist Councillor, Jack Hassard, was upset the Chief Constable and Police Authority, a body tasked with overseeing police behaviour, were refusing to investigate the allegations. Hassard's upset was significant for several reasons. He was a Protestant Unionist Councillor from Dungannon, a person one might not have expected to be concerned with the plight of Republicans. More importantly, he was a senior member of the Police Authority. He had just announced he was resigning from the Authority because he felt the ill-treatment issue merited investigation. Colin Lewis spoke to him, as did Peter Martin, and he agreed to be interviewed live. I instructed Colin to invite the RUC Chief Constable, or anyone the RUC wished to select, to participate in the programme. In that way, conflicting opinions about the issue would be reflected. The RUC Press Office, on behalf of the Chief Constable flat out rejected the offer. I suspected the RUC Press Office believed its rejection would kill off the planned interview with Hassard, which was sure to embarrass the police force. From my perspective, the scheduled dialogue had to go ahead as a matter of public importance. The RUC would be free to respond at a later time if they so wished. There were also plenty of news outlets they could contact to challenge anything Hassard might say. I gave the Peter Martin programme my blessing, and it was broadcast live.

Weeks later, I received the internal Programme Review Board minutes, which showed the programme had been discussed by the Board immediately after it was broadcast. The Minutes read as follows. The text has not been altered.

Mr. Berthon was slightly concerned about some of the items he has heard on the programme. He felt that on some occasions they were almost in breach of the BBC Charter. The programme lacked balance, this morning for instance Jack Hassard was saying some very serious things about the Chief Constable. Last week there had been an item on De Lorean, the attitude seemed to be that John De Lorean had some obligation to supply spokesmen. Audio Manage said this morning's programme had a very fine dividing line between aggressive interviewing and sheer rudeness. People were being constantly interrupted when replying to questions. HPNI was grateful to the Board for drawing his attention to this.

If General Programmes are going to stray on such sensitive matters then obviously editorial guidance is necessary. HPNI asked HRU to make sure he knew the content of the Friday programme at the beginning of each week.

NB: the HRU referred to was Head of Radio, Don Anderson, my immediate editorial boss. These were the actual Minutes, including grammatical flaws.

Cecil Taylor's willingness to accept Berthon's criticism was astonishing as was his comment about 'straying on such sensitive matters'. He not only knew the programme regularly dealt with thorny political issues, but he accepted Berthon's concept of 'balance'. I was perplexed by Berthon's apparent shock that Hassard was permitted to be critical of the Chief Constable. After all, Hassard had just resigned as a senior member of the Police Authority. Neither Berthon nor Taylor appeared to recognise the courage it took for Hassard to speak out on such a controversial topic. The minutes were also a direct attack on me and the programme's integrity. I decided to challenge Taylor and Berthon at the next Review Board. News of my intention travelled like wildfire throughout production offices, and the conference room where the meetings took place was packed a fortnight later. Hawthorne, Taylor, and Don Anderson were present.

Prior to the meeting, I met with Colin Lewis and showed him a statement I intended to read so it would be recorded in the minutes for circulation. I asked Colin, who had been an accomplished actor before joining the BBC, if he would read excerpted sections of the BBC's Charter I had typed for him. He agreed. Though, as he recalled later, he was as nervous as hell because we were putting our careers on the line. Walking into the conference room I felt the tension. I did not know if Taylor would turn up, or if the rumours Hawthorne intended to witness the event were reliable. Everyone expected sparks to fly. When Taylor arrived and sat down, many of my colleagues avoided eye contact with me. After a secretary read the previous minutes, I announced I wished to challenge them. I stood up, Colin at my side, and began reading a prepared statement. Out of the corner of my eye I saw Hawthorne enter the room and remain standing. In a garrulous tone, Taylor interrupted me, demanding to know if I planned to take up much of the Review Board's time. I responded that I would be mindful of the meeting's time constraints. He approved my proceeding and I read the following statement:

> I would like to draw attention to the previous Board Minute on the Peter Martin programme. The programme referred to in the Minute was an excellent programme, and I defy anyone at this Programme Board to question the validity of the interview with Hassard, or alternatively the role played by either the presenter or producer. If the Audio Manager would care to clarify his comments I will be only too willing to listen to a considered and detailed explanation. I would like to ask HPNI before I proceed to the second paragraph of the Minute whether he considers it accurate both in terms of what it implied, and the nature of the language, which is attributed to him.

I paused for Taylor to respond, but he did not. I read on: 'Finally, this Minute is demoralising for a department which has operated under considerable pressure, both financial and technical. Additionally, as someone who has worked in Current Affairs inside and outside this Corporation, I find the implied criticisms in these Minutes despicable, and I would like them refuted in the subsequent Minutes of this Board.'

I then quoted Review Board minutes of 30 June 1978, when lavish praise was heaped on the Peter Martin series and the interviewing skills of its presenter. I asked everyone present to consider if we were in the business of constructive criticism or in a vacuum being subjected to 'glib, inaccurate and destructive comment'. I paused briefly to let all present digest my criticism before addressing the concept of balance and the widely held belief in the BBC that every programme had to exemplify it. At this point, I asked Colin to read from the BBC's Charter.

Here are a few of the lines he quoted:

There are two important qualifications to be made to this concept of balance. First, although it used to be thought essential that every programme dealing with a controversial subject should be balanced within itself, so that all sides of the question were heard together, long experience of working in this way taught the BBC that too much emphasis on balance within a single programme tended to produce a result which was confusing to the listener and more productive of heat and light. A former Director General of the BBC, Sir William Haley, made the point in an article written in 1945 that: Impartiality does not mean so artificially balancing the speakers the listeners can never come to a conclusion on the basis of the argument. More than twenty years later, another Director General, Sir Hugh Greene, developed it further: We have to balance different points of view in our programmes but not necessarily within each individual programme.

Colin read an additional excerpt from the Charter that spoke directly to the balance debate as I understood it. 'The BBC does not feel obliged for example to appear neutral as between truth and untruth, freedom and slavery, compassion and cruelty, tolerance and intolerance.'

Finally, I questioned Taylor's use of the word 'stray', which implied I and my producers were like lost sheep. I challenged his statement about editorial guidance being necessary and the imposition of new controls on the editorial management of the show. I told Taylor if he felt this way about the programme perhaps he should take it off air. He made no comment but my presentation that day killed further publication and circulation of Review Board minutes. I was unhappy my analysis of the balance issue was not published for a wider internal audience but pleased minutes could never be used again for objectionable and uninformed comment.

For too long, the word 'balance' had been tossed around by BBC producers and editors, who had never taken the time to read the

Corporation's Charter. I was glad I had noted that achieving balance was not always possible in an individual programme but could be realised over time. It would not be the last time I would clash with Cecil Taylor over editorial issues.

Three years later, Hawthorne placed me in charge of Radio Current Affairs for a four-month experiment, hoping I might choose to remain in the post. It brought me into direct contact with Taylor rather than the Head of Radio, Don Anderson, because Taylor regarded himself as a news and current affairs guru. One of the decisions I made after I took the job was to change the title of the morning radio and current affairs programme from *Good Morning Ulster* to *Breakfast Special*. I wanted to give the programme a contemporary image and rid it of the old Ulster tag from its Ronald Mason days. I also aimed to broaden the scope of the broadcast material each morning so the show would not be exclusively and reflexively shaped by the conflict on the streets. Overall, I hoped to make it less insular. After the first month, I knew it was going to be a battle of ideas between Taylor and myself. He was old school and saw everything through a 'hard news' prism, which I felt narrowed the range of topics we could present to our audience. When my time with Radio Current Affairs ended, I chose to return to my role as Editor General Programmes. In that post, I was editorially responsible for the majority of the radio output, and I had excellent working relations with my line manager, Don Anderson. I was no sooner back in my old job when I received an annual report written by Taylor. It covered the period when I was in charge of Radio Current Affairs. James Hawthorne, the Controller, read it to me in his office on 15 June 1981. In accordance with the rules, I was not given a personal copy of it. I told Hawthorne aspects of the report displeased me, and he encouraged me to respond to it. He smiled as he lifted a pen from his desk and began writing a summary of my responses. He then read back what he had written and asked me if I wanted it placed on record. I told him I certainly did, and he signed it before instructing his secretary to give me a copy. That was a generous gesture, though I suspected he did it to embarrass his deputy, Taylor. He assured me he would make my disappointment with Taylor's evaluation of me known to him. He sent Taylor a coded signal that if I wanted the Current Affairs Editor job I would be given a fair hearing. Head of Radio, Don Anderson told me Hawthorne wanted me in the post but I suspected his motives. I feared he might seek to use me as a pawn in his disputes with Taylor, so I refused to apply for it.

Instead, I took charge of the Friday programme personally, changing the title to *Behind the Headlines*, and handing the presentation of it to John Simpson, an economist and political commentator. After two years, I replaced him with Brian Garrett, a senior partner in Elliott Duffy Garrett, one of Ireland's most respected law firms. Brian had a history with the Northern Ireland Labour Party and was widely regarded as a fair-minded liberal. We established a fine rapport, and he was happy to take direction from me in his earpiece during live interviews. The format, which was a one-hour live studio broadcast, was central to the programme's success because it enabled me to schedule lengthy interviews in which politicians could be challenged about a single issue or a range of issues. Politicians liked the format because they had enough time to articulate their points of view, which was rarely possible in the sound-bite world of news. From the outset, I advised Brian Garret to apply persistence if a politician refused to answer a question. If necessary, Brian should ask it three times. After the third attempt, the politician's deliberate evasiveness would be clear to our audience.

Media professionals outside the Corporation tuned in to the weekly broadcast and often pulled newsworthy information and commentary from it. Consequently, very few major political figures in the British Isles turned down our requests for interviews. Since we broadcast live at lunchtime, wine and sandwiches were offered to guests in my office when each programme ended. This resulted in a congenial atmosphere in which political opponents exchanged ideas and gossiped. The 'post-programme forum', as I once described it, led to revealing, off-the-record discussions. The more successful the programme became the more resentment it accumulated among some individuals in local BBC news and current affairs departments.

As a result of the programme, I met Katherine Anderson, née Bannon, who gave an interview about women in the fashion industry. She was a former model who ran her own fashion business. She was married to Alan Anderson, the CEO of Century Newspapers in Northern Ireland. We began a love affair, and she and her five-year-old son, Crawford, moved in with me. I subsequently divorced Mildred and married Katherine. We brought our daughter, Nadia, into the world in 1988. Katherine had a keen knowledge of Northern Ireland politics and encouraged me to write *The Shankill Butchers* and *The Dirty War*. My best man at our wedding was the Hon. Roy Bradford, a former Unionist cabinet minister. Guests included a broad cross section of society, many of them leading politicians from both communities, including Jim Molyneaux, leader of the Ulster Unionist Party, and Paddy Devlin, a founder of the Social Democratic Labour Party.

FIFTEEN

Genesis of the Peace Process: Hume v Adams

In my opinion, *Behind the Headlines* will always be associated with one of the major political events of the Troubles, namely the live debate between the two major political opponents in the Nationalist community – John Hume of the Social Democratic and Labour Party and Gerry Adams, President of the IRA's Provisional Sinn Fein. No one thought it possible that the two would agree to appear together in the same forum, but I managed to change their minds after a series of unconnected events. On 1 January 1985, I learned of a political conference due to be staged at Warrenton, approximately 45 miles south of Washington D.C. Considerable secrecy surrounded the conference, which was organised by the well-known American Professor, Padraig O'Malley of the Committee for an Irish Forum. It was scheduled to be held under the auspices of the British and Irish governments, and only a small, selected number of journalists were invited to attend. A source close to the conference organisers told me it would be held under Chatham House Rules, whereby speakers would be guaranteed anonymity.

I tried to get an invitation but was turned down. In fact, I was led to understand no one from BBC Northern Ireland was welcome. My boss, Cecil Taylor, agreed with me it was highly irregular for such an important conference to deny a BBC representative access, especially when British government representatives and the major Northern Ireland parties, Provisional Sinn Fein, excluded, would attend. I proposed to fly to Warrenton on the same flight as local politicians and file a live report into *Behind the Headlines* from the conference centre. As a classic newsman determined to cover a potential story, Taylor thought it was a stellar idea and gave me permission to make the trip. I booked an Aer Lingus flight from Dublin to Washington.

When I arrived in Dublin for the flight, I met John Hume and members of his party I knew well, like Seamus Mallon and Austin Currie. I was greeted by several Unionist delegates who joked they would be in economy class with John Hume's SDLP colleagues, while John occupied a business class seat. I explained my upgrade to first class was a favour from an Aer Lingus friend, not wishing anyone to think the BBC had used the public purse for me to fly in style. On the second leg of the flight, from Shannon to Washington, John Hume, who was in business class, visited me in first class, and we drank champagne while discussing the ongoing political situation back home. He promised to get me an invite to the conference, but I had a feeling it would not be easy even for him. As we talked, I suggested it might be time for a public debate about who represented the political aspirations of the Catholic Nationalist community in Northern Ireland. Was it his SDLP or Gerry Adam's Provisional Sinn Féin? I said I would be happy to devote a *Behind the Headlines* to such a debate were he willing to challenge the oft repeated claim by Adams that Sinn Féin was the true voice of Nationalism.

The more John and I talked about this, the more the prospect of a live debate with Adams appealed to him. I sensed he was confident he would have the upper hand in contentious exchanges with his opponent. After all, he had honed his debating skills over two decades of television and radio skirmishes with tough interviewers and savvy political opponents. He doubted, however, Adams would have the courage to accept the challenge. I felt otherwise. I told him I would phone Adams and make the offer.

When we arrived in Washington, John's colleagues encouraged me to join their party because they were to be escorted through customs without having to wait in line like other passengers. At the airport, his deputy, Seamus Mallon persuaded me to travel on their coach to

Warrenton. He and Austin Currie said they would escort me into the conference and insist on me being accorded press accreditation and accommodation. By that stage, I had no desire to be constrained by the secrecy rules of the conference. I asked the coach driver to drop me at a shopping mall, and I booked into a small motel near the centre. I arranged to meet John Hume in the conference building forty-eight hours later, which left me time to make calls home to check if the conference had made headlines. As I anticipated, newspapers and broadcast outlets throughout the British Isles made no mention of it. On the morning of the second day, I travelled to the conference centre where security personnel placed me in the care of one of the conference organisers, Ruth Ann Harris, a distinguished professor from Boston College. She left me in a hotel suite and went off to fetch John Hume. I spent only half an hour with John because he was busy participating in discussion groups and did not have much free time. He did not tell me much about the topics for discussion, but I left feeling my visit had nonetheless been valuable. Unknown to him, however, I returned to my motel with a conference folder containing the position papers of all the parties at the event. Some of Professor Harris's conference colleagues later accused her of giving me the folder and upset her with the allegation. She wrote to me, asking if I would provide her with a letter indicating it was not the case, and I did so. I should also be clear that John Hume did not give them to me, either.

The position papers provided me with a clear picture of some of the surprising political positions being advocated by the conference participants. Forty-eight hours later, I spoke live by phone on my programme and blew away the secrecy of the conference. I explained how opposing political parties were adopting liberal positions they articulated rarely, if ever, at home. While I was excited to tell the audience in Ireland what some of its political representatives were saying in secret, my two days in the motel were mostly devoted to arranging a live radio debate between John Hume and Gerry Adams. I phoned the Sinn Féin press office in Belfast and spoke to Adams. He thought it was a practical joke. But when I assured him it was not, he asked me to set a date. He expressed surprise that John Hume would actually debate with him live on BBC Radio. I assured him his agreement had just sealed the debate. In truth, I was anxious to get his consent as quickly as possible, fearing if John Hume had too long to think about it he might back out. His SDLP colleagues and friends might pressure him to avoid any public face-off with the Provisionals' political leader, fearing it held unknown risks. I phoned John Hume right away and told him Adams was on board. He seemed surprised at the pace of this development. Judging by his tone I sensed he was having second thoughts, so I advised him if he pulled out Adams would derive political capital from it. The likelihood was that Adams would portray him as too timid to confront the issue of who represented Nationalists. John explained he wasn't having second thoughts. He was merely surprised Adams had taken the bait. This was not an opportunity he would pass up, he assured me. I scheduled the meeting of the two men for 31 January 1985, exactly three weeks after the Warrenton Conference.

In Broadcasting House in Belfast, a strident discussion followed news of my coup. Cecil Taylor insisted that if John Hume pulled out, or fell and broke his leg on the way to the studio, he would cancel the programme. Brian Garrett, the programme presenter, echoed Taylor's concerns, arguing that a programme without Hume would be perceived as providing Adams with a political platform. Brian suggested he might not wish to host the programme in the event the guest was only Adams. I disagreed with both of them. I made it clear if they cancelled because John Hume could not, or would not, participate, it would be up to the BBC to release a public statement, outlining the reasons for the cancellation. I would not wish my name attached to such a statement. The same principle I had outlined to a Programme Review Board regarding the BBC Charter guided my position. I felt, in the event Adams was the only guest, Brian Garrett and I had the ability to produce a broadcast in which Adams would be tested with well-framed questions. I explained to Taylor and Garret, we could interview Hume separately at a subsequent time and give him an opportunity to respond to Adams. Ultimately, this exchange of views, which continued into the night before the planned broadcast, proved irrelevant.

Hume and Adams arrived at the studio on time and participated in a live interview for one hour. It was riveting stuff, and John Hume seemed at first to have the debating edge. As the programme progressed, I felt he began to underestimate his opponent, ignoring the fact he was no slouch in the rough and tumble of political theatre. As the clock ticked down to the end of the broadcast, Hume tried to denigrate him one last time by posing a question to the effect – 'why should I talk to you when you are only the messenger boy for the IRA's Army Council. Maybe I should just talk to the real men.' The question with its inbuilt sarcasm had all the characteristics of a sucker punch that would have left a less formidable opponent reeling. To the programme audience, however, it implied Hume wanted to meet the IRA, yet I doubt that is what he intended to convey. He was simply obsessed with landing a haymaker blow to finish off Adams. Meanwhile, I had spotted Adams momentarily gazing at the studio clock, which showed less than a minute to the end of the broadcast. Suddenly, he fixed John Hume with a stare. 'Do you want to meet the real men?' he asked him. The clock was ticking down, and I am convinced to this day John Hume found himself flat-footed. After all, the politician had earlier opened the door to this possibility and had chastised Adams as a mere messenger boy moments earlier. Adams had delivered his counterpunch with speed and crispness, and in a timely fashion. Hume had no time to craft a clever, perhaps evasive reply. Adams pressed him to answer, saying he was happy to set a meeting between Hume and the 'real men'. Hume managed to agree as the clock ran out. Little did we know, John Hume's decision to meet the IRA signalled a new chapter in the politics of the island.

Gerry Adams left Broadcasting House right after the programme. He looked like a man who had not only held his own but had scored a political victory. John Hume, on the other hand, joined me in my office for wine and sandwiches, appearing perplexed. He wondered if he had done the right thing. As a seasoned political campaigner, it was not lost on him he had just made one of the most controversial decisions of his political life. He phoned Barry White, a fine political columnist with the *Belfast Telegraph*, to get his reaction. Barry said he thought it was an important interview. Brian Garrett phoned his elderly mother, whom he phoned after every Friday programme. She felt Hume had just made a negative contribution to the overall political debate. Leading Unionists shared her view as well and accused Hume of pandering to terrorists. Newspaper editorials took a similar position and lambasted him for providing men of violence with political respectability. A meeting with the IRA leadership was subsequently set up, but Hume walked out of it after heated exchanges in which he called on them to end their terror campaign. In retrospect, the Hume–Adams interview set in motion a dialogue between Hume and Republicans and was the genesis of the future peace process.

I believe Hume acted courageously, and I told his wife so after newspaper editorials and politicians throughout the British Isles condemned him. The criticism was unwarranted and ridiculous in light of the fact British government representatives and the Provisional IRA engaged in secret talks from the early 1970s through Margaret Thatcher's time in office. It was important for John Hume, as leader of the largest party in the Catholic community, to hold a public debate with the Provisionals, who were taking his community down a violent path. By engaging the IRA in dialogue, he demonstrated it was possible to get its leaders to consider an alternative to violence.

From a personal perspective, I enjoyed the company of both Unionist and Nationalist political leaders, including John Hume, Austin Currie, Seamus Mallon, David Trimble, Roy Bradford, Jim Molyneaux and Ian Paisley. I went to lunch with some of them more than once, and I got to know them well. My friend, Roy Bradford, a former Unionist cabinet minister, was an important sounding board and contact when I was keen to know about the politics of Unionism. We co-authored a biography of World II Special Air Service hero, Lt. Col. 'Paddy' Blair Mayne. For years, we frequently had lunch and played snooker in the Unionist Party's Ulster Club in the centre of

Belfast. I thoroughly enjoyed any time I spent with Roy because he displayed a directness, heightened intelligence and transparency unique in the political world. David Trimble, a lawyer and commentator before he became Unionist Party leader, was a good friend. Additionally, I developed a special rapport with paramilitary figures, including the UDA leader, John McMichael. When he was ready to release a document offering a political way forward, he asked me to read it and give him my opinion. I knew several Unionist politicians and advisers who helped him compile it. It provided an interesting addition to the dialogue between leaders in both communities, and I told him so.

John McMichael was anxious for John Hume to read it and wondered if I would ask him to 'give it a nod'. McMichael felt if Hume indicated it was worthy of scrutiny by Nationalists, it might help him convince fellow Loyalists that dialogue was preferable to the gun. I spoke to John Hume and he made a few brief but positive comments about it on a BBC radio programme. McMichael had never met John Hume and asked me to arrange for them to have a 'private chat'. I set up a brief rendezvous between them in a corner of the BBC's private parking area, and they spoke for approximately ten minutes. Their brief get-together was another illustration of John Hume's preparedness to talk to men of violence if he believed it could further the political process. This willingness, I believe, contributed to him jointly winning the Nobel Peace Prize in 1998.

Ironically, events took an even stranger twist later that day when I mentioned to the BBC Controller, James Hawthorne, that I had plans to take McMichael to dinner. He invited us for drinks to his office, explaining he wanted to meet 'a real, live one', meaning a terror boss. After spending an hour with Hawthorne and the UDA chief, I took McMichael for dinner in the restaurant where I had earlier shared lunch with John Hume. The restaurant's owner, Jenny, was shocked that I could have lunch with John Hume and then dinner with a notorious UDA figure on the same day. McMichael, whom she recognised from news broadcasts, particularly intrigued her. As a high-profile figure on an IRA hit list, he was security conscious, and it was unheard of him to visit pubs or bars in Belfast city centre. After dinner, we had drinks with the broadcaster, writer and political commentator, Eamonn McCann. He had spirited exchanges with McMichael, asking him at one point how many killers he had under his command. Eamonn later admitted it was bizarre and frightening interrogating a known killer. A year later, I took a taxi to Lisburn to meet McMichael in a bar he owned. My colleague, Colin Lewis, joined us. After drinks, Colin became nervous when McMichael insisted on driving us back to our BBC offices. McMichael subsequently died when an IRA bomb attached to the underside of his car exploded outside his home.

In the mid-1990s, less than a decade after I arranged the broadcast debate with John Hume and Gerry Adams, I received a call from 10 Downing Street to my home in France. It was an invitation to dinner with David Davis, a senior adviser to Prime Minister John Major. The dinner would be hosted in Westminster. I was intrigued by the offer, but out of caution I asked David Davies to join me for a meal at a central London hotel where I would be staying. He agreed. I knew from several sources that he had taken a keen interest in Ireland. He was knowledgeable about the issues underlying the violence and was trustworthy. When we sat down we were very open with each other. He was an entertaining guest and raconteur. We talked about political personalities we both knew. He shared with me how he threw his support behind John Major's candidacy for the premiership in late 1990 only when Margaret Thatcher declared she would not run again. He admired her leadership and had her personal approval to back Major, he said.

As our conversation progressed, he confirmed that his meeting with me had the approval of Number 10. He was keen to know if I believed there was a possibility of negotiating an end to the Ireland conflict. He wanted my understanding of the personalities and strengths of the IRA's leadership. I knew at the time that John Major's government, like its predecessor, was engaged in secret talks with the IRA. David Davis hinted that Number 10 was anxious to have my opinion on whether some of the IRA's leaders were more open than others to talks on conflict resolution, and if an agreement was reached, could they deliver it to their rank and file. I concluded from some of the things he said that any agreement would involve decommissioning and would not meet the IRA central goal of a United Ireland. The names, Gerry Adams and Martin McGuinness, surfaced prominently in his inquiries.

I knew a lot about Adams from personal encounters and from the observations of people who surrounded him. IRA Intelligence chief, Brendan Hughes, had provided me with important insights formed in his dealings with him. My inside track on McGuinness was based on conversations with sources I had cultivated in the upper echelons of the IRA in Dublin.

I shared with David Davies my belief that Gerry Adams wanted to go down in history as someone who had changed the political dynamics of Ireland. Confusingly, he was an idealist and a realist. He saw himself as a creative revolutionary in the 1916 Padraig Pearse tradition, but he was also pragmatic. Such a person might be willing to engage with the British government in seeking an end to the Troubles, I recall saying. I then offered David this assessment: 'I believe Adams is the most likely member of the IRA's Army Council to propose negotiating a deal with the British government. But Martin McGuinness will have to keep Adams alive before and after negotiations become a reality. McGuinness has the confidence of the IRA's rank and file. I suspect he will support Adams if there is a deal on the table he, too, can sign off on.'

It was my opinion that Adams held the key to any hopes the British government might have had to negotiate an end to the 'Long War'. My reference to the need to keep Adams alive was related to the fact that he was a prime target for Loyalist assassins. I felt I did not need to point out to David Davis that the British government was well equipped to ensure Adams' survival. MI5 and Special Branch had enough influence in Loyalist terror groups to eliminate any risk from those elements. However, Republicans posed a significant threat because they could get to Adams easily. They would kill him if they thought he was selling out. The person who had the military clout to stop that happening was McGuinness.

I did not breach any ethical lines by sharing my thoughts with my Number 10 guest. I could just as easily have penned them for the opinions column of a local newspaper. David Davies later thanked me for speaking frankly and conveyed the prime minister's appreciation of my openness.

It was not the first time a government had sought my expertise. In 1990, when Margaret Thatcher was prime minister, her terrorism advisers encouraged the US government to turn to me for help. They wanted me to be a witness against an IRA gunman, Joseph Doherty, who was seeking political asylum in the New York Federal Courts. Doherty had been the leader of an IRA unit known as the 'M60 Gang'. It ambushed an SAS unit, using a powerful M60 machinegun and killed its captain. When he was caught and jailed, he claimed no prison would hold him because his military expertise was vital to the IRA. He escaped from Belfast's Crumlin Road Prison in 1983 and fled to New York where the FBI tracked him down. He applied for political asylum and quickly became a celebrated figure in Irish-American circles. A street was named after him in downtown Manhattan, next to a detention facility where he was held under lock and key.

From 1983 onwards, Margaret Thatcher was relentless in her determination to return him to jail in Belfast. She was upset by Doherty's international notoriety as a freedom fighter. She privately demanded that President Regan, and subsequently the Bush administration, extradite him. She insisted it would be America's payback for her permission to allow US bombers to use British airspace on their way to bomb Libya in 1986. In her view, Doherty's extradition was central to the proper maintenance of the 'Special Relationship' between Britain and America.

I explained to the Federal prosecutor in New York that it would be unethical of me as a journalist to be a witness against Doherty. Besides, it would carry personal risks for me. I was already under a death threat in Belfast. On the other hand, I was prepared to appear as a friend of the court and answer questions about my published work as it related to the IRA. The prosecutor agreed. He was especially interested in my understanding of the IRA chain of command and how its units functioned. *The Dirty War* contained the most recent and only publicly available copy of *The Green Book*, the IRA's secret rules manual. I spent ten days in New York studying the Doherty case but was not called to give evidence. However, I uncovered the history of Margaret Thatcher's secret pursuit of Doherty. Before I left the Big Apple, I received a special thank you from the prime minister. It was delivered by Sherard Cowper-Coles, her senior diplomat in Washington. I subsequently wrote *Killer in Clowntown: Joe Doherty, the IRA and the Special Relationship*.

On 19 February 1992, Margaret Thatcher was no longer in office, but she must have been thrilled when news reached her that the American military had flown Doherty home, and he was back behind bars in Belfast's Crumlin Road Prison. As he was led to his cell, a prison officer stepped forward and asked him to sign a book. It was my book about him. I subsequently discovered he was unhappy with my account of his terrorist history and his failed political asylum battle.

I suspect Margaret Thatcher would have been unhappy had she, too, read my book. When you write books that do not favour any of the protagonists in a conflict, you often find yourself taking incoming from all sides. The British and American governments were not pleased that I had revealed their secret machinations of over a decade to ensure Doherty was extradited. They had consistently denied publicly that Margaret Thatcher and her advisers were improperly placing pressure on the American judicial process, when, in fact, the opposite was true. Doherty's lawyers and supporters disliked the book because it undercut their portrayal of Doherty as a scapegoat of an unjust British system. In contrast, I exposed him as a prominent member of a murderous IRA unit.

SIXTEEN

Time to Talkback and Natural-Born Killers

On 18 September 1986, I launched a daily, one-hour midday show called *Talkback*. It would break the normal rules of broadcasting in a society in conflict. By then, the large department I had run, General Programmes, had been broken up, and the very successful *Behind the Headlines* had been scrapped without explanation. A year had passed since the implementation of the Anglo-Irish Agreement, which was the centrepiece of Margaret Thatcher's Ireland policy. Unionists bitterly opposed it, and I found myself facing criticism from some BBC figures for allowing Unionists to appear on the airwaves to voice their opposition to it.

One evening, James Hawthorne summoned me to his office to express his displeasure with my coverage of the Agreement. He stressed that I should not forget I was employed by the British Broadcasting Corporation. It should be at the forefront of my thinking when producing programmes reflecting the British government's Anglo-Irish Agreement. Without issuing an editorial edict, he was in effect telling me, in an underhand way, to get in line with British government policy. I knew he would not dare outline his position on paper in the form of a memo. I suspected he wanted to please the British government, hoping it would benefit his career and someday get him a knighthood. I responded that I had a responsibility to reflect Unionist opposition to the Agreement, but he shook his head and sent me on my way, telling me to be more careful how I framed the Agreement in my programming. Years later, Barry Cowan, who had been editor in charge of the television programme, *Spotlight*, told me he was also summoned to Hawthorne's office and given similar advice. It was the kind of editorial interference we both deeply resented. I ultimately chose to ignore it.

Before I created *Talkback*, my editorial designation was changed to Senior Producer Topical Features, and a new Head of Programmes, Arwel Ellis Owen, a Welshman, asked me to create a daily radio show. He wanted it to include a quiz, and my immediate reaction was one of horror. I told him if he wanted a light entertainment show there were other producers and editors better equipped to fulfil that mission. I believed at the time, and still do, there were outside political influences pressing for me to be removed from any news and current affairs programmes. I ignored Ellis Owen's quiz concept and created a controversial, public access show with Barry Cowan as its presenter. He was the most accomplished current affairs interviewer in Northern Ireland, and when I explained to him the new show would be a blend of current affairs interviews, entertaining commentary, satire and a phone-in element to reflect the prevailing political climate on the streets, he was anxious to host it.

My aim was to move away from the narrow confines of news coverage of the conflict to reflect the general atmosphere on the streets and the opinions of all sides on the bitter issues dividing the communities. From my perspective, nothing was off limits. It was time for the society to talk back to itself. We knew the deep prejudices that existed among us, and it was time to hold them up to scrutiny and to encourage people to confront them. I was also determined to introduce a sharp current affairs element in which interviews would focus on all the protagonists, British ministers included, in a manner that tested their positions on issues central to the news. I sensed, as I had when producing *Behind the Headlines*, I was putting my head on a chopping block, and people, including colleagues from the BBC's news and current affairs division, would soon be queuing up to deprive me of it. Current affairs executives believed they alone had the right to reflect the tough issues.

To make the programme appealing to a wide audience it had to be entertaining. I saw potential in using creative writers to attack traditional prejudices by employing humour and satire. For example, a short story writer, John Morrow, created a fictional local council whose characters and meetings tapped into raw, sometimes sectarian issues. We called the town where the fictional council met Ballyturdeen. We also provided entertainment by scouring the world for bizarre stories and conspiracies. A listener famously remarked that some of those stories, including a few from a nutty correspondent in India, proved Northern Ireland wasn't the only crazy place in the world. The style and offbeat content helped to attract a large audience, though I think the political interviews drew the most attention, especially from the local newspapers. The programme was not long under way when it was attacked from within by current affairs editors. They accused me of 'dabbling' in news and current affairs. British ministers at Stormont and local political figures felt we should not be allowing people to express opinions we all knew were reflective of tribalism.

From the outset, I surrounded the presenter, Barry Cowan, with an exciting staff of researchers. They included Leslie Anne Van Slyke, a former Canadian print journalist; Elizabeth Kelly, a trainee journalist; David Malone, a former newsreader and trainee BBC reporters, Stephen Sackur and Karen Munger. Sackur later became a successful international reporter and Munger, an equally accomplished BBC national radio current affairs producer. I chose David Ross, who had been a news reporter with the Irish broadcast network, Raidió Éireann, as my deputy. Another producer was Jennifer Brown, who subsequently swapped broadcasting for a lectureship in Leeds University.

I didn't restrict my range of commentators to local figures. Instead, I tapped into the expertise of creative writers and journalists throughout Ireland, selecting some of the best and most controversial like Eamonn McCann and Nell McCafferty, one of the few women in Ireland who could claim she was 250th in line to the throne of England. Nell lived in Dublin and Eamonn in his native Derry, where he had remained throughout the city's upheaval. I also commissioned weekly talks from writers like Sam McAughtry, Malachi O'Doherty and John Bach, a renowned criminologist.

Talkback had all the ingredients of a daily newspaper. Its charm was that it was thoughtful and provocatively entertaining. It challenged traditional concepts of daily broadcasting. Instead of meekly standing off the major issues by reflexively reporting them, it analysed or parodied them. The paramilitaries, too, were afforded an opportunity to articulate their political views, but were always challenged.

As *Talkback* gained popularity and notoriety, on any given day there was not a politician or government minister unwilling to appear on it. Listeners played a critical role by reacting live on-air to major issues and interviews – a feature some interviewees resented and feared. Some listeners used the freedom of the airwaves to make highly inflammatory comments, which reflected what was being discussed in homes throughout Ireland.

On the second anniversary of the Anglo-Irish Agreement, I took *Talkback* to Dublin to report on Irish government support for it and continued Unionist opposition to it. Other BBC news and current affairs programmes all but ignored the anniversary. That was censorship because it effectively closed off the Unionist voices in Northern Ireland who believed the Agreement was a betrayal by Margaret Thatcher.

Talkback remains the most successful radio programme ever produced in Northern Ireland. I celebrated its thirtieth birthday in 2016. When I left *Talkback*, I was replaced by my deputy, David Ross, and Barry Cowan resigned as its front man.

One event during my time with the programme stands out. When the programme went off-air, I had lunch with my production team. One day, I told my staff I would not be joining them right away at the Arcana Indian restaurant. I could not reveal that, as part of ongoing research for my book *The Dirty War*, I had a rendezvous with Brendan Hughes, a senior IRA counter-intelligence chief. He was a legend in the IRA for having unmasked many British agents in its ranks. He was small in stature and known by the nicknames 'Darkie' or 'The Dark'.

His moniker came from his sallow complexion, which gave him a year-round tanned face.

He had promised to ask the IRA's Army Council to allow me access to notes IRA interrogators made when questioning a British Intelligence agent. I also hoped he would give me a copy of the most up-to-date version of the IRA's internal rules known as *The Green Book*. On my way to see him, I feared I was placing myself in legal jeopardy. A lawyer I had consulted told me the IRA documents I had requested were 'terrorist materials'. Should I be stopped at a military roadblock, and they were found on my person, at the very least I would be put under legal pressure to divulge the identity of the person who gave them to me. At worst, I would be charged with possessing terrorist paraphernalia. I considered the risk worth taking.

Arriving at the rendezvous, two young men took me to see Hughes. I liked him, but he had made it clear to me on more than one occasion if I crossed him he would kill me. On this day, I was in his company only a few minutes when my pager buzzed. Hughes looked at me suspiciously while the young henchmen grabbed me by the shoulders and removed the pager from my pocket. Hughes looked at it and pointed to the message.

'Is this a fucking code of some kind?'

He shoved the pager in front of my eyes, and I had to refrain from laughing because the message on it read, 'Your chicken wings are cold in the Arcana.' The message, I learned later, was from *Talkback* researcher, David Malone. He had ordered lunch for me, and members of the team had goaded him into sending me the message.

I had a helluva time explaining to Hughes the meaning of the message. He only relaxed after I suggested he should phone the restaurant and ask to speak to David Malone or Barry Cowan. Ten minutes later, Hughes sent me on my way with a copy of the IRA's *Green Book* but not the interrogation notes. As he explained privately, months later, a member of the IRA's Army Council, whom I had met with Hughes in the presence of Gerry Adams, had blocked my access to them, in particular to notes on the interrogation and murder of Joe

Fenton, a father of four from West Belfast. Fenton had been a successful agent for British Intelligence. He was seized by IRA Internal Security personnel and taken to a house in West Belfast for interrogation. After he admitted his guilt, he was shot four times in the head. One of his interrogators was Freddie Scappaticci. I will deal with him in more detail in a later section.

British Intelligence could have saved Fenton. They undoubtedly knew from Scappaticci's reports to his Intelligence handlers that Fenton was in danger. The British also had bugs in the safe house where Fenton was being held, providing them with a live feed of the painful final hours of his life. By permitting him to be interrogated, they hoped to learn a great deal about their adversaries' tactics. The questions put to Fenton would have revealed how much the IRA understood about the penetration of its own ranks and how they unmasked Fenton. MI5 knew that any attempt to free Fenton would have led to suspicion falling on Scappaticci, or on another British agent in the IRA's Belfast Brigade.

When I first spoke to Brendan Hughes about Fenton's murder, he speculated that MI5 had let Fenton die to protect a more important agent it had in the IRA in Belfast. By then, Hughes also knew the house in which Fenton had been held had been bugged. He told me the bugs had been removed. Hughes did not suspect Scappaticci, but he was right about the existence of another agent, who was an officer in the IRA's Belfast Brigade. Like Fenton, he, too, was unmasked by IRA Internal Security personnel. However, MI5 launched a mission that freed him before the IRA could execute him. Scappaticci just happened to be at home when the rescue happened. I was told by Brendan Hughes that, unlike the Fenton episode, the second agent had 'privileges'. Once he admitted his guilt, only a member of the IRA's Army Council had the authority to 'put on the black cap'. This is how Hughes explained it:

Only an Army Council member has authority to pass a death sentence on an officer of the Irish Republican Army. In this case, while the interrogation was taking place, notes were written up and sent to a member of the Council who lived in the Falls. The member of the Council was the one you met with me and Adams. He was so angry when he read the interrogation notes he wanted the satisfaction of passing a death sentence in person. He was on his way into the rear of the safe house to do just that when the Brits arrived. He ran into another house.

At the time Hughes spoke to me, he was unaware of Scappaticci's treachery. Over time, Hughes began to believe the IRA cause was being squandered by the political leadership of Gerry Adams and Martin McGuinness. He complained to me on more than one occasion that he feared IRA leaders would eventually 'settle for half a loaf' in their negotiations with the British. Towards the end of his life, he was diagnosed with the cancer that killed him in February 2008. In his final years, he cut a lonely figure, living in seclusion in Divis Flats in the Lower Falls. He drank heavily and was often indiscrete when expressing his dissatisfaction with Provisional Sinn Féin's leaders. A friend who visited him said he complained of nightmares and had difficulty sleeping. I suspected he had a lot of demons. He was a man who had overseen brutal interrogations and sent others to their deaths.

I recall a dinner in New York in 2006 with his niece, the Hollywood actress, Geraldine Hughes, who shared with me her concerns about his health. She had always admired him and was troubled by his loneliness and introspection. After his death, she wrote to me that 'another angel has gone to Heaven'. While he was no angel, he was non-sectarian. He stood up to some of the veteran IRA leaders of the early to mid-1970s when they promoted the tit-for-tat murders of innocent Protestants.

When I subsequently described the Arcana escapade to friends they were amused. Nevertheless, it was a bizarre one that could have cost me my life had I met someone other than Hughes. One man I would not have wanted to meet when he was a functioning terrorist was the natural born killer Michael Stone, the main character in my book *Stone Cold*.

Like other natural born sociopaths I met and wrote about, in particular Lenny Murphy, John Mc Keague, Dominic McGlinchey, 'Mad Dog' Adair, John Bingham, 'The Maniac' Kenny Mc Clinton, Freddie Scappaticci, William McGrath and Billy Wright, Stone was socially dysfunctional. These men could be welcoming and polite, yet they could also express menace in the blink of an eye. The atmosphere was chilly when most of them described their crimes to me. Wright once told me he walked with God but also a lot with the Devil. Thankfully, he did not appear to be with the Devil during my rendezvous with him.

Michael Stone's parents split up when he was young, leaving him in the care of his paternal grandparents. He never saw his mother again, but he created a fictional image of her as a beautiful woman who 'ran off to the big city to seek the bright lights'. It was easier to believe she left him to seek fame – the kind of fame he would later crave. In reality, she wanted a new life in Birmingham. His father left, too, but wrote him letters, which his grandparents kept from him until he was in his teens.

He subsequently met his father, but they were unable to form a bond. He never attempted to track down his mother. Perhaps he knew that meeting her would force him to face the terrible reality that she had indeed abandoned him. He preferred the fiction, which he still cherished four decades later when talking to me. Like Lenny Murphy, Michael Stone lived with a misconception among his Protestants friends and neighbours that he was 'one of the other sort': a Catholic. When I began researching his life, many of his contemporaries mistakenly told me he was Catholic. The confusion about his religious allegiance may have stemmed from the fact a Protestant Stone family with Catholic roots lived in the west of the city.

One of Stone's responses to the misrepresentation of him being Catholic was to date Catholic girls and then boast about how he lured them into sex. He bragged to me that he had a child with a Catholic girl but never provided me with proof. Like Lennie Murphy, he nurtured a flamboyant, man-about-town image, wearing Boss suits to discos. To finance his expensive lifestyle, he became a petty thief. His early influences included two prominent homosexuals, one a theatre impresario, James Young, and John McKeague, a vicious killer with a penchant for torture.

McKeague was Stone's first paramilitary mentor and must have pegged Stone as a young narcissist who could be easily manipulated. UDA leader, Tommy Herron, also took Stone into his tutelage. Herron was rumoured to have Catholic roots as well. But in his case it was true since his mother was Catholic. It is possible Herron believed the stories of Stone having Catholic links and suspected the young man was merely trying to conceal his tribal heritage. At some time during his relationships with McKeague and Herron, Stone began harbouring an all-consuming desire to become a killer extraordinaire: a special kind of killer who would make his mark on the conflict and be lionised by Loyalists.

From the very moment I met Stone, I decided he was a dangerous, manipulative and unpredictable individual. His psychiatrist certified him sane, but I believe she lacked the abundance of detail I unearthed about his personal history. Stone revelled in the minutiae of his murders and killing techniques and basked in the idol status he achieved in Loyalist circles after his violent foray into Milltown Cemetery in March 1988. On that day, scenes of him shooting and throwing grenades at IRA mourners were televised across the globe. Far from being a lone-wolf killer, an image he liked to foster, others used him for their own gain, including British Intelligence. Nevertheless, the portrayal of him as a public avenger, like the character played by Charles Bronson in the *Death Wish* movies, appealed to his grandiosity and made him an instant celebrity. In prison, he cut off locks of his hair and posted them to female admirers. He did daily workouts to build a powerful physique and boasted to me he could snap the neck of any Republican prisoner who crossed his path. I took this for nothing more than bravado. He knew the killing of a Republican would lead to an open war behind bars. In prison, there was an unwritten agreement terrorists would not target each other. The murder of Billy Wright, however, broke that rule.

In 2000, under the terms of the Good Friday Peace Agreement, Michael Stone was released back into society. Before long, he began marketing himself as an artist. Though garish and amateurish, his oil paintings were snapped up by collectors because of his notoriety. He quickly became a celebrity and featured in Belfast newspaper and magazine articles, as well as in gossip columns. Some journalists ignored the fact he was a narcissistic killer desperate for the limelight. His efforts to reinvent himself as a talented artist and reformed killer testified to his chameleon-like personality. I knew the adulation he was receiving would not satiate his craving for greater fame. I predicted to friends he would return to killing because he needed to be in the headlines and not a footnote in a gossip column. I worried I might run into him in Belfast. I had been reliably informed that he told his associates he wanted revenge for what I had written about him in *Stone Cold*. Besides, he was aware I possessed disturbing information about him, which I did not include in the book in order to protect innocent people close to him.

During the first half of 2006, I received a phone call from a BBC Northern Ireland television producer. She had just recorded interviews with Michael Stone as part of a 'reconciliation' series in which killers met the families of their victims. She claimed Stone was now denying some of the killings to which he had previously admitted. His denials had upset the families, and she wondered if I would fly to Belfast for a face-to-face interview with him. She suggested it would be an opportunity for me to defend what I had written about him. I told her I stood by my writings about Stone and felt no obligation to publicly defend them. I had no desire to meet him, but I was prepared to talk to the families of his victims if it would help them come to terms with the true character of his crimes. I cautioned her she was in danger of according Stone the status of an honest witness to his own crimes. He desperately wanted to re-write the past in order to whitewash his history, and I was not going to enable him. She should not try to play that role either, I told her. Her naïveté concerned me a bit. Nevertheless, I restated my willingness to speak to the families. I then gave the producer an off-the-record warning: I believed Stone was a ticking time bomb with severe mental problems, and the courts had made a serious miscalculation by not confining him to an institution like Broadmoor, where he would have been given the mental health care he needed.

I never heard back from the producer, but on 24 November, I got an interview request from Al Jazeera. Stone was back in the news, this time for trying to enter the Stormont Parliament buildings armed with an axe, nail bombs, two knives, a garrotte and a fake pistol. His intention, he said, was to assassinate Sinn Féin leaders Gerry Adams and Martin McGuinness. When courts subsequently tried and found him guilty of attempted murder, Stone claimed his actions were really 'performance art' not intended to cause harm. Stone's sentence of over 600 years, which he received in 1988, was reinstated. I never heard again from the BBC Northern Ireland producer.

SEVENTEEN

The Joker Club

While *Talkback* was undoubtedly a controversial programme, my final project for BBC Northern Ireland created a much bigger public stir. It was a television programme called *The Show*, which attracted the wrath of the Churches, the mainstream political parties, the security forces, the Northern Ireland Tourist Authority and British civil servants at Stormont. I tend to believe political pressure led to the BBC hierarchy in London killing off the programme, but not before it made its mark on broadcasting. *The Show* was the only BBC light entertainment programme in the United Kingdom taken off-air for several weeks during the start of the first Gulf War. One has to ask, even now, how one could reasonably have concluded that a local programme remotely posed a threat to national security or the war effort. It posed no threat whatsoever.

It first took shape after the Head of Television, Ian Kennedy, and Controller, Dr Colin Morris, persuaded me to move to television to create a weekly programme of my choice. They knew I would bring some of *Talkback*'s irreverence to the project, but I guess they, like me, never anticipated the opposition it would face. Ian Kennedy was the most highly talented manager I ever worked with. He promoted innovative programming and was respected by his staff. Dr Colin Manley Morris was the most sophisticated Controller boss I had during my BBC career. He exuded finesse and possessed a fine intellect. As a young man, he was a Methodist minister, working for years in the African missions. Before he replaced James Hawthorne as Controller, he served as the BBC's Head of Religious Broadcasting, based in London. In his first conversation with me, he expressed astonishment that a programme like *Talkback* existed, given the BBC's preoccupation with balance and the fact Northern Ireland was a war zone. From that moment, he gave me his backing. He was the antithesis of his predecessor.

Dr Colin Morris and Ian Kennedy were confident I could create a television version of *Talkback*, although they never said so. It took me the best part of a year, with Colin Lewis as my deputy, to put together *The Show* concept, focusing on the use of creative writing and an innovative approach to television. When Norman Jenkinson, a *Belfast Telegraph* features writer, reviewed the first episode, he compared the experience to 'looking through the gates of Hell'. The front page of that edition of the paper carried the headline: 'The Show Must Go'. Lower on the page was an announcement that the Berlin Wall had fallen, followed by a report of a sectarian murder. Within twelve hours of the first broadcast, every church leader and major political party in Northern Ireland had issued press releases condemning the programme. Unionist leaders declared they would go to the Westminster Parliament to table a motion demanding the BBC apologise and pull the programme from its schedules.

So how did a live television programme generate such heat from all sides of the political and religious divides? The answer lay partly in that a society in conflict was not ready for satire, and the forces of religious and political conservatism were alive and thriving in both communities. The piece that fired up the Churches was a song, 'Baby, should I have the baby or not', sung by a young American singer. The lyrics defended a woman's right to choose, a topic that sent conservative Catholic and Protestant church leaders into a frenzy. Fundamentalist Protestants were especially angered by a sketch of a fundamentalist preacher, played by Dublin actor, Tom McLoughlin. In one sketch, he delivered a dreamlike sermon, interspersed with bizarre Biblical references and pseudo-sexual overtones from a pulpit designed for the set. A wooden, half-nude mermaid, reminiscent of figureheads on pirate ships of old, adorned the front of his lectern.

The set had been built around what we called 'The Joker Club'. It was designed like a very large nightclub to include seating, a bar, a stage, special lighting and garish oil paintings of large nudes. Actors portrayed patrons such as an American reporter, a former Vietnam veteran high on drugs, an elderly couple having an affair, members of paramilitary organisations, dancing police officers, British Intelligence figures and British diplomats. The audience had access to a functioning bar, and drinks were also served at tables, adding to an overall sense of a regular club. Before the first edition kicked off, it was suggested lights be removed from the cameras so members of the audience would not act self-consciously when featured in exchanges between characters. That proved unnecessary since the audience instinctively played along with the deception. In reality, we were operating a real club because Colin Lewis and I signed a Belfast City Council permit to allow us to have a working bar on the set. Of course, we hired a company to run the bar and provide waitresses. Before long, many young people in Belfast believed The Joker Club was a private venue and phoned the BBC to get its location and tickets. The availability of alcohol on the set did not create problems, and before long some members of the audience wandered in and out of live camera shots with the kind of performance skills I admired. Some people were hired to dress extravagantly so they could weave from time to time into live shots. One such individual was my friend, the lecturer and criminologist, John Bach, who claims a connection to the famous family of that name.

When I began creating *The Show*, I set out to find the right team. I chose Colin Lewis as my deputy. At the time, he was working in television in London, but I persuaded him to return to Belfast. He eventually became my director. His assistant producer was Philip Mc Govern, who like many of the staff went on to run their own production companies. Philip's was called Big Mountain Productions. I encouraged David Malone to leave *Talkback* and join me as a researcher, and soon he was also producing as well. Eina McHugh, who worked for me as a researcher, was subsequently appointed to a senior role in the administration of the Irish film industry. David Malone was especially important in booking local and internationally famous music acts to perform live and in tape scripting/editing. To assist him I hired Crispin

Avon, a fixer and researcher I met on the *Terry Wogan Television Show* in London. I soon had a very creative grouping that included Hamish Hamilton. He went on to be a top music director, working with U2, Madonna and Robbie Williams.

I then focused on finding writers, who could produce exciting satirical pieces. Colin Lewis and David Malone came up with Tim McGarry, Damon Quinn, Martin Reid, Nuala McKeever and Michael McDowell who became famous as *The Hole in the Wall Gang*. They later changed their name to *Give My Head Peace*. Malachi O'Doherty, who had been a regular *Talkback* contributor, joined the writing programme team, as did my friend, Martin Lynch, one of Ireland's finest playwrights.

After the first programme, a hurricane of political and religious protests engulfed the show and encouraged predictions it was dead in the water. Rhonda Paisley, daughter of the Rev. Ian Paisley, whom I had recruited as an interviewer, resigned within hours of the first broadcast ending. I felt sorry for her, realising how hard it must have been for her to face the wrath of her father. Political figures in Northern Ireland inundated BBC executives with complaints and calls for my head. But my bosses, Ian Kennedy and Colin Morris, held firm to the principle that the show had potential and we would weather the storm of criticism. When religious leaders, Catholic and Protestant, declared the programme was blasphemous, we had our own in-house theologian to respond. Dr Morris publicly dismissed the blasphemy charge, and few of our critics were prepared to challenge him. Still, he made one concession to them. The pulpit with the female nude on it would be struck from the set, and there would be no more appearances by the fundamentalist preacher character. I agreed, as did Colin Lewis, but our director, Dubliner Gerry Stembridge, resigned. I was not sorry to see him go. The show was more important than an individual, and I replaced him with Martin Shardlow, a veteran London director I had met on *The Wogan Show*. Before long, Colin Lewis took over direction and brought greater stability to the project. The pulpit returned to the set after several broadcasts but without the nude on it. She adorns one of the walls in my apartment nowadays, reminding me of a turbulent past.

The Hole in the Wall writing team, as well as our other writers, produced excellent satirical material. They were assisted by a range of superb Irish acting talent. When I learned the British government was secretly talking to the IRA, I commissioned a satirical piece portraying a member of the IRA's Army Council and a British diplomat drinking and discussing terms for a ceasefire at a secluded table in The Joker Club. We also broadcast a Vaudeville routine with actors dressed as English cops singing about how they brutalised the Birmingham Six: Irishmen wrongly accused in 1975 of bombings in Birmingham. They were treated harshly and jailed until 1991 when the Court of Appeal ruled their convictions had been 'unsafe'. They each received financial compensation from the British government.

During the series' second year, an audience of young people packed The Joker Club every week. My friend, Van Morrison, performed twice and after one show treated the audience to a twenty-minute rendition of his hit 'Gloria'. During one of Van's visits, we received a bomb threat intended to force BBC executives to take the programme off-air, but Van courageously announced he would not leave the club and played live.

At the end of Season 2 of *The Show*, an impeccable political source informed me that 'people with clout' had told the BBC's hierarchy the programme was 'subversive'. Its main critics were British government advisers at Stormont Castle, as well as security figures. By then, complaints from local politicians, the RUC and Churches had dwindled, but rumblings of discontent rose from security circles, especially after we satirised ongoing collusion between elements of the RUC and Loyalist paramilitaries.

The only threats we received were aimed at me and were related to matters I had dealt with in my book, *The Dirty War*. I was threatened by several young men on *The Show* set one evening. They were not armed, but I was troubled they had sought me out and had known my whereabouts. BBC security personnel escorted them off the set, and they were not seen again. I chose not to make an official police report, fearing if they were arrested they might seek me out in different circumstances with the aim of killing me. Judging by their words, they were affiliated to the Provisional IRA. I mentioned the matter to a source who advised me to be vigilant. From past experience, I knew the threat against me was real. I had revealed damaging information about paramilitaries on both sides, making more than my fair share of enemies as a consequence. When driving in and out of Belfast, and through other parts of Northern Ireland, it was difficult to avoid areas where those enemies lived. An example was the Markets, a mere three-minute stroll from my office. I had written that Brendan 'Ruby' Davidson, an IRA commander and hero in the Markets, had been a double agent for British Intelligence. I unmasked him after he had been murdered by a Loyalist hit squad and honoured by the IRA as a hero. Ruby's funeral had all the trappings given to a senior terrorist, and to ensure his legacy he was buried in the IRA's special plot in Belfast's Milltown Cemetery. It is easy to understand why so much anger flowed in my direction after his demise, since a wall mural commemorated him as an IRA martyr.

His reputation was jealously guarded in the years after his death by supporters and later by his nephew, Gerard 'Jock' Davidson, who also became the IRA's commander in the Markets. He spread a tissue of lies throughout Belfast to discredit my revelations about his uncle Ruby. Jock, like many of Ruby's admirers, denied Ruby had a secret sex life. Jock suffered his uncle's fate when he was shot dead in the Markets in 2015. Suspicion immediately fell on Loyalists, but IRA sources claimed he had been murdered by someone from his own community with a personal grudge against him. I have since discovered his life was much more complex than what I imagined when I first wrote about him.

EIGHTEEN

Agent Ascot: Paedophile, Terrorist and British Spy

Over decades, the Markets area cultivated a reputation for being bohemian. Charlie Chaplin resided there for short time in the 1920s when he was performing in a visiting circus. It was particularly celebrated for its indoor market. When I was child, my mother shopped there for fish and vegetables every Friday morning. While there, she rubbed elbows with all sorts of characters, including those with backgrounds in hare coursing and horse racing. Others made money from selling scrap metals and used clothes, deploying carts pulled by donkeys to transport their merchandise throughout the city. My friend, Peter 'A', who was a police constable in the Markets, remembered it was 'a wonderful neighbourhood of friendly people until the young became radicalised by the IRA'. When searching a house in the early days of his Markets' beat, Peter spotted a photograph of Sir Roger Bannister, the Englishman who ran the first sub-four-minute mile. He asked the elderly lady of the house how she acquired the photo. 'Sure he's my cousin,' she replied. For Peter, it was a classic example of a fascinating place, but in the shadows men with a history of honouring the gun in Irish politics were busy influencing a new generation. Radicalisation dominated life throughout Catholic districts with the emergence of the Provisionals in January 1970.

The Markets, traditionally an Official IRA stronghold, was gradually taken over by the Provisionals. Peter told me he never felt ill at ease patrolling the area even though he was Protestant. He developed important relationships with locals and, as a consequence, he built up his own small network of informants. The majority of them were grandmothers angered by the way the Provisionals sucked young people into their violent world. He recalls a bizarre episode when a local priest discovered a cache of weapons in St Matthew's Catholic Church behind the pipe organ. The priest knew nothing about the weapons, which had probably been there prior to the Troubles. According to Peter, the church was saved embarrassment when newspapers reported that the arms had been stored in a house, not in the church. How the truth was concealed from the media remains a mystery.

Yet, for all Peter's confidence in the relationships he developed with locals, he risked being ambushed or kidnapped at any moment. He credited his survival to Brendan 'Ruby' Davidson, convinced Ruby kept him off the local IRA's target list. It is unclear when Ruby began betraying the IRA. A trusted source told me a policeman who hailed from Joy Street in the Markets recruited him. If that is true, one has to ask how Ruby became an asset for British Intelligence, in particular for a group known as the DET – the 14th Intelligence Company. It acquired the abbreviation DET because it had three detachments operating in Northern Ireland. The one that took control of Ruby was based in police headquarters in Ladas Drive, Belfast. I believe that DET worked closely with MI5 and Special Branch, which had operational assets in the same facility. DET had considerable financial resources. It bought information with hard cash and recruited spies from terror groups in both communities. While investigating the recruitment of informants and terrorist agents by police Special Branch and British Intelligence outfits such as DET, I discovered the most persuasive tools were money and blackmail. In working-class areas with high unemployment, money was the perfect inducement to extract information from ordinary people. Even so, IRA operatives rarely changed sides for money or for ideological reasons. When detained, they were often treated to rough interrogations, blackmail, or the promise of having charges reduced or dropped in exchange for spilling secrets.

In Ruby's case, blackmail was the main factor in his recruitment. A police Special Branch file on him noted he was a secret homosexual who visited public toilets and had sex with men in a massage centre. By leading such a life, Ruby flirted with danger in a society that had criminalised homosexuality. Had either his sexual preferences for young men or some of his bizarre sexual behaviour been exposed, he would have been equally at risk for retaliation from the religiously conservative Provisional IRA. I am convinced his sexual choices made him vulnerable to recruitment by British Intelligence. At some point, probably at the start of the Troubles, his first recruiter lost control of him to more senior RUC figures, but they later handed him over to Special Branch, which subsequently shared him with British Intelligence. Eventually, he became the exclusive property of MI5.

The process developed incrementally, but when informants were deemed vital to strategic security plans, MI5, the prime mover in all major intelligence operations, took charge of them. It had the oversight to regulate how intelligence from agents like Ruby should be coordinated and exploited. MI5 possessed a secret legal authority, allowing it to withdraw police and army from civilian areas. It used the authority to aid assassination squads, comprised of Loyalist terrorists or secret military units, when they were targeting known Republicans for death. Clearing areas of police and army ensured that assassins were not arrested while carrying out their hits. In the early 1970s, a British military undercover unit, the MRF – Military Reconnaissance Unit – assassinated people, many with little or no connection to paramilitaries. Many MRF assassinations were carried out under the cover of a sectarian war that claimed a large number of innocent lives. Most of their murders were wrongly attributed to sectarian gangs. The MRF's assassination strategy provided a policy template that continued throughout the Troubles. Often, agents like Ruby facilitated state-sponsored assassinations by identifying potential targets, and by providing intelligence on those targets for their British Intelligence handlers. I believe the MRF was responsible for over twenty extrajudicial killings. The figure may be even higher.

Peter 'A', my constable friend, told me money hadn't motivated Ruby's betrayal of the IRA, even though £12,000 in cash was found in his home, along with a loaded gun, on the day he was shot dead. According to witnesses, 'funny guys in suits' seized the items. Ruby had assured Peter that he had never been 'financially driven' to become an agent, and that everything he had earned as a terrorist agent had gone to a 'worthy charitable cause'. Peter first encountered Ruby when he searched his family home and flat. To Peter's surprise, Ruby was not a typical thug.

'He was kind and gentle. He was not the killer he was often portrayed as. He was an intelligent and thoughtful man who read deeply. I searched his flat and parents' house many times and was always struck by his quality of reading from Orwell to Solzhenitsyn and Shakespeare.'

Ruby may have begun feeding information to the police in his teens. He was notably respectful to uniformed police in the area, a trait not often seen in his contemporaries. There are residents of the Markets who never shared Peter's admiration for him. On the contrary, many people feared him. He was muscular, six feet two inches tall, and he had acquired a reputation for being able to 'handle himself' in a fight. Locals said he took offence easily and became difficult to control when drunk. He was typical of many of the young men who filed into the ranks of the Provisional IRA after January 1970. He had the physical stature to impose his will on others and possessed a native cunning. His artfulness served him in his double life as he rose rapidly in the IRA, displaying talents for planning terror and finding new recruits. One night, outside the Trocadero, a bar on the edge of the Markets, he found himself in a violent brawl when Peter and a fellow constable arrived on the scene. They cuffed him after he refused to comply with their request to stop fighting and took him to Musgrave Street Police Station to book him for disorderly conduct. In the station, Ruby gave Peter a number to call.

'Tell the person at the end of the line you have Ascot in custody,' he told Peter.

Peter made the call. Thirty minutes later, a senior police superintendent, accompanied by an MI5 officer, arrived at the station. They released Ruby without charge. Superiors formally instructed Peter to never discuss the matter. Ironically, the episode deepened Peter's respect for Ruby, now aka Agent Ascot. Peter and some of his colleagues, realising Ruby was an important intelligence asset, personally devoted some of their spare time to watching over him. It was an unusual, if not risky, endeavour. Ruby was happy to know Peter had his back. The two began spending more time together, discussing politics and history. During one conversation, Ruby told Peter that he decided to betray the IRA because he was appalled by the IRA's brutal murder of two young British soldiers lured to their deaths in a honeytrap operation in Belfast. He shared with Peter that he had expected the IRA to abduct and interrogate the soldiers, but not to kill them.

In my view, Ruby may have been genuinely horrified by the double murder, but it is inconceivable he would have expected the IRA to kidnap two soldiers and later release them. His justification of betrayal did not make sense. It may have been a ploy to endear himself to Peter, or to evade questions about the complex process that had led to him becoming Agent Ascot.

In the early 1970s, with the Provisional IRA at the height of its power, Special Branch and British Intelligence had an urgent need to recruit spies within the IRA. The fact that Ruby had a history as a common police 'tout' and that he was suddenly rising through IRA ranks must have brought him to the attention of Special Branch. That is how he would have begun transitioning from a run-of-the-mill police informer to one of the most significant terrorist agents in Belfast. Besides, Special Branch shared him with DET and MI5. It was not an uncommon practice, but one often resented by uniformed police and RUC detectives.

When writing *The Dirty War*, I came across an instance of the procedure after it led to the cynical execution of several members of a criminal gang by members of a specialist military intelligence unit. The execution resulted from the fact that an informant in the gang, who had been run by RUC detectives, was 'appropriated' by Special Branch, DET and MI5. When that happened, the gang became the focus of government and military agencies devoted solely to combating terrorists. As a consequence, the gang members were deliberately marked as terrorists and shot dead, execution style. I have always believed that they were executed because DET/MI5 wanted to send a message to the crime fraternity not to cross over into the Intelligence world. Their deaths had been preceded by a theft of weapons and intelligence files from the parked car of a DET agent. The thieves then passed the files to the IRA to endear themselves to an organisation that often kneecapped criminals. One of my major security sources concurred with me that the killing of the gang was an example of extrajudicial murder.

Ruby had been a police informant too, like those in that ill-fated gang, but his meteoric rise through the ranks of the IRA marked him as a precious asset for those leading the counterterrorism war. By some accounts, he began feeling invincible when he became the IRA's commander in the Markets. He treated the area like his personal fiefdom, knowing the IRA and British Intelligence protected him. He confidently pursued his secret sex life, unaware Special Branch had video of him having sex with young men in a sports centre. I contend Special Branch wanted to be able to blackmail him should he ever stray from his agent role. I doubt Special Branch knew how he was treating young criminals, some of them boys, arrested by the IRA in the Markets. They were brought to his flat where he made them drop their trousers and underpants. Then he told them to bend over while he spanked them with a wire brush. He may have abused some of them in other ways. He would not have been the only abuser in IRA ranks. In 2006, a man originally from West Belfast told me he was one of several boys in the Beechmount district of West Belfast who were forced to give a young man oral sex. The abuse began in the late 1950s, and the abuser subsequently became a leading Provisional. Haunted by the experience, the victim said it was more than likely his abuser exploited his terrorist role to select new victims in subsequent decades.

Ruby's pursuit of young men was an aspect of his life Peter 'A' knew nothing about. He believed Ruby was a hero, risking his own life to save others.

'Had he been a British soldier he would have been awarded the Military Cross. In my eyes, he was a modern-day Michael Collins, the Irish revolutionary hero, who was assassinated by the IRA after he made a deal with the British. Ruby saved many lives and probably took a few. On that we challenged each other daily, but we shared a mutual respect. I have no doubt he saved many civilian, police and army lives. He could talk politics and history as much as I could. He loved Carson as a leader. He hated de Valera as a traitor. If Ruby had been in the British Army he would have been a Field Marshall. He was a decent man,' Peter said to me.

Peter's admiration confirmed his deep respect for Ruby. As for Ruby's professed love for Sir Edward Carson, founder of the Ulster State and the man who prosecuted Oscar Wilde for sodomy, this was somewhat bizarre, if not ironic. The admiration for Edward Carson may have been Ruby's way of trying to please Peter, who, as a Protestant would have been expected by a Catholic like Ruby to have considered Carson an exemplary historical figure.

Ruby was a complex figure. Aside from his commander role in the Markets, he was prominent in the Provisionals' Internal Security apparatus. He was privy to the outcomes of the interrogations of IRA members suspected of betrayal or of ordinary people believed to have passed information to soldiers patrolling neighbourhoods. In this position, he had access to what the IRA knew about British Intelligence at any given time. For example, if a terrorist agent was captured, Ruby learned what the agent, under torture, had divulged about his British Intelligence links and the identities and tactics of his Intelligence handlers. Ruby's IRA rank also enabled him to acquire considerable intelligence on the IRA's most senior figures. He might have known the identities of senior Belfast Brigade staff. He had a seat on the IRA's General Headquarters Staff in Belfast, a role that brought him into contact with operational planners across the city.

I have often been asked about Ruby's double life as a terrorist agent. When researching for *The Dirty War*, I met a source connected to the intelligence community who passed me documents, one of which contained the startling revelation that the late Brendan 'Ruby' Davidson had been a highly placed British Intelligence agent. At the time, I didn't give the material much credence. Information of a dubious nature was often fed to journalists and authors. Such 'leaks' had the appearance of truth, but in reality were bogus. A British Intelligence department skilled in deception and disinformation regularly fed intriguing, but fictional, tales to the media because the war against the IRA was also a 'hearts and minds struggle'. The details about Ruby's betrayal seemed too good to be true. According to my IRA contacts, Ruby had been a genuine Republican hero murdered by Loyalists. Although the IRA excelled at feeding lies to the media, I had grown to trust my sources over time.

'Do you really think if Ruby Davidson had been a top Brit agent, the Brits would have let Loyalists assassinate him? C'mon we all know the Brits control the Loyalist hit squads,' one senior IRA figure said when I asked him if it was possible Ruby had been an informer.

Still, I needed to test the Ruby material against the knowledge of one of my best security sources – a man I respected and called my friend. He worked closely with the Intelligence community, but he was not part of the 'wide-boys' network of Intel units in the business of assassination and disinformation. Like Peter 'A', he respected the rule of law. I turned to him after I became increasingly convinced the Ruby material might well be genuine because all the other revelations in the documents I had been given had proved true when I had checked them with a wide range of reputable sources.

'Why should the Ruby story be a deception?' I asked myself.

'Where the hell did you come across this stuff?' my friend said when I showed him the documents.

'I can't reveal the source,' I replied. 'I just need to know if I was being conned.'

'It doesn't look like you're being conned,' he responded. 'But I'm puzzled why someone would provide you with such a wide range of highly classified information.'

He was not only alluding to the Ruby revelation. There were other equally eye-opening items in the documents, but they were not related to my book research. Therefore, they were of no use to me, and I was not the kind of person to pass them to other journalists or publish them in newspapers just to get attention. I stressed to my friend the only story in the documents which mattered to me was the one about Ruby. The rest I would shred.

'You might be better to forget you ever had any of this material, especially the Ruby references,' he retorted. 'It could get you killed if you publish it. The IRA will not take kindly to you ruining the reputation of one of its dead heroes. Remember, in their eyes, Ruby is a gold-plated hero. Think twice before you do anything with this stuff. You might want to ask yourself why this was passed to you. My guess is that those who ran Ruby want the revelation about him published, and they know you have credibility as an investigative writer. People will not be inclined to dismiss Ruby's betrayal as black propaganda if it comes from you. These people who have targeted you know you are writing a new book about their business. They are confident you will check all the material and discard the stuff that does not concern your investigations. They know you well, Dillon. They thought this out.'

'Why would it be beneficial for them to make it public?' I asked.

My friend smiled. 'It will set the cat among the pigeons, creating paranoia in the IRA's ranks. It will also damage the IRA's reputation among its rank and file, as well as its supporters. The IRA gave Ruby a classic Republican funeral in Milltown Cemetery, and you will be saying they were conned and buried a traitor with pomp and ceremony. That makes a mockery of the IRA leadership.'

I pointed out that the IRA's likely reaction would not deter me from ignoring such an important story. I planned to publish it.

'On your head be it!' my friend concluded.

One thing that struck me about the Ruby issue was how it reflected a classic example of the modus operandi of the intelligence world.

'You came to me to verify the information you were given was kosher,' my friend said. 'Those who made the information available to you hoped you would check it out with your best sources. To convince you to do that, they inserted juicy stuff into the documents even though it was not exactly what you were looking for. Nevertheless, they expected you to check out the juicy stuff, knowing once you learned it was accurate, you would be more inclined to zero in and pursue the Ruby material. Their game was designed to draw you closer to the story that really mattered to you, and to them. They were confident that once you confirmed from sources that 99 per cent of the material leaked to you was spot on, you would accept the veracity of the Ruby revelation. I can't confirm the Ruby story is true, but I believe it probably is because the documents are clearly from an impeccable source and only 1 per cent of the Ruby material is hard to verify. Would I publish? Not on my life, and not on yours either!'

He proved to be right about the risks I would likely face. After I published the Ruby revelation in *The Dirty War*, I acquired more dangerous enemies than I needed. But my friend did not see the whole picture, and neither did I at the time. There was another reason the 'men in suits' wanted me to expose Ruby as a British agent. It helped shift the spotlight away from 'Stakeknife', the code name for Freddie Scappaticci, one of the most prominent British agents inside the IRA. He and Ruby shared a survival instinct that would cost others their lives.

NINETEEN

Murderous Choices: Getting Rid of 'The Monkey'

Freddie Scappaticci also hailed from the Markets but lived in West Belfast. He enjoyed his reputation for ruthlessness. When I met him in the 1980s, his professed love for Italian ice cream and his Italian heritage amused me. I developed an instant fear of him. He had cold eyes and a hair-trigger personality. Running the IRA's Internal Security structure in Belfast meant he had a close working relationship with members of the Provisional IRA Army Council, and in particular a member of the Council living in the Lower Falls. Scap, as he was sometimes called, had a lot of contact with Ruby, but I doubt either of them knew of the other's secret affiliations to British Intelligence. Contrary to rumours in the Markets, Scap was not related to Ruby through marriage. There was, in fact, little real closeness between them, though they were often in each other's company. Scap maintained an address in the Markets area and was sometimes seen there with Ruby and other senior IRA figures.

A secret and constant concern for both was maintaining the cover of their double lives. They tried to make sure they did not fall under suspicion during investigations into blown IRA operations. Ruby was more vulnerable to being exposed as a traitor than Scappaticci because he was closer to the Belfast Brigade's active service units. This made him privy to bombing strategies, in particular the IRA's plans to obliterate all businesses in the city centre. Since the Markets served as the virtual centre of Belfast, bombing runs from West Belfast to the heart of the city's business sector were coordinated from the area. This required

Ruby's involvement. In some instances, bombers launched attacks from the Markets or found sanctuary there after their bombs exploded.

According to Peter, Ruby passed valuable information about planned bombings to MI5. I believe that not all the information would have been actionable. In order to maintain Ruby's cover, MI5 would have had to allow some bombings to take place. For example, if a small circle of IRA operatives, including Ruby, had access to the same information about a planned bombing it would have been deemed unwise to interdict the bombers without casting a shadow of suspicion on Ruby. Many times during the dirty war, information that could have protected innocent lives was purposely ignored to protect agents. The principle was explained to me as follows by an Intelligence officer: 'Sometimes you had to protect an agent by not using information. You had to choose the long-term perspective. It was a case of allowing a terror attack to go ahead, sacrificing maybe two or more innocent lives, in order to protect dozens of lives down the road.'

Ruby was ruthless when it came to insulating his agent role. We may never know how many people he ordered to be killed to divert attention from himself. I suspect Scappaticci killed many more in the same pursuit. The more successful Ruby became as an agent, the greater impact he had in helping the security forces interdict IRA shootings and bombings. According to Peter, Ruby persuaded the IRA's top brass to confine its bombings of the city centre to Sunday nights, thereby lessening the risk of civilian casualties. His success in providing information that led to the arrests of IRA operatives, generated paranoia in IRA ranks. The organisation's spy hunters concluded that there was a mole in their midst with access to insider info. They launched a determined effort to ferret out the traitor, and no one, including Ruby, escaped scrutiny.

Internal Security teams began peeling away the layers of involvement of IRA personnel linked to blown operations. Throughout this process, they determined who had access to critical intelligence, and who might have passed it to the British. Even if Ruby felt confident that he was too big a fish to draw scrutiny from the IRA, MI5 would not have wanted him in the IRA's crosshairs. Fortunately, MI5 had their man, Scappaticci, to keep them updated on the progress of the IRA's spy hunters.

Ruby would also have been assured by his handlers that if he were unmasked, they would ferry him to safety before the Internal Security's 'nutting squad' came for him. He was familiar with IRA interrogation methods and knew he would never be able to keep his secrets if tortured.

Ruby or Scappaticci and his handlers, designed a cynical, murderous strategy to ensure suspicion fell on someone else. One of them likely chose a patsy to be offered up as the mole. When I consulted Peter about this issue, he pointed an accusing finger at Scappaticci. That made sense because Scappaticci ran IRA mole hunting probes. It would have been easy for him to select a scapegoat.

I believe, however, the culprit in this twisted scheme was MI5, guided by Special Branch. MI5, known as 'The Box' to insiders, would have been anxious to protect its two major agents, and Scappaticci was ideally positioned to take the lead in finding a sacrificial lamb. Still, others have pointed the finger at Ruby as the prime mover, claiming he was anxious to silence a person spreading gossip about his sex life. That person became the scapegoat.

After I wrote *The Dirty War*, two of my sources fingered Ruby as the person who chose the patsy. Still, it is possible Scappaticci may have helped Ruby. Scappaticci, as head of IRA Internal Security, had the authority to approve the selection of anyone fingered by Ruby, especially if the individual was a fully-fledged member of the organisation. In this particular case, the scapegoat was a member of the IRA, so it is likely Ruby and Scappaticci discussed the matter.

The fall guy was Anthony 'The Monkey' McKiernan, a happily married man from West Belfast. He worked in a large bakery, mixing dough. He acquired his moniker because he had been an expert climber of backyard walls in his youth. He was a funny, talkative individual. Some said he had a loose tongue after drinking heavily in 'sheebeens' – illegal drinking clubs. When he joined the IRA, he adapted his bakery skills to mixing large quantities of fertiliser for making bombs and, by all accounts, he became an expert bomb maker, taking great pride in his work and boasting about the damage done by his explosives. Some Intel reports placed him in Libya for a short time. If so, he travelled to improve his bomb-making skills and to learn how to use Semtex, a plastic explosive the Gaddafi regime made available to the IRA in large quantities.

I never believed The Monkey was a British agent. While he was cunning, he was never flush with money. The selection of him as a patsy removed a skilled bomb maker from the battlefield. Perhaps MI5 encouraged Ruby or Scappaticci to get rid of McKiernan to lessen civilian body counts in the future, and to avoid any suspicion falling on Ruby for the capture of IRA bombing teams. While I have never been able to confirm it, I was told by a source that McKiernan suspected Ruby was a 'tout' and threatened to out Ruby as a paedophile. Had any of this reached Ruby's ears or MI5, it would have been enough for Ruby and his handlers to mark The Monkey for death.

IRA operatives seized The Monkey and detained him in a house in West Belfast. IRA interrogations were often tape-recorded and made available to a member of the IRA's Army Council in the Falls area of the city. It took only one member of the Council to pass a sentence of death, sometimes making the time between a death sentence and execution a matter of thirty minutes.

In The Monkey's case, operatives attempted to disguise the manner of his death. They held him over a bathtub and waterboarded him with alcohol until he admitted he was a mole. Once he confessed, his interrogators poured a very large quantity of alcohol down his throat, effectively ending his life. A source told me that Ruby attended the interrogation, and that he later played a taped confession to a select number of Provisionals. The Monkey was such a popular operative the IRA leadership did not wish to publicly brand him a traitor, believing some in its ranks would dispute the claim. The bottom line, however, was that the IRA, always conscious of its public image, did not wish to announce that it had killed a mole in its ranks, especially when it was the organisation's leading bomb maker in Belfast. Portraying his death as suicide, caused by over drinking, was the preferred storyline circulated throughout West Belfast.

Years after *The Dirty War* was published, a nervous young woman approached me on one of my trips back to Belfast. It turned out she was The Monkey's daughter. She was eager to talk to me about her father's murder. She made no effort to hide the fact her father had been a bomber but felt he did not have to die being tortured by his own people. She said she had learned the cause of death from an autopsy report. The IRA had, at the time of her father's death, tried to disguise it as suicide, she claimed. She wanted to know if Ruby had been her father's killer. I shared with her that there was evidence linking him to it.

The Monkey's forced confession shifted any lingering suspicion from Ruby being the person betraying IRA bombing operations. Some in the IRA heralded Ruby a hero for exposing a major mole on the organisation. This allowed Scappaticci to put the lid on the mole hunting operation. If Ruby was not present when The Monkey was murdered, I have little doubt Scappaticci was present during the interrogation. After all, his 'nutting squad' carried out the killing. Since the victim was a serving Provisional, the member of the IRA's Army Council, based in the Lower Falls, would have passed the death sentence. It is possible he did it in person.

Ultimately, Ruby's demise was not determined by the IRA, but seemingly by his prominence as a terror figure in the Markets. Because of this, Loyalist paramilitaries targeted him. In 1987, he survived an assassination attempt, but was not so lucky on 25 July 1988, when a gunman armed with an AK47 assault rifle shot him nine times at point blank range. Incidentally, the gunman and two associates wore police uniforms.

Different opinions circulated about who murdered Ruby. The IRA was convinced the UVF targeted him because he was a leading Irish Republican. They pointed to the fact that the weapons used to kill him were part of a consignment of CZ 58s, South African versions of the Russian AK 47 Kalashnikov assault rifle. It is notable that the

FRU, a British military undercover outfit that operated in Northern Ireland, trained South African Special Forces at Potchfestroom, in the North West Province of South Africa. The FRU also ran senior UDA and UVF figures responsible for tasking assassination teams that carried out many controversial killings of Republicans. Throughout the Troubles, there was a South African link to Loyalist paramilitaries. For example, Loyalist gunmen targeted an academic in Belfast who was a prominent critic of South Africa's apartheid regime. The quid pro quo for Loyalists agreeing to kill the academic was the promise of weapons. The Loyalists shot the wrong target.

Another scenario for Ruby's killing is that he was murdered by the UDA from East Belfast. Its leaders were familiar with his status as a well-known Republican. The Loyalist angle is, nevertheless, somewhat complicated. British Intelligence knew everything there was to know about UDA/UVF hit lists. For example, Brian Nelson, a British soldier employed by the FRU, MI5 and Special Branch, ran the UDA's assassination teams out of East Belfast. The FRU and Special Branch supplied Nelson and his hit squads with weapons and vital intelligence. Nelson died mysteriously from a brain haemorrhage in April 2003, aged 55. He was just weeks away from a scheduled appearance before a British government inquiry looking into his activities. His sudden death ensured that he took his secrets to the grave. So would the FRU leadership, or MI5, really have permitted the UDA or UVF to assassinate Ruby so that his secrets would also be buried? They might, had they considered him a liability.

When I asked Peter 'A' about Ruby's murder, he made several interesting observations. He recalled Ruby was very security conscious, rarely staying more than one night in any house or flat. On the morning of his death, he received a telephone call to his flat. The caller purported to be a representative of the Northern Ireland Housing Executive, wishing to confirm that Ruby would be at home to receive a visit from inspectors who would check the flat's heating system.

'How Loyalists would have known Ruby's exact whereabouts and how to find his flat is beyond me,' said Peter.

Ruby's killers were cool and clinical, and this confirmed it was a well-planned hit that required intelligence from people with access to Ruby's entire lifestyle. For example, during the time of his murder, a young man was staying over at his flat.

According to Peter, Loyalists might have assassinated him, operating on intelligence provided by the IRA in the nearby Short Strand. Ruby had become vocal in his denunciation of Provisional leaders like Gerry Adams. His open disdain for the Adams leadership would have raised questions about his loyalty among senior IRA figures. Besides, his behaviour in a Short Strand Social Club, following the election of Gerry Adams to the British parliament, could have sealed his fate. Peter said Ruby had stood on a table and shouted, 'Today, we have achieved a great victory at the ballot box, but mothers will have to bury their sons tomorrow.' A fight ensued, but Ruby, at six feet two inches, came out on tops. He was referring to a soldier who had been shot dead, something Adams gloated about on his selection as an MP. Peter suspected Ruby was doomed thereafter.

My personal belief is that Ruby was marked for death by his Intelligence handlers. He had become openly antagonistic towards the Provisional IRA leadership. That eroded his status in the IRA and therefore his potential as a major British agent. His handlers would have been told by Scappaticci that there was loose talk among IRA personnel in the Markets and the nearby Short Strand, that Ruby was a 'loose cannon', leading a gay lifestyle that left him vulnerable to Special Branch recruitment. There was also increasing gossip in the upper ranks of the IRA that he was possibly the mole that betrayed the IRA's planned bombing of Gibraltar. The betrayal led to the SAS – British Special Air Service – wiping out the IRA's Gibraltar unit. Scappaticci would have been aware of that gossip and could have passed it to his MI5 handlers.

Did MI5 conclude it was only a matter of time before Ruby was unmasked, and having the Loyalists kill him was a preferable end? In the world of Intelligence even the dead have a purpose. In my opinion, outing Ruby was designed to create paranoia in the IRA. When I named him as a British agent in *The Dirty War*, a lot of IRA operatives who believed my findings became nervous. They were constantly looking over their shoulders, wondering who else in their ranks was working for the British. The truth about Ruby was a blow to those in the IRA who were trying to convince the rank and file the organisation was impenetrable. My evidence that Ruby was a high-level mole implied that British Intelligence had insider knowledge of the workings of the IRA's Belfast Brigade, and its active service units. That caused the kind of confusion that was valuable to the IRA's adversaries. Ironically, Scappaticci angrily accused me of deliberately damaging Ruby's memory, telling others Ruby was a hero and I had been conned. In perpetrating the lies about The Monkey and Ruby, Scappaticci allayed any possible suspicions about his loyalty to the IRA. His and Ruby's role in the undercover war raised other issues about fighting secret wars in a democracy.

TWENTY

Counterterrorism's Moral Ambiguity

There are a host of complex moral issues surrounding Britain's use of terrorist agents. For example, they were permitted, if not encouraged, to commit terror to maintain their bona fides in groups like the IRA, UVF and UDA. Intelligence sources I spoke to claimed that if their agents in the IRA had impressive 'terror résumés' their loyalty was rarely questioned by their IRA bosses. It was, therefore, necessary for agents to commit acts of terror to burnish their credentials with their paramilitary colleagues. There is truth to that logic. A competent IRA bomber or shooter was unlikely to be suspected of being a British spy if he killed on the orders of his IRA commanders. In light of that, we have to conclude that those running counterterrorism operations in Northern Ireland engaged in a moral trade-off. They permitted the terrorists they employed to bomb and murder in the belief it was for the greater good. I once asked my late friend, the celebrated RUC detective, Jimmy Nesbitt, if moral ambiguity was prevalent in the intelligence world. His response was as follows:

> You have to suspend the normal rules of policing in this game. It means putting aside moral reservations about working with men who are killers. That's the trade-off. In the movies, MI5 plants its people in terrorist organisations, but that doesn't happen in the real world. In fact, the best agents are bona fide terrorists in the real world. They have the advantage of being already on the inside. They don't have to pretend to be terrorists. The problem is you can't

control them the way you control guys you work with. Terrorists can be unpredictable informants. Of course, it means you have terrorists on your payroll, and at your disposal. It is as simple as that, no matter what some people might tell you. When you give them money, they consider it a salary. You might have to ignore the fact some of them are sexual perverts. If a terrorist tells you he has been ordered to kill someone, you will want to know the target, though you'll not discuss the rights and wrongs of him killing the person. That's a discussion for you and your bosses. His job is to provide you with intelligence. You don't have moral discussions with him. All a handler needs to know is what an informant's IRA unit is up to, the identities of its members, its interaction with other units, where weapons are stored and what operations are planned. Handling terrorist agents is a stressful business because many of them are unstable. You can never fully trust them. They are likely to lie to you if they feel they may risk too much by telling you the truth. Still, knowing their personal secrets – extra-marital affairs, sexual perversions or links to prostitutes – is vital to controlling them. You cannot let yourself get too personally attached to these guys because the time might come when you have to sacrifice them or arrest them because of the danger they present to you or themselves. They are tools to defeat terror. The objective drives the means.

In another conversation with him, he shared his opinion on trade-offs:

A trade-off that nobody in this business wants his fingerprints on is the decision to ignore intelligence that could save lives. You know if you act on it, you will expose a highly placed informant. Let's say your informant is one of two IRA operatives who know when a bombing is due to happen. Acting on this intelligence will allow the IRA to focus on those operatives, and the chances of your informant being fingered as the traitor becomes a real possibility. Those running the show have to decide sometimes if they should let an IRA operation happen knowing an innocent person or persons will die. Protecting an agent's cover means he will be able to continue to provide critical intelligence. If you have to let your agent kill someone on the IRA's orders, that's one of the unfortunate aspects of the intelligence game. That's life. No one wants to see innocent people die, but in some circumstances there has to be a trade-off of one life or a few lives to save many. I imagine people who make those decisions have a hard time living with them later.

Jimmy never admitted he had faced trade-off choices, though I knew he ran highly placed sources in Loyalist terror groups. One of those was the West Belfast UDA leader, James 'Pratt' Craig, infamous for his 'champagne lifestyle' and extortion of money from local businesses. Craig even took his enforcers and bodyguards on continental holidays. Jimmy hinted to me that, at some stage in his relationship with Craig, the UDA leader became the exclusive property of Special Branch and MI5.

In his role as a criminal mastermind, Craig struck racketeering deals with some Republican splinter groups. He also collaborated with the Provisional IRA to plan the murders of prominent Loyalists who opposed his criminality. The UDA's Inner Council leadership assassinated him on learning of his treachery. I believe there is enough evidence to conclude that his handlers knew or helped select some of the Loyalist paramilitaries he set up for assassination.

Jimmy once described for me a classic case of a trade-off when a terrorist agent presented his handler with an RPG7 rocket launcher wrapped in a blanket. He had been storing it at home on the orders of his IRA commander, but he thought his handler would want it removed from the battlefield. The handler ordered him to take the launcher back home, fearing suspicion would fall on him if the IRA found it was missing. The handler assured him he would not be in trouble if he fired it under IRA orders, but he should try to let him know the target in advance.

Terrorist agents were undoubtedly the most effective tools in the war against the IRA. Men like Ruby and Scappaticci were spies working at the heart of the IRA's operational structures. They were also vicious assassins. My friend, Peter, would argue forcefully, and with some justification, that the State was morally justified employing terrorists if they saved lives. Proof of Peter's claim about Ruby saving many lives is hard to come by, though I have no reason to doubt it. In fact, others in security circles have confirmed it for me.

Still, it is hard to accept the fact that Scappaticci was encouraged by his handlers to run the IRA's 'nutting squad', which tortured and killed men suspected of betraying the IRA. He also, I believe, had men killed to remove suspicion from him. His agent role highlighted the moral ambiguity at the core of counter-terror operations. He could have saved his fellow agent, father of four, Joe Fenton.

In a dirty war, nothing is as it appears. Sometimes, I had difficulty separating the good guys from the bad when interviewing some of them for my books. I continue to wonder if Scappaticci could provide me with convincing evidence that he saved many lives, and that his reign of terror was necessary to maintain his cover as an agent. That is unlikely to happen since his handlers placed him in the British version of the FBI's witness protection programme, where I expect him to remain in hiding for the rest of his natural life. There is little likelihood any British government will let him spill the beans about his role in a very dirty war.

There is another aspect of the undercover war that interested me as an investigative writer. It was the history of extrajudicial murders that began in the early 1970s and continued throughout the Troubles. I am referring to murders committed by Loyalist assassins who were agents of the State, and by members of secret British Military Intelligence outfits. The existence of some of those outfits has been scrubbed from classified files. Their targets included militant Republicans, people loosely or wrongly linked to Republican terror groups through bogus intelligence, members of Sinn Féin and innocent Catholics. I believe that, beginning in 1971, people in the higher echelons of the British government's security apparatus knew Loyalist assassins run by the State were slaughtering innocent Catholics. The soldier, Albert Walker Baker, a UDA assassin of the early 1970s whom I wrote about in *The Dirty War*, was an example of a terrorist agent permitted to torture and murder innocent Catholics while spying for MI5 and Special Branch on the UDA's leadership. For over two decades, Loyalist hit squads were provided with intelligence by Special Branch, MI5 and British Military Intelligence to target and kill Republicans. Not all their victims were members of the IRA. Some were Catholic solicitors. Murders were often dismissed as the work of crazed sectarian assassins when they were in fact part of a state-sponsored proxy war aimed mostly, but not exclusively, at the IRA. Loyalist leaders were also targeted.

This undercover war impacted innocent Catholics and Protestants. For counterterrorism bosses, it conveniently intersected with tribal bloodletting, leading to the mistaken attribution by the media of many state-sponsored murders to tribalism. It is an aspect of the Troubles that demands greater scrutiny by everyone concerned with civil liberties and justice.

In the years since my book *The Dirty War* was published, I have been contacted by many people: the loved ones of victims, students studying the period, journalists, authors and academics. The latter always amused me because of their presumption I would fill out detailed questionnaires and hand over my sources to aid their research. Some of them, I was convinced, had never met a terrorist, much less observed a street riot.

Instead, I preferred helping families anxious to find answers to the murders of their loved ones. When I did not possess the expertise to assist them, I was fortunate to have my trusted detective friend, Jimmy Nesbitt. He was the most accomplished investigator I had ever known. We formed a close friendship, and I believe he may have saved my life on several occasions by alerting me to threats from terrorists. On one occasion, when I was due to fly into Belfast from abroad, he warned me about chatter in Loyalist ranks about a plan to kill me. In other instances, he advised me to avoid certain areas. After I wrote *The Shankill Butchers*, he warned me a police informant had overheard associates of the Shankill Butchers discussing a plan to kidnap and butcher me. Jimmy frequently reminded me to examine the underside of my car in the mornings before driving to work, in case an explosive device had been attached to it by the Loyalists or Republicans.

'You have made a lot of enemies on both sides. Never let your guard down,' he used to say.

Over the years, even after he retired, he continued to counsel me about my security during my return trips to Northern Ireland. I first met him while writing *The Shankill Butchers*. He was the senior detective in charge of the murder squad in Tennent Street Police Station, off the Shankill Road. He was calm, authoritative and willing to share secrets with me provided I did not compromise him and his fellow detectives. He was a chain smoker who led a very stressful life. He and his staff had more than one hundred unsolved murders in their files. He spent long hours chasing down leads, examining tortured bodies in dark alleys and interrogating dangerous men. He led one of the tightest detective squads in policing.

As he rose through RUC ranks, higher-ups asked him to supervise the security and relocation of 'supergrasses' – terrorists who had given evidence in court against their former comrades. MI5 secretly appointed him to the role of negotiator in the event of terrorist kidnappings. Some Special Branch bosses disliked my friendship with him. He shared with me that a senior Special Branch figure, concerned about our closeness, tried unsuccessfully to limit his access to intelligence.

Jimmy was an honourable man who would never have betrayed the RUC, though he had a genuine mistrust and dislike for parts of the Intelligence community. He believed 'outfits' like 14th Intelligence Company acted like cowboys. After he retired, he remained attached to his former colleagues. Top brass in the Police Service of Northern Ireland and the Intelligence community often sought his advice.

He was always willing to work with me on cold cases. One such case involved the murder of an innocent Protestant man, who was abducted, beaten and shot dead by Loyalists in West Belfast in the early 1970s. The victim's daughters appealed to me to find their father's murderers, and I enlisted Jimmy's help. He persuaded former colleagues to go back through old files and track down information on people Jimmy and I felt might be the perpetrators. I told the victim's daughters that I would do my best to get them closure, but cautioned that success might prove elusive. The daughters had a terrorist culprit in mind as their father's killer. It was a man I had met and written about. Based on research I had done on him for my book, *The Trigger Men*, and interviews Jimmy recalled that he had conducted with this individual, we were confident he might be the killer. After several weeks of digging into the particulars, we ruled him out. While the murder fit his modus operandi, it turned out that he had been in police custody at the time of the crime.

I was handling the investigation from New York where I was living, and Jimmy was in Belfast calling in favours for access to intelligence. We spoke by phone constantly, trying to connect the dots. After two months, we decided that we had run out of options. By then we had discovered there might be two, possibly three killers. Our only hope was that, at some point in the future, one of the perpetrators would turn himself in and give up the identity of his accomplices. We were convinced the victim had probably questioned the actions of the violent men running the streets of the Shankill during a lawless, bloody period when many innocents lost their lives. He disapproved of political violence and had a reputation for being outspoken. Such traits, especially in Shankill bars would have attracted the attention of violent men. A witness last saw him alive on the Shankill Road, presumably drunk. His murderers shot him in the head and dumped his body in the Glencairn district, a spot used by Loyalist hit squads to dispose of victims. We suspected vigilantes patrolling the Shankill abducted him and then handed him over to paramilitaries. There were many sadistic Loyalist killers in the Shankill area at the time.

Jimmy and I suspected that one person mentioned in the detectives' files about the murder knew more than he admitted to the police. This gave way to a new theory: someone close to the victim betrayed him or withheld important details about his last hours. The victim's daughters thanked me for our efforts but held tight to the belief that the killer they had in mind from the outset was their father's assassin. I realised it was hard for them to abandon their theory. They were courageous young women who had kept their father's memory alive. They would never give up hope of getting justice. I hope they will get their wish one day.

Jimmy and I felt we had done our best. We admitted, however, that pursuing cold cases involved a host of emotional challenges. The loved ones of victims inevitably expected closure, but to bring that to them was not always possible. In the final years of Jimmy's life – he died of cancer on 27 August 2014, aged 79 – we talked often. He was battling cancer with the kind of courage he displayed when confronting terrorism. At one stage of his illness, he told me he believed he had defeated cancer, only to discover months later it had metastasised and found its way into his bones. He never despaired during periods of excruciating pain. We were working on the above-mentioned cold case while he was undergoing chemotherapy.

I discussed with Jimmy the prospect of writing a book on his life, but each time we thought we could cut out time to meet up he had to endure more chemo treatments. I was unable to see him in his final days, but I arranged for my friend and fellow author, Hugh Jordan, to bring my best wishes before he died.

Many times in our conversations, Jimmy expressed his deep regret that he was unable to bring Lenny Murphy, the leader of the Shankill Butchers, and his two closest associates to justice for mass murder. One of those associates, Lenny's brother, John, died in a car accident. The other associate was alive at the time of Jimmy's death.

Lenny Murphy was shot dead by the Provisional IRA on 16 November 1982. In Jimmy's opinion, the IRA had timely intelligence on Murphy's whereabouts. It came from British Intelligence via a Loyalist terror agent. Prior to the killing, MI5 used its special security authority to remove all police and military units from the area where Murphy was due to be shot. It allowed the IRA hit squad unobstructed access to and from the murder site in a predominantly Protestant area.

Armed with an assault rifle and a pistol, two gunmen shot Murphy twenty times. He died not far from the Glencairn location where he had often dumped his victims.

Jimmy was the most decorated policeman in the history of the UK with sixty-seven recommendations. I miss his dry wit, intelligence, thoughtfulness and the loyalty he showed to his friends and colleagues.

TWENTY-ONE

In the BBC's Crosshairs

In 1991, the sudden departure from BBC Northern Ireland of Ian Kennedy and Dr Colin Morris, *The Show*'s biggest defenders, signalled the series' limited life span. The BBC hierarchy in London encouraged the two men to accept posts elsewhere in the Corporation. Before long, their replacements were Pat Loughrey, a former Schools producer whom I had once rejected for a *Talkback* production post, and Robin Walsh, whom I had worked under in my BBC news days. BBC bosses in London had me in their crosshairs at this time. I was told as much by Don Anderson, a former Head of Radio Ulster, who heard it from a BBC executive on a flight from London. Before long, Walsh and Loughrey asked me to take early retirement; a euphemism for asking me to resign.

From the outset of his arrival in Belfast, Walsh insisted, unlike his predecessor, Dr Morris, or for that matter, Ian Kennedy, that every satirical script should be read to him before it could be cleared for broadcast. Colin Lewis and David Malone were often the 'readers'. Walsh pulled *The Show* off-air for a short time during the first Gulf War. I believe it may have been the only television programme in the UK to suffer that fate.

With Walsh in charge, I felt that the third season would usher in the death of *The Show*. When Walsh and Loughrey made it clear to me they wanted me to resign, they did not know that Ian Kennedy, who was then Head of the BBC's South East Region in England, had approached me to join him and produce two major television documentaries about origins of the Troubles. Once I accepted Walsh's retirement package, I took the Kennedy offer. I could have challenged the BBC's attempt to end my career in Belfast, and it would have proved highly embarrassing for the Corporation. However, I chose not to have a public dispute and took the redundancy package. Loughrey subsequently succeeded Walsh as Controller. I later learned that archived tapes of *The Show* were not easily accessed by staff. I found that somewhat amusing in a strange sort of way. It was as if someone in the Corporation thought their content was subversive.

I have often been asked why I took the BBC redundancy package and left Northern Ireland for good in 1991. I was reticent to open up publicly because it would have required me to expose some of the darker secrets that informed my decision. Having faced some hostility from executives, I was already disillusioned with the leadership in the BBC, and I wasn't surprised they didn't want me around anymore. I was exhausted from petty programme squabbles and unnecessary constraints on my editorial freedom. I also regretted putting my wife and stepson through a lot of stress by writing controversial books, and I worried about my three-year-old daughter, Nadia. Katherine and Crawford knew about death threats delivered to me, and my friend, Jimmy Nesbitt, persistently cautioned me to be alert to dangers lurking in the shadows.

Irrespective of my efforts to be objective in my writing and broadcasting, I nevertheless angered a lot of dangerous people from within both communities. I was cavalier about death threats, but I now realise this was a defence mechanism. Deep down I was often genuinely terrified. I tried not to show it to my parents or my family. I later discovered, when some of my siblings married, they were uneasy about me visiting their homes. I had become a risk to those around me.

My stepson, Crawford, was a courageous boy who attended Campbell College. He followed an important routine when we lived at Donaghadee outside Belfast and later in Ardara House, Comber. He would keep a list of the number plates of suspicious vehicles seen near our home. In the mornings, I would look under my car to make sure it was not wired with a bomb. At night, I had a loaded gun at my bedside.

I tried not to think too much about the episodes when I was threatened at gunpoint, but those experiences found their way into my nightmares. How could I erase my memorable meeting with John Bingham, a prominent UVF Commander who was also a pigeon fancier? On finding out I was inquiring about his terrorist role in the organisation, he became angry because he had never been successfully prosecuted for his crimes. He lured me to a meeting with promises he would talk openly about the UVF, but when I got to the agreed location, he jammed a gun in my mouth. Coldly and calmly he warned me that, while he could never harm a pigeon, he would have no hesitation in killing me if I crossed him. Later, he phoned to apologise, insisting I join him for drinks at his place. I find it difficult to understand, even to this day, why I accepted his bizarre invitation. Perhaps I intuitively reckoned it was safer for me to iron out my issues with such a violent terrorist as John Bingham, even if it meant walking into the lion's den. The alternative was to reject his drinks offer and risk him sending a hit squad after me or putting a bomb under my car. Unable to dissuade me, a detective friend offered to put a tail on me. I rejected his offer, fearing if Bingham suspected I was arriving with cops in tow, he might just shoot me anyway. It was a peculiar sit down. He offered me Scotch, which I refused. He grinned when he said if I was hoping to drink something Irish I was out of luck because he 'never touched anything Irish'. He even showed me a gun he had concealed under a cushion, claiming it was like a work of art, and he even offered to let me hold it. I wondered if that same gun had been the last thing some innocents had seen.

I was also targeted in Dublin, where I had set up an interview with a member of the IRA's Army Council who cancelled at the last minute. Late that night, in O'Connell Street, two men jostled me into a doorway, and one shoved a gun in my face. They ordered me out of Dublin. When I tried to investigate the incident, a senior IRA Intelligence source suggested the gunmen were British Intelligence agents who did not want me 'sniffing out' ongoing secret talks between the Provisionals and the British Government. It was possibly true, but my presence in Dublin might just as easily have made some IRA people unhappy.

These, and similar incidents, took a toll on me and those around me. In 1991, I decided that it was time to move my family to a safer environment. We chose to settle in Tingewick, a picturesque Buckinghamshire village.

For the following eighteen months, I worked on contract for Ian Kennedy as a producer with *Timewatch*, a television documentary unit based at the former Elstree Film Studios outside London. When I took up the post, I began planning a major two-part series on the Troubles and persuaded many of my contacts in Ireland to allow me to interview them. At this time, I did not have much contact with senior editorial figures in Elstree like Paul Hayman, who regarded himself as an expert on the Troubles. My only knowledge of him was that he had once made a programme with political figures in Northern Ireland. When Ian Kennedy moved to Elstree he became Hayman's boss and had a heated exchange with him. Ian's view was that Hayman in the past had shown a reluctance to commission documentaries from Northern Ireland-based producers. Hayman responded that producers, who lived or worked in BBC Belfast, were not qualified to make balanced programmes about the Troubles. Ian quickly chastised him, pointing out how London-based producers had only been able to make successful documentaries about the Troubles because of contributions by BBC news and current affairs staff in Belfast. Some London producers, presenters and reporters shared Hayman's perspective, yet it amused me how they could pay infrequent visits to Northern Ireland and consider themselves experts.

After one year with *Timewatch*, I complained privately to a senior BBC editorial figure about my concern that emails were circulating, some from at least one figure in Belfast, questioning my involvement with the two Troubles' documentaries. In the BBC there was always a level of secrecy one could not breach, even when one was the subject of discussion. I spoke to an executive who confirmed that some BBC bosses were displeased when they learned *Timewatch* had contracted me. Before long, my position became untenable, and I made it clear to the BBC through emails and legal representation that there was a campaign to marginalise my role and force me out of the Troubles project. Before the matter could be litigated in the courts, the BBC reached a financial settlement with me. Peter Taylor, a BBC correspondent, subsequently used important interviews I conducted when working for *Timewatch* for a programme he made about Ireland. Taylor's programme was credited with unearthing new historical facts about the early days of the Troubles.

In 1992, after taking my leave from *Timewatch*, I continued contributing as a terrorism expert for the BBC and other networks, especially Sky TV and Channel 4. Unfortunately, when threats from paramilitary figures in Belfast reached me in England, neither I nor my family felt we had moved far enough from Northern Ireland. I shared my fears with Jimmy Nesbitt, who remarked that 'the wrong types of people in Ulster have long bloody memories'. It was time to move on again. I relocated with Katherine and Nadia to the south-west of France, while Crawford remained at school in Buckinghamshire.

Two years later, in 1994, I wrote and presented *The Last Colony* documentary for Channel 4 television. It was exactly the kind of programme I had planned to make for *Timewatch*. Ian Kennedy, who had left the BBC, produced it. He was running his own production company. *The Last Colony* was broadcast four times by Channel 4 and the Irish network RTÉ. Interviews I conducted with the late Field Marshall Lord Michael Carver and Prime Minister Edward Heath made news at the time of the broadcast and formed part of my witness statement to the Bloody Sunday Tribunal in September 2002. Lord Carver's revelations exposed many policymaking flaws within the British Army and 10 Downing Street between 1970 and 1973, and nowadays form an important part of the history of the period.

Many exciting, disappointing and even bizarre moments filled my career with the BBC. One of them stands out today even after so many years, and it concerns a trip my colleague, Colin Lewis, and I made to West Belfast during a violent riot. I was editor of Current Affairs Radio at the time and off-duty when I learned about confrontations between mobs and soldiers in the Falls and Whiterock areas. In one incident, an exploding petrol bomb had set a young soldier alight.

When I phoned my staff, it dismayed me to learn that no reporter was covering events on the ground, and they were relying on the police and army to keep them updated. It was a familiar case of not having a reporter on duty who knew the Catholic Falls areas or was prepared to go there during a riot. Many of my BBC colleagues over the years had become desk bound and lacked the experience of working on the streets. Some were genuinely apprehensive and that was understandable. They were a different breed from print journalists, who cut their teeth in conflict areas during the early days of the Troubles. It is equally true the BBC had its fair share of excellent news reporters, local and national, but they were few and not always available. That was especially true of the local radio and television output. In this instance, I asked Colin Lewis, who just happened to be with me, if he would accompany me to West Belfast to see what was happening. Colin was a fine programme producer, who had never visited the Falls much less witnessed a riot, but he expressed his desire to join me. Knowing no taxi driver in his right mind would take us there, I picked up a BBC staff car. As I was leaving Broadcasting House, two staff members bound for a late-night party asked if I would be kind enough to purchase several bottles of wine and a bottle of vodka for them. Before driving to the Falls, I bought the alcohol and put it in the boot of the car.

I drove slowly through streets littered with barricades and rubble to the Springfield Road. It was a main thoroughfare, and I realised if I could travel unhindered as far the Ballymurphy–Whiterock Road junction, I could negotiate a route to Andersonstown and back to the city. When we reached the perimeter of Ballymurphy, the scene was a familiar one. Riot debris blanketed the streets, and British Army personnel carriers were angled across the main road with soldiers crouching beside them. I stopped the car and got out to talk to locals. They confirmed there was a temporary lull in the rioting.

Ballymurphy's rioters were notorious for their organisational skills. They operated a shift system whereby they could declare a temporary stoppage from time to time to let them rest up and enjoy a snack. During their breaks, others trickled onto the streets to relieve them.

This was the case when we arrived, and I decided it would be unwise to hang around too long in a large shiny BBC Ford.

I drove off citywards, down the Whiterock Road to the Falls. We were relieved exiting the riot zone, but our mood changed when we spotted a barricade of burned-out cars blocking the Falls Road at Beechmount Avenue.

'That's us screwed,' said Colin, like a man resigned to a death sentence.

I had been in this situation before and realised we faced a stark choice. I could do a U-turn and find an alternative route, but the goons manning the barricade might suspect we were undercover military and open fire. If we got away without being shot, they would radio IRA units in the area, making escape impossible. We had no option but to drive slowly to the barricade and display our BBC credentials. I told Colin to wind down his window, and I warned him not to reach into his pocket or make any sudden movement.

'Let them come to us,' I said as I stopped the car.

Several men wearing balaclava masks walked towards us from a crowd standing at the Beechmount Avenue junction. They moved with the deliberate pace of men confident we were not going anywhere. I whispered to Colin to let me do the talking, adding the worst that could happen was they would take our car and set it alight.

'Who the fuck are you?' asked one of the men.

I replied we were BBC producers and asked if it was okay to show him our passes. He grunted and I handed him mine and told Colin to do likewise. The man looked at it and threw it back in my lap. Instinctively, I decided to add a little humour to lighten up the proceedings.

'If you're gonna take our car would you mind if I got my wine and vodka out of the boot? We're going to a party tonight,' I said with a smile.

'Are you trying to be fucking funny?' barked the man closest to me.

I gingerly replied they could open the boot to see for themselves. There was a method in my apparent crassness. I wanted to assure them we posed no threat and had nothing in our car to imply we were anything other than what we claimed to be.

One of the goons, whom I took to be the leader, pointed his finger menacingly at us. 'Stay in the fuckin' car,' he said, while motioning to his associates to follow him back to the crowd on the corner. A heated discussion ensued between them all, some of them pointing from time to time at us.

'They're deciding whether to shoot us. Maybe we should make a run for it,' whispered Colin.

The thought occurred to me, too, but there was nowhere to run and I was determined to be casual. After all, I had been stopped by paramilitaries many times. In a few instances I was detained while they checked me out. Some threatened me, but usually when they established I was a journalist they permitted me to proceed unharmed. Paramilitaries, especially in Republican districts, tended to respect the media, though I knew there were always exceptions to the rule.

'It'll be okay,' I assured Colin, adding they would likely liberate the booze before burning the car. He didn't think that was funny. After what seemed like an eternity, two goons ambled back to our car, and one of them leaned in towards me.

'You're fucking crazy!' he said with a grin.

'Now, fuck off and consider yerselves lucky,' his companion added.

As I drove out of the area, Colin let out an audible sigh of relief. 'Dillon, you really are crazy,' he joked.

It may well have been my craziness that allowed us to drive away unharmed.

TWENTY-TWO

Legacies of Home

We who left become sentimental. We remain attached to songs about leaving, soil between our toes, and tears waiting to be shed in a parting glass. Everywhere we settle, Ireland lurks in the folds of sadness like the bog wood bleached white. History hides in the layered texture of the land. Open the turf bog like a coffin, and the spade cuts steps into the softness of yesterday. The earth is blackened as a hessian hood and the air dries it hard for the burning. Woven, the tapestry shrivels in the heat with broken fragments and images in the charred strands.

Stones Don't Die – Martin Dillon

The first time I truly felt Ireland's embrace was the evening I sailed out of Belfast as a boy to begin my studies in Montfort College seminary. I can still recall clinging to the rail of the Liverpool ferry, gazing at the mountains holding tight my city. At that moment, I felt a special attachment to Ireland, which I have nurtured with all my faults in the years following. Those of us who left Ireland to settle abroad eventually come to the realisation we miss its gentleness. No matter where I have travelled and lived in the past two decades, Ireland and its people have never been far from my thoughts and affections.

Any time I fished the Salmon River, one of the world's best rivers at Pulaski in Upstate New York, my mind would wander back to the days I used to cast into rivers like the The Ownea, The Bush, The Shimna, The Ballynahinch, The Newport and The Moy. Ballynahinch held a special place in my heart. I loved the Castle Hotel and Mikey

Conneely, the head ghillie. He was a short, barrel of a man with a warm smile and a sharp brain. He guarded the river like it was his child, ensuring people fly-fished it according to the rules. I taught my stepson, Crawford, to fly-fish on that river.

New York was a city I had never imagined I would call home when I flew into Kennedy airport from Paris, in January 1998, with all my worldly possessions in two suitcases. I chose New York due to personal circumstances. My marriage to Katherine had collapsed, and she had chosen to remain in France with our daughter, Nadia.

Ireland was still not the safest place to go back to. New York seemed like a good alternative when my trilogy – *The Shankill Butchers*, *The Dirty War* and *God and the Gun* – was published in the US. For the first couple of weeks I was booked on a publicity tour that took me from the East to the West Coast. I was pretty familiar with New York, having produced radio programmes for the BBC in its Manhattan studios in the 1970s and 1980s. The city also had an Irish lineage, which put me at ease. Suddenly, I had peace of mind and a sense of security: two things that had been missing in my life.

I was in Manhattan for only a week when I met my future wife, Violeta Kumurdjieva, a Bulgarian translator and journalist. She had relocated to the US with her daughter, Natalia, at the invitation of William Meredith, a Pulitzer Prize winner and celebrated poet. He had persuaded Violeta to come to the US to help with the translation of the second volume of his anthology of Bulgarian poets. After Violeta visited one of my readings in a Manhattan bookstore, she asked me for an interview. As a Foreign Press Association member, she later introduced me to her journalist friends and invited me to media events. We struck up a friendship and were married in 2003. She has been an enormous support to me and my work.

Ireland still finds its way into my thoughts as easily as it did on a warm August morning in 1998. I was driving from Bulgaria's capital, Sofia, to Bourgas on the Black Sea coast when two donkeys strolled aimlessly across a barren field reminding me of Connemara and Donegal. On 15 August 1998, I was pruning roses on my mother-in-law's terrace in Bourgas, just days after her death. In keeping with tradition, a black silk bow and a photo of Dora were attached to her front door and would remain there for forty days of mourning. I was placing the rose clippings in plastic bags and tying them tight, certain life had left them withered and choked by neglect, when a friend phoned me. The Real IRA had bombed Omagh and there was utter carnage and horror – twenty men, women and children were dead and over 200 were injured or maimed. On that tragic and bloody day, I looked at the plastic bags of severed stems and felt Omagh's roses had been ruthlessly severed as well.

'The killers will blame it on the phones,' I told myself, remembering the July 1972 bombing of the village of Claudy nestled in the Sperrin Mountains. Little Katherine Aiken was washing father's shop window, and Mrs Brown was in an alley looking for her cat. That's how my late friend, the poet Jimmy Simmons, in his poignant song, *The Ballad of Claudy*, depicted life unfolding before the bomb went off. Jimmy described the mundane lives of ordinary people as 'they waited to die'. In his mind's eye, he saw Artie Hone on his way to a neighbour's door, and Mrs McElhenney was serving petrol. I can't remember the name of the fifth person Jimmy placed on Main Street, but he noted it wasn't 'pigs squealing in the village square when a strange car exploded, leaving the dust and the terrible dead'. The killers later claimed they had tried to phone a warning about the bomb but the lines to Claudy were engaged. No one believed them. I saw remnants of victims' clothes still attached to overhead wires in Claudy's main street five years later. I was the first to reveal that one of the perpetrators of the Claudy massacre was a Catholic priest. No doubt, here too, amidst the bloodshed and backlash of Omagh, phones would be blamed, and it sickened me to the core.

Two days after the Omagh massacre, I stared at a newspaper image of the carnage and wrote the following:

STILL LIFE – Omagh 1998

It was not tiles slotted into rooftops,
warming in a midday glow.
A darkened place screamed out,
reset by a Cyrillic headline.
Could it have been the bonnet of a Ford,
gleaming somewhere in the wreckage,
stripped down to a soft top,
edges severing sinews?
Away from the lens, an assembly of
bodies was spray painted in dust,
ready for wrapping in foul smelling rubber.
It could have been a shameless installation.

The Omagh and Claudy images, and so many more I saw, were testaments to historical madness, which often characterised our island's history. Some believe you should forget the past, but it would be wrong to deny the horror. Through understanding it we may be able to ensure terror does not revisit us in the cyclical and vicious way it has done for centuries.

Colourful landscapes and even more colourful people are what I prefer to remember of Ireland. We all have warm memories of our past, of the people we loved, the places where we were raised and the richness of the land. When friends ask me if I miss Belfast, my answer is I do. It is hard not to love a place where I spent many happy years. It was more of a town than a city, with easy access to countryside, rivers, lakes and mountains. Belfast people have much too often taken those blessings for granted.

The longing to reconnect with Ireland often prompts a common response from those of us living abroad. We reminisce about our childhood, the beauty of the Mournes, Connemara, Kerry or Donegal. Out of sentimentality, we may attend a St Patrick's Day parade or pay occasional visits to an Irish bar. With the help of a whiskey or a pint of Guinness, we might be encouraged to wallow a little in self-pity, knowing what we have lost we may never regain.

During the 1970s and 1980s, the political violence in Northern Ireland touched too many families on both sides of the religious divide. Each morning, my mother prayed to God and her favourite saints to protect her husband and children from the sectarian gangs roaming the north of the city. In the mornings, after my young brother, Patrick, and dad left for the day, she was terrified they would never return home. She imagined them being abducted, tortured and murdered. Her fears grew stronger in winter months when darkness descended by late afternoon, enabling killers to move unobtrusively. I believe the sectarian violence took its toll on her physical and mental health, as it did on many other mothers during that period.

In the autumn of 1978 nothing suggested she was in ill health or facing an impending health crisis, yet she suffered a massive stroke that left the right side of her body partially paralysed. Fortunately, she didn't become speech impaired, but she had to spend a considerable time undergoing physical therapy. She decided the partial paralysis to her left arm and leg would not lessen her love of life or weaken her faith in God. Her greatest challenge, she later admitted, was convincing her family and the outside world she was capable of making financial decisions and returning to her role as matriarch of the family.

When she embarked on her road to recovery she was determined to move around freely up and down stairs with the aid of a heavy plastic contraption on her left leg. Even though her left hand was paralysed, she became skilled in using a long metal device with two prongs to lift food from a plate. The stroke's damage to her hearing caused her the greatest distress because hearing aids failed to filter out extraneous noises, leaving her to make sense of cascading sounds. Over-eating was another side effect of her illness, and it increased her stress level, especially when she was alone waiting for her children to come home. She had a difficult time controlling her desire to eat, and her skill at raiding the refrigerator when alone did not help. My father threatened to put a lock on the fridge if she didn't curtail her appetite, and his words upset her greatly.

If he followed through with his threat, she said she would apply to legally change their address from 19 Chestnut Gardens to 'Stalag 19'. And, if he and several of my sisters did not desist from terrorising her because of her eating habits, she would write a poem about Stalag 19 and send it to the *Belfast Telegraph*. Since I had once worked for the *Telegraph*, she expected my influence with the editor would result in her poem being published 'prominently on page three'. It would, she declared, expose the way she was being 'brutalised like a prisoner of war forced to survive on meagre rations'.

During that period, she often sat alone in the living room overlooking a small garden dominated by a big rosebush my father had woven over a wooden archway. For a woman whose life had been filled with crying babies and demands for everything from food to clean clothes, pocket money and a cuddle, she was suddenly faced with silence.

However, by the autumn of 1979, with no school-aged children left to brighten her day, she avoided the lure of abject depression and began to take charge of her life. She used her good right hand and the metal device to prepare the evening meal and listened to the radio, watched television and wrote notes, always with a pencil.

She often talked about how God 'tests us' and how, sometimes through suffering, we get closer to him and understand 'his sorrows'. She likened her deepening faith in God to her ability to survive the stroke. She claimed God had helped her overcome affliction by allowing her to reclaim her life. She pointed to the fact she had travelled extensively with my father after the stroke and eventually wrestled back control of her roles as wife and mother. By 2000, she had developed angina and severe intestinal problems, but she retained her liveliness, humour and deep Christian belief. Above all, her romantic attachment to the past was as vibrant as it had ever been.

In 2003, I flew to Belfast with my wife, Violeta, to spend Christmas with my parents. They had moved to a very comfortable apartment in the south of the city. During our stay, my mother suffered a heart attack and was hospitalised but discharged a month later, proving her fortitude once again. On 10 March 2006, she was rushed to hospital suffering from acute angina. Most of us were sure she would pull through, but on the evening of 16 March, her bladder and several other organs showed signs of failure. The only option was surgery, and in keeping with legal requirements, her surgeon told her she had a 40 per cent chance of surviving an operation. If she chose to proceed with surgery, he would require her signature on a document. My mother calmly took a pen and signed the legal paper. 'I hope you can read that old signature of mine,' she told the surgeon, before turning to chat to my father as though nothing important had taken place. After the surgery, she was lucid, but her organs suffered a fatal shutdown, and she died six hours later.

A month after she passed away, I asked my father what it was like to lose the woman he had known for 65 years.

'There's a large hole in my thoughts where she used to be,' he replied.

Two months after her passing, one of my sisters was rummaging through a box of old family photos and came across a sealed envelope. Inside was a valentine card my mother had addressed to my father but had never given him. The valentine bore the date of 17 February 1995 and read:

Dear Gerry, love, you are still my Valentine. I've had so many happy years with you – 52 to date – and we'll be 40 years married this month on the Feast of Our Lady of the Snows. Ever since the awful stroke I suffered in 1978, I've enjoyed every moment of my life with you. You've cared for all my pains and aches and all the love you've shown me touches this old heart of mine. If I should ever pass on before you, you can be sure that every word was written with deep sincerity. I hope you can read my writing because this old hand of mine has taken its toll over the years.

All my love Gerry, Maureen.

Sixteen months later, my father suffered a heart attack and found himself recuperating in the same hospital room my mother died in the previous year. It could not have been easy for him to spend weeks in a room where he had watched his wife die. At first, he thought he was fit to undergo a triple bypass operation, but it was not to be. He died on the morning of 18 July 2007.

His funeral should have been a celebration of his life, but it was transformed into a bitter charade and I did not attend it. Unfortunately, my mother's prediction that 'the family that prayed together stayed together' proved to be a fiction. I was not informed of my father's final illness or the fact he was hospitalised. I had to learn the news that he was ill from a relative.

Family disagreements had begun to surface forty-eight hours before my mother's funeral, but I had dismissed them, realising it was a stressful time for all of us. There is much I could write about this topic, but, out of respect for my late parents, I decided to limit my comments to one or two matters.

On 7 December 2007, I met the executors of my father's estate, my brother, Dr Patrick Dillon, and my sister, Ursula Mc Laughlin, in the Radisson Hotel in Belfast. They arrived with my sisters, Frances Gibson and Imelda Feinberg. I was accompanied by my sisters, Attracta Fay and Monica Graham. At the meeting, I reminded the executors that I understood that my father had kept an extensive archive that included letters, photos, slides of our Uncle Gerard's work, and short stories he had written. I had seen many of those items in my father's possession over the years. In fact, he had loaned part of the archive to the late James White when he was writing his book on our Uncle Gerard. White subsequently returned the materials. I knew a lot about my father's possessions because of my closeness to him and Uncle Gerard. The executors told me that there was no archive in existence, to their knowledge, and had no details of many matters related to the artworks.

While writing this book, I emailed the executors, and kindly asked them to provide copies of documents related to my late Uncle Gerard's estate. I did not receive a reply, nor did I receive replies regarding other items in my father's possession before he passed away. The executors did not even consult me or my sisters, Monica and Attracta, about the inscription on our parents' headstone. My father was buried in the Milltown Cemetery grave that held the remains of my mother and Uncle Gerard.

After the breakdown in family relations, it troubled me that my father's role as a guardian of the Gerard Dillon legacy ended with his passing. He had always been available to respond to questions from galleries, auctions houses, academics, publishers and others who sought advice about my uncle. Since there are many fake Dillons in the Ireland art market, I believe it is vital the family fulfils the same type of same guardianship that my late father provided. Often, auctions houses ignore a glaring fake because they are guided only by a desire to profit. Those responsible for fakes usually create small pieces that generate good revenue. They are careful not to produce larger pieces whose high monetary value would likely be reflected in media coverage of auction sales. The Dillon family has an obligation to monitor the sales of our uncle's work so auction houses and those organising exhibitions to honour his legacy might be more circumspect in what they show.

While writing about my family, which my parents held together for decades, I couldn't help thinking its disintegration was inevitable. I always thought my family would be different since my mother had ten children, an extraordinary feat in itself. She wanted the family united, always placing her children's needs above her own. Her life's struggle was to raise them to become valuable members of society; doctors, nurses, teachers. She was happy she 'married her daughters well'. In a way, I am glad she is not around to witness the family divided in such a fashion.

In respect of Dillon matters I mentioned Leo Smith and James White several times in this book, and it would be unfair not to end with some personal thoughts and observations about them. I liked and respected both men as formidable art experts. Each admired my uncle's work. James White was a highly respected international art expert, and

Leo Smith brought to the Dublin art scene a wealth of knowledge he acquired while working in galleries in London's Bond Street.

I have been asked many times why James White never explored my uncle's sexuality in his book about him. He had discussed my uncle's 'secret life' at length with me before the book was published, and once remarked how he was bewildered when he learned that his brothers, Joe and Vincent the priest, were gay, too, and so was their sister, Molly. I had expected revelations from him and was somewhat shocked when his book ignored the topic. Perhaps, his conversations with me had been his way of getting things off his chest while he debated with himself how to handle this very sensitive material. I was aware that he had avoided the topic of my uncle sexuality when talking to my parents. In retrospect, I believe, he was certain if he published what he had discovered about Gerard's life, in particular, revelations from Gerard's contemporaries in Ireland and Britain, he risked a barrage of criticism from living Dillon family members and many of Gerard's friends in the art world. In 1994, when his book was published, there was a general reluctance among many members of the Dillon clan to accept my uncle's homosexuality. Most of them have remained in denial to this day. The prospect that three of Uncle Gerard siblings were also gay would have horrified them then, and may still do now. My mother and Madge Campbell both refused to admit Gerard was gay. In contrast, my father rarely discussed the matter but was clearly not in the denier category.

I never reproached James White for turning his back on his research, convinced, he had secretly wanted to explore Gerard's personal life in the context of his art. He later hinted to George Campbell that he had been prepared to do it, but in the end, he got cold feet. He never publicly acknowledged the reasons for his actions. He may have worried Irish society was not ready for such revelations at that time, even though many of us recognised in my uncle's Pierrots portraits his inner debate about his sexuality. White cleverly chose instead the easy option in his book, using carefully coded words and phrases to hint that Gerard was socially unconventional: 'His psycho-sexual nature was formed when he was still quite young, and apart from keeping up appearances to please his mother, he gave up the practice of his religion. He also seemed to reject intimate relationships and to grow up in a very private, solitary environment, always living alone or seeking isolation during the periods when he shared quarters with another friend.'

A loving and generous man, my uncle addressed the world with a childlike sense of wonder. I have always felt, we who knew him, owed him no less than to be honest about his life. It will help others fully appreciate his engaging art and lasting images, many of which speak to the beauty of the natural world, suppressed sexuality and the uniqueness of humanity.

While I have been critical of James White's role in undervaluing my late uncle's estate to benefit Leo Smith, I nonetheless admired both men. White is personally credited with making the National Gallery of Ireland one of the finest during his tenure as Director from 1964 to 1980. His prediction that Gerard Dillon would be recognised as one of Ireland's greatest artists of the twentieth century came true and much faster than many expected.

Epilogue

When I left Ireland over twenty years ago, I never expected to feel homesick. I continued to write and broadcast about the Troubles, and I made a few brief return trips to promote my books, host a television documentary and attend my mother's funeral. With each succeeding trip, I observed major changes in the fabric of life in Belfast. Nowadays, the town centre resembles a modern European capital, something I had always wished for in the years I lived there. Optimism permeates many of my discussions with relatives and friends, and the city's night life is a far cry from the days of the Troubles, when only a few restaurants dared to stay open, and pubs were unsafe to visit after dark. Several generations that missed out on a normal life for most of the 1970s and 1980s are now enjoying a new, refreshing environment.

But I would be naïve to think the tribalism, which plagued parts of the island for centuries, has miraculously vanished. A lasting peace will require more than a desire for change. It will need a re-evaluation of Ireland's diversity and troubled history. It will require honesty, transparency, tolerance and respect for the views and aspirations of all its citizens. It is encouraging to see some of the mental barriers that defined a half-century of the Troubles have been replaced by a new realism. Who would have thought in 1969 that Martin McGuinness and Ian Paisley would have shared a political stage? That being said, the Ireland of today is nowhere near perfect, and Belfast's dividing walls remain a testimony to fear and suspicion. Across the island, there is still an outward flow of people seeking jobs and new lives in Europe, Australia, Canada and the United States. There are still those in the shadows, perhaps now smaller in number, willing to press an historical button generating animosity and resurrecting the cult of the gunman and the bomber. It is noticeable, however, that the majority of people throughout the island have moved on from the days of hunger strikes, sectarian tit-for-tat murders and a depressing conviction that nothing would ever change. There is a young generation that knows little about the Troubles. One would like to think, with all that has happened since 1969 and the subsequent peace, the keepers of history will encourage young people to believe that what has gone before should never define them or their future.

The view of Ireland from America, where I have lived these past 18 years, has changed dramatically, too. Within the Irish-American community, the mythologised images of the Famine Ireland, of IRA heroes of the 1916 Rising, and of Bobby Sands and the hunger strikes have been replaced by an awareness of a peaceful Ireland with part of the country weighed down with financial burdens and the dark spectre of emigration. There is also a growing recognition within the Irish-American community of the significant role played by Ulster Scots in building the United States of America. They left Ireland well before those who came after the famine, and, like all exiles, they felt the same sadness and loss.

An awareness of Ireland's diaspora has broadened the historical narrative about my native country. I recall in 2008 discussing the Ulster Scots-America link with my friends, Paul Tweed, a media lawyer with a stellar international reputation, the late Liam Clarke, a fine journalist, and Brendan McGinn, a president of one of Ireland's most reputable accountancy firms. Paul rightly reminded us that people in Ireland needed to see the Ireland-America historical connection in its totality and not merely through a prism shaped by the nineteenth-century famine exodus. There are millions of people with an Ulster Scots heritage across the length and breadth of the United States trying to reconnect with Ireland, and Ireland has to reach out to them, too. Israel provides the model for the way Ireland must address its diaspora. Israel benefits economically and intellectually from its dispersed sons and daughters, and they number much less than the 80 million people worldwide claiming a connection to Ireland. If one thinks for a moment of the talent, wealth and resources that lies beyond Ireland's shores, one can well imagine the benefits to Ireland once that link is nurtured.

It would be foolish of me to disregard or underestimate some of the underlying problems still existing in Northern Ireland. A significant amount of prejudice remains, but I believe it can and will be eradicated through education.

The Troubles defined many of us throughout the island over decades. We, journalists, historians and students were all on a learning curve, seeking to understand the conflict we were writing about while making efforts to put aside inherited prejudices. While I may have been critical of some of my contemporaries in this book, I nevertheless recognise that we were individually, and sometimes collectively, trying desperately to get to the same place: a place where openness and freedom could flourish in our writings and broadcasts. My abiding feeling is that each of us working in journalism and broadcasting loved the island of Ireland with all our faults.

Before finishing this book, I was rummaging through boxes in my study when I came across another symbol of Ireland: my Orange sash. It was folded neatly into a pouch with a label confirming it had been made by Alexanders, Regalia Manufacturers, 27 Castlereagh Road, Belfast. In 2007, my friends, the journalists, Jim Mc Dowell and Hugh Jordan, had it specially made for me. It was a testimony to Jim's tradition, which he hoped I would remember kindly in exile. It made me aware that had I been born on the Shankill Road, a short walk from my childhood home in the Lower Falls, I would have been Protestant and a proud supporter of the Orange Order tradition. I might even have become the Worshipful Master of an Orange Lodge, leading my neighbours in the annual 12 July parade. In Ireland such small matters of slim dividing lines between communities generated so much upheaval.

AN ORANGE SASH IN MANHATTAN – Martin Dillon

Even if the Pope says no,
I'll put my lips to it like a stole,

slipping it over my head,
until it falls gently on my breast.
I may need a bowler.
Perhaps a darkly pressed suit, too,
and shiny leather shoes.
I must be straight as a rod,
mouth and shoulders tight,
ready for the Lambeg roar.
I may choose a fine March Day,
a sweet lily in my lapel,
a Scottish ditty on my lips.
There will be no flamenco in my step,
just arms swinging like a metronome,
keeping me in line,
Uptown on Fifth.

Index